PRAISE FOR
BIRD WATCHING

"Courtside seats to one of the game's greatest. . . . The book is endearing for its humanity, [and] there are enough descriptions of Celtics and Pacers games, and playing against Michael Jordan, Magic, playoff teams, and their coaches to keep basketball enthusiasts happy. . . . [An] articulate and candid book."

—*Kirkus Reviews*

"Surprisingly revealing. . . . There are anecdotes from his playing days, insights into his coaching philosophy, and even some details of life in French Lick. . . . When Bird talks basketball, people listen."

—*Booklist*

"The Hick from French Lick solidifies his reputation as a straight-talker unimpressed with his own legend."

—*Publishers Weekly*

"Lays out Bird's coaching philosophy in an accessible manner."

—*Newsday*

"Excellent . . . intelligently written."

—*Library Journal*

Bird Watching

On Playing and Coaching the Game I Love

LARRY BIRD

with Jackie MacMullan

Foreword by Pat Riley

WARNER BOOKS

A Time Warner Company

WARNER BOOKS EDITION

Copyright © 1999 by Larry Bird
All rights reserved. No part of this book may be reproduced in any form or by any electronic or mechanical means, including information storage and retrieval systems, without permission in writing from the publisher, except by a reviewer who may quote brief passages in a review.

Cover design by Tom Tafuri
Cover photo by Glenn James/NBA Photos

Warner Books, Inc.
1271 Avenue of the Americas
New York, NY 10020

Visit our Web site at
www.twbookmark.com

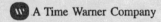 A Time Warner Company

Printed in the United States of America

Originally published in hardcover by Warner Books.
First Paperback Printing: October 2000

10 9 8 7 6 5 4 3 2 1

To my parents, Georgia Marie and Joe Bird
—Larry Bird

To Michael, now and always
—Jackie MacMullan

Acknowledgments

I would like to thank my wife, Dinah, and my family for their ongoing support in everything I do; to Jackie MacMullan and her family; to my editor at Warner Books, Rick Wolff; to Jill Leone; and to Donnie Walsh, for giving me the opportunity to coach the Indiana Pacers.

—Larry Bird

To Rick Wolff, Jill Leone, and Karen Bolton for their professionalism; to Dan Dyrek, Dave Gavitt, Donnie Walsh, Rick Carlisle, and Dick Harter for their insights; to Tim Edwards, Mary Kay Hruskocy, and David Benner for their assistance; to Fred and Margarethe MacMullan, Sue Titone, and Karen O'Neil for their unwavering support; to Alyson, Douglas, and Michael for their love and their patience; and to Larry Bird for his candor.

—Jackie MacMullan

Contents

Foreword

I had the opportunity, as a player and coach for the Los Angeles Lakers in the seventies and eighties, to be around some truly great, great players. I played on teams with Jerry West, Elgin Baylor, Wilt Chamberlain, and Kareem Abdul-Jabbar, and later in the eighties coached both Kareem and Magic Johnson. What I grew to realize is that all the great ones have an underlying subtext to them. You don't always sense it from their exterior public persona, but it's there. It's something totally unique that lies underneath, and drives them to exceptional accomplishments.

When Larry Bird was named head coach of the Indiana Pacers, I was neither shocked nor surprised. I was not aware of his plans, but I had felt it was only a matter of time before someone with a great will to win and compete against the best would return to the game he loved. Larry never walked away from any challenges. He needed this. After all, there were more Lakers, 76ers, and Bulls to beat.

I vividly recall the time Larry Bird revealed to me the unique competitive perspective and quality that was part of those great players who always won. It was during the

1987 Finals in Boston Garden when Magic hit that famous baby hook to put us ahead in the final seconds of Game 4. The Celtics called time-out, down by one, to set up their crucial play. We knew in the huddle it would be Bird getting a pass from Dennis Johnson in the corner—it was a play they ran all the time. Sure enough, when they came out of the huddle to inbound the ball, Bird cut to the sideline from the free throw line and pushed James Worthy off, so that he could get free. Bird then cut sharply to the corner. As he sprinted to his spot, looking back over his shoulder at D. J. to make sure he was focused on the ball, Larry's face was looking toward our bench.

When Bird caught the ball, he was directly in front of me, and he was wide open. My basketball life flashed in front of my face. This was death. It was one of those rare moments when time stood still. Even though he had to catch, turn, and shoot very quickly, I knew he was going to get a good shot. As he faded back and let it go, Bird fell out of bounds. With my heart in my throat, I watched the ball, and it was as straight as an arrow, but it was long. The ball bounced off the back rim and we won the game that propelled us to the world title.

Our bench was going wild when Bird walked past us. He was both unfazed and unaffected by the missed shot and taunting opponents. He would not show us any emotion other than "It ain't over yet, we'll get you on Sunday." But he knew I knew this—Bird looked directly at me. He didn't say a word. The expression on his face showed exactly what he was thinking. While everyone else in Boston Garden was in despair over the loss, Bird's piercing lethal look into my eyes said, "I can't believe you left me wide open like that! You lucked out, Riley." He was right. I did. There's no question it pained Bird to miss that shot, but I think it pained him even more that he missed a chance to put the dagger right between my eyes. Boy, did he love to win and let you know it.

When Larry played for the Celtics and I coached the Lakers, we were involved in knock-down, drag-out battles for the ultimate prize—the championship. People talked about the level of dislike, or even hatred, among our two teams, but it was more about a fierce attachment to the same goal.

I can still remember every play of that great Lakers-Celtics rivalry. I have never forgotten how Larry Bird affected the outcome. When you are striving for the same kind of greatness, you develop a lifelong respect for your adversaries, even though you rarely articulate it. I have always admired the level to which Larry Bird would go to fulfill his commitment to winning, the game, and his teammates. His commitment was sacred, and he made sure yours was too. If you wanted to play for rings, both teammate and opponent had to surpass his commitment.

I used to challenge Michael Cooper and anyone else who was charged with defending Bird. I told them, "You must raise the ante or this guy will embarrass you. He will take your heart out, stomp on it, then walk off the court with that sly grin on his face. He won't stop until he whips your ass." They had to hear that in order to have the respectful fear and alertness one needs to compete at his level. Come to play or Bird would bring you to your knees.

I found it interesting to learn that when Larry retired to Naples, Florida, in between golf rounds and a few cold Millers he spent some of his time tuning in to the Miami Heat games and watching me go through my coaching misery. I was flattered that he mentioned me favorably but also knew that if Larry got into coaching, my old Boston Celtics paranoia would alert me that these kind words were simply a way to soften me up and give him an edge. The truly good coaches and players always observe those they compete against. They study, they watch, they listen, they look for ways to beat them and their game. I've spent eighteen years studying all kinds of coaches, trying to identify the common denominator that makes their game work. I believe it's a *sincere, competent, reliable,* restlessly competitive *disposition* to dominate all aspects of the game. All good coaches have the knowledge, but it's their disposition and attitude that sets them apart. Bird reeks of it. It's not conjured up; it is simply there.

This disposition becomes the crucial conduit relating to your players. The players watch you like a hawk. It's like that Marvin Gaye and Tammi Terrell song many years ago, "Ain't Nothing Like the Real Thing." We saw the real thing in Bird. Right away you could see Larry Bird understood, from experience, what his players needed, wanted, and would tolerate. Larry's innate wisdom as to how to relate to his players was fascinating to watch. Some coaches never get it.

As an example, when Reggie Miller hit that big shot in the final seconds of Game 4 in the Eastern Conference Finals against Chicago in the 1998 playoffs, everyone on the Pacers team was going crazy except Larry. He coached. While his inner emotions were jumping for joy, he just stood there, devoid of any exterior emotion. The question is, was it conscious, or unconscious? He was coaching consciously to show the calm and collected demeanor he knew his players would require to close out the win. He knew they would look to him in that situation, and he knew there was still time on the clock, so he provided what they needed most—composure—just like he needed when he played.

When I look at how Larry has coached the Pacers, there's nothing complicated about it. What you see is what you get. He keeps it simple. His offense, defense, and rebounding operate on solid, basic principles. His team takes tremendous pride in playing extremely hard and doing the little things well. Bird's team rose to the occasion every night because he made them. I have also taken note of the comments Bird made to the press his first season, and it seemed as though everything he said was the right thing at the right time, for the right reason—not too much, not too little, but of *great impact.* It's obvious that his players respect and trust him and draw from his completeness as a former player, present coach, and honorable fair man. They know Larry Bird has no agenda other than to win and make them better.

That's why, when my team competes against his team, I know my guys better be in the right frame of mind, or they'll get their asses handed to them. Larry Bird is going to get you, just like he did when he was playing.

I have deep respect for Larry Bird. Our paths have crossed countless times in competition, but we have rarely talked at length. As a coach who wants to win, I don't believe in creating those kinds of relationships with people you are competing against, and from what I've been told, neither does Larry. One day when the competitive gloves come off for both of us and we can raise a couple of cold ones to help us along the way to the "remember whens," I believe we would enjoy each other's company. He reminds me of what the great warrior Tecumseh said: "I am a Shawnee. My forefathers were warriors. Their son is a warrior . . . From my tribe I take nothing. I am the maker of my own fortune." Yes, yes, he was a Celtic. He was proud to be a Celtic. While he may be a Pacer now, you get the feeling he came from a long line of warriors. His sons, daughters, and players will also be warriors. They will be taught to take nothing from their tribes. They will be taught to be the makers of their own fortune and, damn it, they will do it together.

I am proud to have competed against one of the greatest of all time. He has forced me to fear with respect, and that has forced me to prepare to get better. To teach my players that when we play his team the encounter will be for men only, and you better get ready to take the hit in all ways, shapes, and forms. But there will always be a quiet relief on my part as coach. That I won't be stupid enough to leave him wide open again, ever. I know better.

Pat Riley
Head Coach, Miami Heat

CHAPTER 1

On Retirement

On August 18, 1992, I announced my retirement from the Boston Celtics.

It was one of the happiest days of my life.

You have to understand how screwed up my back was at that point. I had been playing through back problems for almost ten years, and I just couldn't take it anymore. The pain was relentless. No matter what I did—whether I was standing up, sitting down, lying down, leaning over—I couldn't escape it. It had completely taken over my life. There were some days I couldn't even bend over to pick up a basketball, never mind try to shoot one. Some nights, I had to eat dinner sitting on the floor. Even lifting up my son, Conner, hurt so much that I had to stop doing it. When I'm hurting, and not able to play the way I want, I can be a pretty miserable person to be around. I don't know how my wife, Dinah, lasted through that last season of my career, because I was in pain all the time, which meant I was in a bad mood all the time too.

Maybe that's why when I walked up to the podium at my press conference in the Boards and Blades Club at

Boston Garden and finally said out loud that it was over, I felt like the weight of the world had been lifted off my shoulders. I can't tell you what a relief it was not to have to push myself through all that pain anymore.

I can honestly say I hated basketball at that point.

As soon as that press conference was over, me and some of my good friends, including my physical therapist, Dan Dyrek, went out and celebrated. There was nothing to be sad or sentimental about. It was time for me to be done.

I had known for months before the actual press conference that I wasn't going to play anymore. When my back started flaring up in training camp, before the start of the 1991–92 season, I knew that was probably it, but I don't think I actually admitted it to anyone—probably not even to myself, really—until January or February of 1992. I wasn't afraid of life after basketball. It was more a matter of finishing a job. I don't believe in giving up in the middle of anything. But it really wears you out when you are in constant pain. I had what they call a nerve impingement, which meant the L-4 vertebra was sitting twisted and compressed on the L-5 vertebra, and there was a nerve trapped in between the two. It left my spine very unstable. The bone kept pushing itself into the nerves in my back, and it was just terrible. Dan Dyrek would work on it so he could temporarily push the bone off the nerve, but before long I'd be feeling that burning pain shooting down my leg, and I'd be in serious trouble all over again.

By this time Dan had been treating me for almost a decade, and he was really concerned about the permanent damage I might be doing to myself. There were a whole bunch of times we had serious discussions about retirement. We came to a compromise, and worked out a system where we'd make decisions from game to game. Dan would examine me, and if my back was really "hot," or agitated where the disc was, he would tell me I had to sit out. If Dan gave me a thumbs-down, that was the final word for that night. Neither the Celtics nor I questioned him—most of the time. Looking back, it was a ridiculous way to finish my career, but at the time I just put my head down and tried to get through it.

I missed 37 games in my final season. People knew I was hurting, but very few of them had any idea how bad it really was. It got to the point where I was wearing a brace almost all the time except when I was practicing or playing. I even had to wear it to bed. I really hated that brace. It was made of a quarter-inch of fiberglass and went from my chest all the way down to my hips, and it was really uncomfortable. But I knew it was necessary. One thing is for sure: I wasn't going out much at that point. I didn't want anyone to see me in that thing.

The day I finally didn't need that brace anymore, I took it outside and destroyed it.

Even though I knew I was playing my last season, I kept it to myself. The last thing I wanted or needed was a big commotion at every city we went to. I had no interest in a retirement tour. Our team was still pretty competitive at that point and that's all I wanted to concentrate on, getting as deep as we could into the playoffs and, if we caught a break or two, maybe into the Finals. Of course the media was speculating on how much longer I'd play, but I wasn't saying a word.

Well, not publicly anyway. I do remember walking into Dan's office early in 1992 and telling him, "Dan, the back is really bad. Just get me through this season and I'll quit."

Dan said what he had been saying for over a year: "Larry, you should quit right now. Your back is unstable.

Every day you go out there, you are risking further damage. It's over. You have to stop playing."

I knew Dan was right, but I couldn't see quitting in the middle of the season. I promised myself I wouldn't do that, because people had bought season tickets that year thinking they were going to see me play. Most of them knew my back was bad and I might miss some games, but they were counting on seeing me at least some of the time, and I didn't want to let them down.

For the rest of the season I lived on anti-inflammatory drugs and wore that stupid brace. Both Dan and the Celtics trainer, Ed Lacerte, did the best they could to hold me together. It seemed we'd be talking every two weeks or so about retiring, but then I'd have a period of ten days or so where I felt okay, and that would be the end of it. Then, like it always did, the pain would come back. Both Dan Dyrek and Ed Lacerte have told me I played that last season in a state of unconsciousness.

The truth is, I should have retired a couple of years earlier, after I had my first back surgery in the summer of 1991. We had played Indiana in the first round of the playoffs that spring, and I was in really bad shape. The burning down my leg was so bad I couldn't feel my toes. I couldn't sit down, I couldn't stand up. I was in shock, really, but how could I stop in the middle of the playoffs? I remember after we lost Game 4 in Market Square Arena, it was about the worst I had ever felt. I wanted so badly to be healthy, because we had to go back to Boston for a deciding Game 5, and there was no way I could let that team beat us, because I didn't want to hear about it all summer from my friends who lived in Indiana.

I went to see Dan, and he started feeling around, and he said, "There's nothing more I can do for you." I left his office thinking, "Boy, this really is it." I got in the car and started driving, but the pain was so intense that I had to stop after about a mile and get out and walk around.

Somehow I managed to play Game 5 at the Garden. A lot of times I would feel lousy heading into the game, but after Dan worked on me a bit, and all my adrenaline got pumping, I could block it out. I knew I'd pay for it later, but that was later. We beat the Pacers in Game 5 and won the series, but not before I banged my head on the parquet floor chasing after a loose ball. I don't remember much of it, to be honest, because when they took me into the locker room I was in a daze. But I do remember one thing: after all I had been through with my back, no lump on the head was going to keep me out of the playoffs. I remember sitting in the locker room with our team doctor, Arnie Scheller, and after my head started clearing a little bit, I said to him, "Do I have a shot? Can I get back in there?" He said, "Hey, you've done enough. That's it for you." So we sit in that training room some more, and I keep hearing the crowd. They're chanting, "Lar-ry! Larry!" I look at Arnie, and I said, "Aw, hell!" and I get up, I run through that tunnel, back onto the court, and the place goes absolutely nuts. Later, when I got hired by the Pacers, Donnie Walsh said he knew I would play. He said he knew I'd come back, and the place would go crazy, and we'd win the game, which is exactly what happened. Even so, we couldn't sustain the momentum. We ended up losing to Detroit in six games in the next round, and a couple months after that I had my first back surgery.

The procedure involved shaving the disc, as well as widening the canal where the nerves that led to my spinal cord sat. I knew the surgery was not going to solve all my problems. In fact, the pain was back within a couple months. Fusion surgery had been an option, but the surgeons warned me that very few professional athletes had ever played again following fusion surgery, and I wasn't interested in being a guinea pig. The truth? I was just trying to buy myself some time.

The same day I had my first surgery, I went out and walked ten miles. My surgeon was very optimistic. He said, "You should come back in January and I'll take another look, but I think you are going to do just fine." Well, Arnie brought the surgeon to one of our first games of the season. This doc knows nothing about basketball—he's an old hockey player. He came in after the game and he said to me, "Larry, the way you play this game, you're not going to last another month. I had no idea you did all this stuff. Hell, you don't spend any time on your feet." He looked kind of worried, but I didn't pay much attention. I was feeling great!

At the time, we were 28–5, and on our way to the best record in the East at the All-Star break. Not very long after that, I was shooting around before the game, and I turned a little funny, and boom! There goes my back. I couldn't believe it. I knew right then that was the end of it. I was in and out the rest of the season.

Once I realized my back was still going to mess me up no matter what, I seriously considered retiring right then and there. Dave Gavitt, who had come to the Celtics in 1990 to run the team, kept talking me out of it. Not too many people can change my thinking when my mind is made up about something, but Dave was different. We hit it off from the first day we met. Dave had a lot of innovative ideas about how to help the team, and I loved talking about basketball with him. You can tell he was a former coach—he had some really good Providence teams back in the seventies—because of how he approached people. He understood how a player saw the game, and understood that a team needed to have an identity, and that whatever went on in the locker room, or on the floor, was something that should be shared among each other, like a family.

I was really excited when Gavitt took over as the team's CEO. We needed someone with his basketball expertise making personnel decisions. I was sure he'd be the one that would win us our next championship—until my back interfered.

I went into Dave's office about four months after my first back surgery and told him, "Dave, I don't think I can go on like this. I'm not the same player I was. I can't play the way I want to anymore, and I'm thinking I should retire." He put his arm on my shoulder and said, "Larry, I didn't come here to throw you a retirement party. I came here to help you win a championship." He gave me a little pep talk about how special our team was, and how the NBA would probably never see another front line like me, Kevin McHale, and Robert Parish again, and then he got into the whole thing about the Celtics tradition and what it meant to the city of Boston, which was why he had given up his job as commissioner of the Big East to take over the Celtics. I'm telling you, Dave was a pretty persuasive guy. He could get you all fired up. I knew he would back me up, whatever I decided, and I guess I didn't want to let him down. Besides, I agreed with him on one thing: we still had a chance to win a championship. As long as we still had a crack at that, it was going to be hard—impossible, really—for me to give up playing.

The last championship we won was in 1986. It was a dream season. Everybody played at the top of their games—me, Robert, Kevin, Dennis Johnson, Danny Ainge—and we had a great bench. We also had the two best centers in the league. That was the year Bill Walton played with us, and he was just phenomenal. He is the best passing big man I've ever seen, and I marveled at the things he could do, even though his feet were a mess and he wasn't anywhere near the player he had once been. That didn't matter on our team. Bill did what he could do, and that was more than enough. But what people tend to forget is that one of the big reasons Walton was able to have that kind of success was because of Robert Parish. Robert was an All-Star center, and he started every game, but there were many times when it was Walton, not Parish, who was on the floor in the fourth quarter. On a different team, with a different guy, that could have caused all sorts of problems. Some players get really protective about minutes, or when they are on the court and how much credit they're given, but not Robert. He was a true pro. He really didn't care how much he played, or when, as long as it worked for the team. That's why that year was so great, because it was all about winning. I'm sure there were some days that Robert wished he was out there, but he would never have said so. I'm sure, also, there were times Robert got tired of all the media attention Bill got—and believe me, it was a lot, which I appreciated, because it took some of the spotlight away from me—but in the end, Robert knew his team respected him, and that's all that really mattered.

Those are the kind of things I told my Indiana team when I took the Pacers job. Never mind what the outside world thinks—what do the guys who are on the court with you, day after day, think? Because they are the ones who know whether or not you've given them everything you have. I used to laugh when I read things in the paper about how important this guy was to our team, or how that guy wasn't helping us. Because many times they had it all wrong. Take Greg Kite. He was a center from Brigham Young who got drafted by the Celtics in 1983, and Bob Ryan, a sportswriter for the *Boston Globe,* was constantly killing him. He'd say things like, "He's a twelfth man that doesn't belong in the league, this and that," but what people don't understand is that most fans only see the games. They don't see practice. I always thought the practices were so important—I still believe that—to prepare other guys to play. That's why our 1986 team was so successful. We had Walton going against Parish every day. We had Scottie Wedman going against me for a number of years, pushing me every day. To the second unit, those practices were their games, especially to a guy like Kite who didn't play much. He wanted to beat us every day in practice. He never took a day off. He couldn't afford to. He was excellent for our team. He was a smart player, he knew everything we were doing, and he understood exactly what his role was. I wish I could find me a Greg Kite right now for the Pacers.

After that 1986 championship, everything fell apart. Walton stuck around another season, but he was hurt almost all of it, and he retired after playing only ten games in 1987. The Celtics drafted Len Bias that spring, and he died of a cocaine overdose. That was a real shock. I was taking a shower, and my mom came in and told me. I thought it was somebody's idea of a cruel joke. Then Kevin hurt his foot the next season, and by the time we got to the Finals against the Lakers, he was playing on a broken foot. It just seemed like we couldn't catch a break.

Just before the 1988–89 season, both of my heels started

really bothering me. This wasn't a new injury. I had always had some pain down there. Dan said it didn't help matters that I never stretched those Achilles tendons. He also said there had been some inflammation in that area for some time. But what took this pain to an unbearable level was that, over time, with repeated trauma to that area, I developed bone mass in both heels. There shouldn't be any bone anywhere near there, and it was embedded in the tendon. I tried to play through it, but it wasn't going to happen, so they decided to do surgery on both heels and take all that bone out. Dan was against the surgery. He thought he could treat me without it, but I wanted the pain to stop. I told him, "Let's just get the stuff out of there and worry about the rest of it later." Originally the doctors said I would miss about three months, but I ended up missing the whole season. I was miserable. It's no fun watching your team struggle while you're sitting there on the bench in street clothes.

When I started my rehab that summer I knew I would never be the same. My legs felt different. The surgery took all the life out of them. I did all the exercises and all the workouts they gave me, but I couldn't move the way I used to. I could still score and rebound and all that, but defensively it really affected me. I didn't have the same lift, or side-to-side movement. It was very, very frustrating, but there wasn't much use in talking about it. I could either play on or give it up, and I figured I had a lot more playing to do.

Of course, that was before I had any real idea of how bad my back would get. I guess I should have known. The doctors had told me I had congenital problems. I was born with a narrower canal than normal where the nerves lead to the spinal cord. Then there are the joints in my back, called the facet joints. They are supposed to be aligned a certain way. The left and right joints should be parallel to each other, but the ones on my right side were at all sorts of different angles. What all of this meant was my disc was going to slowly break down over the course of my life. Dan says I would have had back problems whether I was a professional athlete or not. Just through the wear and tear of every day, my spinal area was deteriorating, and the disc was degenerating. And the worse that disc got, the more excessive motion it caused in my back. That created a wobbly area that had very little stability.

All of that may have been true, but when you are a kid running around playing basketball and baseball and everything else, you don't want to know that stuff. I didn't have any major injuries as a kid growing up, unless you count a broken ankle that I got playing basketball. I had no way of knowing my back was going to give out on me.

My first real back problems cropped up in 1983, when I went home to my house in French Lick for the summer to do some work on my property. One of the first things I wanted to get done was to install some tile around my basketball court, to help with the drainage. I was never much on hiring people to do work I was perfectly capable of doing myself, and this job shouldn't have been a problem. I needed some gravel to seal it, so I got my brother and his friend Eddie to help me spread it. They weren't doing it the way I wanted, so I said the heck with it, and I took that truck full of gravel and did it all myself. It wasn't the best idea I ever had. I woke up the next morning and I said, "Something is wrong." My back was killing me. I couldn't walk around, much less work out, and I was worried. I had only been with the Celtics for four seasons at that point, and we had already won our first championship, but I knew that if we were ever going to win another one I was going to have to be even better than I was the year before.

I didn't want to have to tell the team I was hurt, so I didn't do anything for about two or three weeks, hoping the rest would make it all better. But by then it was July, and I knew I had to get moving with my conditioning and everything for the season, so I called the Celtics team doctor, Tom Silva, and told him what had happened. He told me to put lots of ice on it. I did that for the rest of the summer, but it wasn't helping much.

I remember really suffering through training camp. Doc Silva would alternate with heat and ice, heat and ice, but it wasn't working. I remember after we played Philadelphia in an exhibition game at home, the pain was so bad I went to Silva again and said, "We've got to try something else." He said, "Larry, I don't know what else to tell you." He called in Dr. Robert Leach, who examined me, then recommended I be seen by this physical therapist, Dan Dyrek, who he thought could help me. I agreed to see Dyrek at my house the next day.

He examined me in my living room, with Doc Leach and our trainer, Ray Melchiorre, watching. He was twisting me this way and that way, and digging into certain areas of my back, and everything he did hurt a whole lot. He explained what he was doing as he went along, and I was listening to everything he said, but I kept looking at Ray and Leach, because I knew them, and I wasn't sure what the hell was going on. I was only twenty-six years old, and I didn't like the looks on their faces.

My first impression of Dan was pretty good. At least he wasn't telling me I needed heat and ice, heat and ice, because it was pretty obvious that wasn't going to work.

I remember about an hour after they all left, I got up to turn on a light, and they were all standing in my driveway, still talking. I went back and told Dinah, "They're still out there. You know what that means. My back must be pretty screwed up."

Dyrek called me the next morning and explained that there was what he called a real "hot spot" in my back around the disc that he wanted to treat by mobilizing the tissues and tendons around that area. The idea was to manually manipulate that area to restore normal motion and take pressure off the disc. I said, "Let's start today."

That's how my relationship with Dan Dyrek came about. It started out as professional, but he's become one of my close friends. When you spend that much time with somebody, you find out what kind of person they are, and Dan was always a professional. I never worried that he would be talking to anyone about my treatments. And I could tell early on he knew what he was doing. When I first started seeing him, I was getting these major pains in my side that would last for more than ten seconds when I sat down. It was brutal. But after two or three weeks of seeing Dan, that pain gradually started going away. I ended up receiving treatment every other day for two years.

A couple of months after he started helping me, I offered Dan a couple of my tickets to a Celtics game. I knew he'd never ask for anything. I didn't even know if he was a sports fan until I saw his face when I gave him the tickets. He looked so excited, and surprised. I'm not the type to just go out and give my tickets to anyone, but I really appreciated how much Dan was helping me. So I gave him two tickets to each game for the rest of the season. We spent so much time together that our pregame treatments turned into little challenges. Just before it was time to take the court, Dan would ask, "How are you doing?" and I'd say, "I'm feeling like I can score forty-three points tonight." If I actually got to 43 points, we'd have some kind of prearranged signal, like a salute, and I'd turn and give it to him.

It was really important that I could trust Dan not to discuss my injuries. I didn't want the fans and the media to know every little thing that was wrong with me, but even more important, I didn't want the teams we were playing against to know! That's why nobody knew about the neck problems I was having about this same time. But that was nothing compared to my back.

My next serious back episode was in the summer before the 1989–90 season, when I went to a fund-raiser that the singer Kenny Rogers put on each year. I love Kenny Rogers's music, and I had been doing his charity event for three years or so and it was a lot of fun. He got four pro basketball players, four fishermen, four tennis players, and four golfers, and we all tried to play one another's sports.

I was still having some trouble with my back, but Dan had gotten me to the point where I had long stretches of being pain-free. I was feeling pretty good about the upcoming season.

We were in the final minutes of this charity basketball game when I went up for a rebound and came down a little sideways. Michael Jordan was going for the ball too, and he landed on my back. Right away I knew I was in trouble. My back started tightening up, and I could feel the pain coming on. The game was almost over, which was a good thing, because I was done. I just kind of stood there until it ended, and then I walked off the court without telling anybody what had just happened. Dinah was there with me, and she got on the phone to Dan and told him we needed to come up to Boston to see him. It was awkward, because the fund-raising people kept asking me to play tennis, but I couldn't, and I really didn't feel like explaining why.

Within a couple of days we were in Dan's office, and I could tell right away the news wasn't good. I had torn additional portions of the disc wall, and my back was really traumatized. I didn't know it then, all the way back in 1989, but that was the beginning of the end. Dan was able to treat me so I got better and was able to play, but I never came all the way back. For the rest of my career I had to rely on Dan to continually treat me and put things back in their proper place. We told the Celtics what had happened. They took it pretty well. The truth was, my back was so unstable, it was going to give way sometime. It wasn't like it was this violent collision; Michael didn't even land on me that hard. I was just at the point where I was an accident waiting to happen.

Nobody ever found out about that charity game—until now—which was good. There was nothing I hated more than talking about my injuries. It never helped them feel any better, and to me it always sounded like an excuse. Also, I found myself getting kind of superstitious. I remember one time, I had just finished practice at Hellenic College, which is where the Celtics used to hold all their workouts, and I was feeling fantastic. Peter May, a reporter who covered our team for many years, asked me how my back was feeling. I answered him, "Great!" I drove home from practice, lay down to take a nap, and I woke up with that horrible burning pain down my leg again. The next day, I was at the hospital getting injections. That's when I decided, "That's it. I'm not talking about my injuries anymore." I know it was hard for the reporters covering the team, but they got used to it. They knew that if I was cranky, it meant something was hurting. Near the end, that was every day.

It was just a grueling process. Dan would check my back to see if it had lost its alignment, because things were so unstable, the bones were prone to shifting, and that set off all sorts of spasms. But the worst part about it was that my back prevented me from practicing, and without all that time in the gym, my skills were deteriorating. I loved to practice, and I needed to practice, and my game really suffered when I didn't.

That played a part in my decision to retire, too.

My last game at Boston Garden was on May 15, 1992. We had beaten the Pacers 3–0 in the opening round of the playoffs and had Cleveland next. The Cavs were a good team, and had us down 3–2 heading into Game 6. It wasn't a memorable performance for me. I remember feeling a little off balance all night. My shot didn't feel the way I wanted it to feel, and everything was a little out of sync. But Reggie Lewis hit some foul shots at the end, and we won to tie the series 3–3. I wasn't thinking it was the last time I'd play in the Garden, because I truly believed we were going to beat Cleveland and come back home for the next round. But that didn't happen. The Cavaliers beat us at their place, and then—boom!—all of a sudden the season was over, and so was my career with the Celtics.

I hadn't told any of my teammates I was done, so there weren't any hugs or handshakes or anything like that. I'm sure some guys suspected, but nobody said anything. I just grabbed the game ball, stuffed it in my bag, and went home.

The official announcement didn't come for about another three months, because I had to play for the United States in the Olympics in Barcelona. When we decided it was time to let everyone know I was retiring, we called up everyone that morning and told them. I didn't want it to get leaked out ahead of time and have people camping out in front of the house. Better to get it over with all at once. Dinah decided to go back to Indiana. There was something going on in French Lick, and I think she really didn't want to be around to see it end. I remember she called me the night after the press conference and said she was getting her hair done at the beauty shop when the announcement came on over the radio. She said it got her all teary-eyed and everything. It was a big change for both of us. We had gone through all this pain and sweat, and now all of a sudden it was going to be over.

There were a lot of reporters at the press conference, even though we hadn't given them much advance notice. They wanted to know how I had spent the previous night preparing for the announcement. I told them I sat in my house in Brookline by myself, and watched old tapes of myself and cried. But that was crap, of course. I don't know why I said it. It just came out, and it sounded good. I remember I did sit home and I started thinking about it, and said to myself, "My God, this is really over. I'm really out of here." Then I started thinking back to when I first got there, and how I went in and saw the house that I really liked, and how much fun we had in that house, and then I started going through in my mind everything that happened during those thirteen years. More than anything, I was so thankful to have played in one place my entire career. That's something I believe is truly special, and I'm so glad it was with the Boston Celtics. I used to tell people, if you haven't played for the Boston Celtics, you haven't played professional basketball. I suppose that's a little bit of bull too, but it felt that way to me. I never tried to imagine wearing another uniform, because I couldn't have. I would have retired first.

Some of my friends think it's too bad the fans didn't know which one was my final game, because they didn't get to say goodbye, but they did. The Celtics held a retirement night for me, and it was one of the greatest things I've ever experienced. It was Dave Gavitt's idea. At first I didn't want any part of it. The way the Celtics usually retire jerseys is at halftime of a game, but Dave said it would be almost impossible to get the ceremony done in such a short time, and it would be disruptive to the game. His idea was to sell tickets to a Larry Bird Night, and donate all the proceeds to charity. The way he envisioned it was to have me onstage, in uniform, and have various people who were important throughout my career come up and talk with me. He also wanted to fly in Magic Johnson from L.A. to be there, which I thought was a great idea, because the two of us were so closely connected throughout our careers. Dave thought Magic should be in his Lakers warm-ups, and I should be in my Celtics warm-ups. I fought him a little on that, but I finally gave in. Dave also thought I should take one last shot, but there was no way I'd agree to that. I told him, "Dave, I've already taken all the shots I'm going to take."

Anyhow, once I said yes to this Larry Bird Night, I got concerned about it. Who would come? There wasn't any game being played. But once it was announced, it sold out in a matter of minutes. Everyone got pretty excited about it. Mark Lev, who worked in the marketing department for Boston, came up with the idea of selling 1,033 limited edition Leroy Neiman prints, signed by both Neiman and me, for $1,033 each, with that money going to charity as well. (The additional 33 was for my uniform number.)

The night itself is one I'll never forget. I still can't get over all those people showing up, just to cheer for me. When they cheer for you in a game, you never know if it's because of the play the whole team just made, or because they love the Celtics, or what. But that night, I really appreciated their applause. Bob Costas, who agreed to fly in and be the emcee at no charge, was great. Magic was his usual charming self. My mom made a rare appearance in Boston to attend, and my son, Conner, who was just a baby, helped me raise my number to the rafters.

We raised over $1 million for thirty-three different charities. We gave money to everyone from Celtics Wives Save Lives (to benefit breast cancer research) to Shriners Hospital for Crippled Children. It wasn't easy choosing where the money should go, because there were so many worthy causes. I remember that at the time, Conner loved the show *Barney,* so I asked that we give something to the public television station that aired it. I wanted to make a donation to the Colonel Daniel Marr Boys and Girls Club, because I had seen for myself all the good they had done, and I wanted to make sure we gave a new van to a homeless shelter in town called Rosie's Place. Some of the donations involved personal connections too. We gave money to an Alzheimer's foundation named after M. L. Carr's father, who died of the disease, as well as to the Red Auerbach Youth Foundation. I also wanted New England Baptist Hospital, whose staff had taken care of me all those years, to receive a donation.

People ask me all the time if I regret playing through all that pain, and if I would do it over again, knowing what I know now. When I list all of the things that went wrong with my body, it sounds like I'm whining about my injuries, and I hate that. That's why you didn't hear me talking about them when I was playing. It was the *last* thing I wanted to talk about.

I will say this: I should have retired after my first back surgery. I wish I had. But the mentality of our team was to play through anything, to do whatever it takes, and most of us did that. Like when Kevin had that broken foot. We knew it was bad, and if he had decided he couldn't play, we would have lived with it. We would have understood. But the truth is, we all knew Kevin wasn't going to sit, because he knew we had a chance at a championship that season, and those chances don't come too often. I'm sure McHale has some regrets. We lost to the Lakers in the Finals in 1987, and from what I understand, all these years later that foot still gives Kevin some trouble. You hate to hear that.

I think one of the problems with our league today is that guys will sit out more now if they're injured because they don't want to ruin their reputation of being a great player, and it's hard to perform at your top level when you're injured. The other thing is that guys whose contracts are up figure they stand to make a lot of money, so why push it if you don't have to? Then there's the agents. These young kids are letting other people make their decisions for them, and that's too bad. A kid like Marcus Camby, he's got all this talent, but he's hurt so much it doesn't matter. You feel like telling him that if he tries to play through some of the nagging injuries he might actually feel better. I played some of my best games when I had a muscle pull or I was sick. You come in that night figuring you can't feel any worse, and when you finally get out there and run around a little bit, you tend to forget about what was bothering you.

One thing I've tried to understand as a coach, though,

is that everyone handles pain differently. Some people know how to play through it. Others just can't. You have to be realistic. I like to see guys play through twisted ankles, stuff like that. When it gets to more serious injuries, though, only you can decide how far you want to push yourself. My whole thing is, if you don't think you can play, then don't. And if you can, then go out there and do it, but don't spend a whole lot of time talking about it. Nobody else knows your pain threshold but you. Sometimes I'd complain privately to Dan Dyrek and say, "Why isn't this guy playing tonight? We could use him." But Dan would always tell me, "Larry, you have an unbelievably high threshold of pain. You can't expect other people to have that same threshold, because they don't. It's not fair to question how much people are willing or able to put themselves through. That's just not fair." I've tried to remember that in dealing with my own players.

So was all that suffering worth it? When you look around Boston Garden and see 15,000 people there, then it's worth every minute. I loved looking around and seeing every seat filled. That's a special feeling I'll never forget.

There are some other things I would rather forget. A few years after I retired, I was in Boston with a friend of mine who was having back trouble, and I called up Dan Dyrek and asked him if he could take a look at him. Dan's offices were in a new place, but even so, the minute I walked in there and started remembering all the pain I had gone through, I felt sick. Dan looked at me and said, "Larry, you look pale. Are you all right?" I took one look around and answered, "As long as I never have to come back here, I'll be fine."

CHAPTER 2

On the '92 Olympics

I can't think of a better way to end my career than to play for the United States in the 1992 Olympics. Ever since I was a little kid, I used to love it when the Olympics were on television. I really wish my father would have been around to see that gold medal put around my neck. I can remember way, way back, always watching the Olympics with my dad. They'd play that national anthem, and he'd perk right up. He fought in the Korean War, and he was really very proud of our country. He'd watch that flag go up, and he'd say, "God, that must be a great feeling."

Then all those years later, there I am in Barcelona, getting my own gold medal. He would have loved to see that. So would Mom. She watched it all on television, but she didn't come over to Barcelona with us.

It never occurred to me that I might get to be in the Olympics. Back before our 1992 team was chosen, and nicknamed the "Dream Team" because it was full of so many big NBA stars, the Olympic basketball team was always made up of college players. The problem was that the Olympics were only every four years, so if you were, say, a sophomore in college in an Olympic year, and you were coming on but were not quite the player you were going to be, chances are you'd miss out, because the Olympic committee was going to pick guys who were at the top right then and there, usually upperclassmen. So by the time the Olympics came around again, you'd be in the pros. That's pretty much what happened to me. I went to Indiana during the 1974–75 season, but left school before the basketball season even began. The following season, 1975–76, was an Olympic year. By then I had transferred to Indiana State, but had to sit out a year before I was eligible to play. By the time the next Olympics came around in 1980, I was just finishing up my rookie year with the Celtics.

Like a lot of guys, including Magic Johnson, I figured the Olympics was something that just wasn't going to happen for me. So in 1991 when I started hearing talk that they were considering adding pros to the competition, I didn't pay much attention. I figured I was too old. By the time the Olympic team went to Barcelona, I would be thirty-five years old. Besides, my back was as bad as it had ever been.

At that time Dave Gavitt was the CEO of the Celtics, but he was also president of USA Basketball. He told me they had been quietly working for some time with the NBA to make the Olympic team available to professionals. Nobody was sure whether anyone would be interested, but Dave figured if he could convince the best players to commit to playing, then everyone else would follow suit. Dave was smart. He went after Magic first, because at that point Magic was "retired" because he was HIV-positive, but was still itching to play. Magic said yes right away.

Then Dave came to me and told me Magic was playing and they wanted me on the team. My first reaction was, "No way." I told Dave, "Look, I'm too old for that. It should be a chance for some younger guys." But Dave wouldn't let it drop. He told me I was being given a chance to play for the Olympics, for maybe the best team ever assembled in basketball history. Then he started talking to me about the team spirit, and the fellowship and patriotism and all that. In the meantime, once the word got out that I had this invitation, the phone started ringing.

It seemed like everybody I knew wanted me to go to the Olympics. They didn't understand why I was hesitating. But the reason I was trying to get out of it was because I knew my back would be just awful, and I had been through enough pain. I just wanted to retire and forget all about basketball for a while. But all these people kept calling me and telling me I should do it. They all said the same thing to me: "You've worked your whole life to get to this point. You've earned this." That might have been true, and I really did want to play, but under the circumstances I just didn't feel I could do it.

There was another thing bothering me. I wanted to make sure they wanted me for the team because they felt I was still good enough, not because they wanted me in some kind of honorary role. I never wanted to take a spot that I didn't earn. I looked Dave Gavitt in the eye and told him, "You better tell me the truth. Do you want me because I can still play, or do you want me because I'm Larry Bird?" He looked right back at me and said, "Larry, in international basketball they play zone defense. How many guys can pass and shoot the ball like you?" He made a pretty good point.

I thought about it some more, and decided I'd give it

a try. Then Gavitt went to work on Michael Jordan. He told him he had me and Magic, and didn't Michael want to be a part of history too? Next thing you know, Michael signed on. By then, everybody really started clamoring to play. Before long, Patrick Ewing, Karl Malone, John Stockton, Chris Mullin, David Robinson, Scottie Pippen, and Charles Barkley had agreed to be on the team. The good thing about it was they didn't have any tryouts, because that could have gotten really ugly. The original plan was to have eight pros and four college players, but the response from the NBA guys was so overwhelming that the committee decided to pick ten pros and leave two spots open. The idea was that if one pro had a really unbelievable year, he'd be added, but if no guy emerged, they'd take two college players. In the end, the pro who had the great year turned out to be Clyde Drexler. He was put on the team along with Christian Laettner, the only college player, who had just finished up a great season at Duke. He beat out a big center from LSU, a kid by the name of Shaquille O'Neal, for the final spot, in part because his team had more success, and in part because he had put more time into playing international competition through USA Basketball.

Of course there was going to be some controversy over who didn't make it, and the one guy most people were talking about was Isiah Thomas. I know he must have been hurt by it. Hell, Isiah was one of the top players in the league. He helped Detroit win two championships. He was one of those special players and, to be honest, I wondered myself why he wasn't on the team. The problem with a selection process like that is a lot of guys are going to be left off. You always know somebody is going to be left unhappy.

For those of us who did make it, we all understood it was an honor. Even Michael, who had played on a gold medal Olympic team before, said how great it was to be part of the Dream Team. Our first training camp was in San Diego, and it was amazing to see all these players in one gym and on the same team. Right away, the atmosphere was loose. The first day, Magic was busting on everyone in sight, and that set the tone for the whole Olympic experience.

Magic liked to tease the other guys about all his rings. I never said anything about it. Magic did all the talking about the championships. One day me and Magic were shooting around at one basket and Patrick Ewing came over. Magic took one look at him and said, "Get out of here." Patrick said, "What's with you?" And Magic said to him, "You don't belong at this basket." Patrick is all confused, and he says, "Why not?" Magic says to him, "Hey, you haven't won nothing!" So then he shouts over to Barkley, "Hey Charles, you might as well just stay over there too, 'cause you haven't won anything either!" That's Magic for you. So now he's got everybody in the gym going. I'm getting all embarrassed about it, but Magic says, "Hey, if you've got championship rings, you can shoot at this basket. Let's see. I've got five of them, and Larry's got three. We've got eight championship rings over here. What do you guys have?" Next thing you know, Michael is coming over, and at that time he had won two titles. So Magic starts shouting, "Okay, then. Now we got ten rings." He sees Scottie Pippen laughing, and he says, "Hey Scottie, you want to come over and shoot with us? Then we'll have an even dozen. You don't want to be over there with all those losers, do you?" We were all cracking up.

Everyone got caught up in the Olympic fever. Everywhere we went, people were urging us on. I remember one night in San Diego, me and Ed Lacerte, the Dream Team trainer, who had also been my trainer with the Celtics, went out with Bill Walton. Bill lived in San Diego, and he took us to this restaurant where he thought we might not be bothered too much. So we're sitting in this Mexican place having dinner, when these people come up and ask us for our autographs. Ed is sitting in between us, so after I signed the paper, he took it and passed it over to Bill. After Walton signed, the people said to Eddie, "Can we have your autograph too?" Ed said to them, "No, you don't want my autograph." The people said, "Oh yes we do, John. Please?" They thought Ed was John Stockton. Eddie kept saying, "No, really, you don't want my autograph," but these people were persistent. Finally I said, "John, just sign it for these nice people." So Ed signed Stockton's name, and the people left. I turned to Eddie and said, "If you're going to hang out with us, you've got to remember one rule: sign it and move on."

We really did have a lot of laughs. The best part about it was nobody tried to pull any star treatment. If you needed to be taped, it was first come, first served. No egos involved. I remember one day in San Diego, Charles Barkley was carrying coolers out to the truck for the medical staff. It was that kind of atmosphere. Michael Jordan was treated the same as all the rest of us, and he didn't mind, either.

It's funny, because I've gotten to know Michael so well in the last few years, but I never did any of my commercials with him until after I retired, so I didn't know him all that well in Barcelona. Michael played golf every day. We hardly ever had practice, so he'd be gone first thing in the morning to play eighteen or thirty-six holes. He'd play on game days too. He'd finish up like an hour and a half before it was time to get on the bus and go to the arena. I did play golf with him a couple of times. Me, Michael, and Magic got together one night too. They had a room downstairs from our hotel with everything in it, and the three of us went down there with Michael's buddy Ahmad Rashad, drank a few beers, and talked. It was a nice change, to be all on the same side like that, something I'm sure none of us ever dreamed would be possible. We talked a lot about basketball, and the times we played against one another. As usual, Michael and I were cracking on Magic. At one point Ahmad asked us who we thought was the best basketball player ever. After a lot of discussion, we all came to the conclusion that Michael was the best—not every night, though.

One of the things that was really disappointing to me was I wasn't able to march in the opening ceremonies of the Olympics. The problem was that the whole thing, from start to finish, was going to take around four hours, and my back wouldn't have made it. I couldn't stand for more than a half hour without stiffness and pain. Dave Gavitt tried to arrange it so I could slip in and out of the march, but they wouldn't let us do that, for all sorts of security reasons. I wish I could have done it. Magic and Charles and David Robinson and some of the others marched, and they said it was a great experience. But I knew the fact that I was in Barcelona at all was stretching it, so I had to take what I could get.

One night, the people of the city of Barcelona arranged to have a restaurant closed down, and the whole team went there for dinner. That was one of my favorite nights. Everybody showed up, and we had a lot of laughs, and nobody could get to us because they had police stationed all over the place, inside and outside the restaurant. It was always fun to be around that team, because the guys always had something going. I can remember Scottie and Clyde going at each other. One little joke could turn into one big hoot on somebody, and everybody would put in their two cents worth. It reminded me a little bit of our 1986 Celtics championship team. We had a lot of big personalities—Kevin McHale, Bill Walton—and it seemed like somebody was always getting it.

For all the fun I had, the basketball was very, very tough. I really shouldn't have been playing. I was hoping the rest I had since May, which is when the Celtics were eliminated from the playoffs that year, would help, and it did for a while. When we had that training camp in San Diego I was surprised at how good I felt. I even actually worked out a little bit. I couldn't go out and practice for two or three hours, but I could go out there for forty-five minutes and do some things. We played our first game, and I felt great. I was talking to the press about how exciting it all was, and then I felt it. It was that awful burning pain again, shooting right down my leg. I was devastated. Right away, I went to Dave and said, "Look, you might as well replace me. I can't do this."

He said, "Look, Larry, I know you're hurting. You don't have to practice to be on this team. You've come this far. Try to hang in there. Think of all you've been through to get here."

That much was true. I was really in bad shape finishing up the season with the Celtics. I needed a lot of treatment, and a lot of anti-inflammatory drugs and painkillers to make it through. One of the things we had to be really careful about was monitoring the medication they were giving me. The Olympic committee had very strict rules about what kind of drugs were allowed in an athlete's system.

One of the drugs that was banned was steroids. When my back got really unstable and my nerves got extremely inflamed, one of the treatments we resorted to was a steroid injection in my back. Once I decided to play in the Olympics, we had to be careful about using that as a method of treatment, because we were concerned residues of it could show up in a drug test. Everyone kept telling me it would probably be fine, but the truth was we couldn't be 100 percent sure, so a lot of times I didn't take the shot, even though I really could have used it.

By the time we went to Portland for what they called the Tournament of the Americas, I was in agony. I didn't think I could keep it together much longer. I flew home to Boston from that tournament in my back brace. As soon as I got home, I got in my car and drove to Massachusetts General Hospital to see Dan Dyrek. When he saw me walking down the hall toward him, I know he was shocked, because I never, ever saw him without an appointment. I barely said hello. I told him, "I need to talk to you." We went into his office, and I said, "Dan, I'm not going to the Olympics. I tried to fight through this, and I can't." He knew I wasn't exaggerating. If I couldn't even get out of bed, it was a waste of time for me and the Olympic committee to go all the way over there. Dan was quiet, because he knew how important it was for me to be part of that Dream Team. I finally said, "There's only one way I can do it. You have to come with me." It was a really big thing for me to ask him, I knew that. We were leaving for Monte Carlo in a few days for our last leg of training, and Dan was a busy guy. Aside from his patients, he was teaching a graduate school course. But I wasn't going to the Olympics unless Dan Dyrek came with me. Simple as that.

Dan really didn't know what to say. I could tell his mind was going a mile a minute, trying to figure out how he could make this happen. He finally said, "Okay, listen. I'm going to have to change a few things around. Let me see what I can do." He smiled, and then he said, laughing, "You better send my secretary about two hundred red roses, for all the work she's going to have to do in the next twenty-four hours."

The next day, when Dan Dyrek's secretary showed up for work there were two hundred red roses waiting for her in the office. Dan called me up and said, "Hey Larry, about the roses. I was only kidding." I told him, "I know that, Dan, but I also know how much work it took to get this done."

Dan ended up coming with me to Barcelona, and I think it must have been a great experience for him. Of course, once the guys all got to know him, he was helping them out with their little problems too. In the meantime we were falling like flies. I had back problems, Patrick dislocated his thumb, then John Stockton broke his leg. I guess at one point there was a meeting among USA Basketball and NBA officials, and some people wanted us injured people replaced on the roster. But Dave Gavitt and some others got up and reminded everyone that it wasn't like the gold medal was in jeopardy. The truth was, and everyone knew it, we were much better than any of the other teams, whether Patrick, John, and I played or not. To Dave it would have been suicide to alter the Dream Team at that point. Dave told the committee, "These players are the ones our fans want in Barcelona." And that was the end of that.

According to Olympic regulations, the numbers on our jerseys had to go from 4 to 15. I wore number 7. The protocol for drug testing there was kind of old-fashioned. We'd be in the middle of a game, and this drug official would walk down to our bench and have Eddie Lacerte pull three numbers out of a box. If one of the numbers matched your uniform, then you were the one tested, whether you played that day or not. It was a random test, but for some reason the first two times it was done, my number came up. I remember the first time, the game had ended, and I was running off the court, and this guy came up and grabbed me. Another guy grabbed Chris Mullin, and they took us in the bathroom and stood there with us while we gave them a urine sample. I remember standing there thinking, "First time out. Just my luck." I was a little nervous taking that first test, but it came up clean. When it happened the second time, and my number got picked again, I said to Eddie, "What are you trying to do to me?"

The funny part of it was that I wasn't really worth testing. A lot of games, I spent most of my time on my stomach on the floor in front of the bench, trying to get comfortable watching while everyone else kicked butt out there. There were some games I didn't play in at all during the Tournament of the Americas in Portland, my back was so bad. In one of those games, I was at my usual spot on the floor when this Latin American official ran by our bench. I hadn't played at all, and as he ran by he said, "Mr. Bird, Mr. Bird, please, you must come in the game." I was looking at him, wondering what he was talking about. He said, "I must be able to tell my family I refereed a game in which the great Larry Bird was playing." Of course, it was my luck Magic and Michael were sitting on the bench with me at the time. Next thing I know, they're pulling off my warm-up jersey and telling Chuck Daly to get me in there.

Being part of that Olympic team was one of the best times I've had in my life. The guys were always up for a good time, and somebody was always busting on somebody else. We lived in this building that had really small hotel-style rooms, and it was protected by a whole bunch of security guards. There was always a huge crowd of people waiting for us to come out the front door. Day or night, it didn't matter. Everybody wanted to see the Dream Team.

The whole time I was in Barcelona, the one thing I wanted to do was go watch the United States play baseball. So one morning I got up and I told Dinah, "I'm not going to lay in bed today. I don't care how bad my back is feeling, I'm gonna go out and watch a baseball game." It was hotter than hell, but I didn't care. I told Dinah, "I'm going by myself and people aren't going to bother me. I'm just going to do this." No matter what happened, I was determined to see the baseball game. So I grab my things and I go down to the lobby, and sure enough, there are thousands of people just standing there, waiting. They were mostly roped off by police, but it was a certified mob scene and I didn't want any part of it. I was starting to get upset, because I needed to get a break. I go to the back, and I find this security guy, and I say, "How can I get out of here? I know there must be another way out. If I go out that front door I'm going to have people all over me, and I really don't want that. Please. I know you must know a different way." The guy looks at me, and says, "Just go out this door right here, walk up one block, take a right, and hop on the subway. That's the best way to get to the baseball stadium." I couldn't believe it. I said to the guy, "You're kidding! You mean all this time I could have just walked out that door?" He said, "Sí, señor." So I said, "Adios!" and grabbed my bag and I was off. Once I got on the subway, I knew people would recognize me, but they were great about it. They said, "Hey Larry, where you going?" and I told them I wanted to see some baseball. Everyone was really nice. They even showed me which stop to get off at. So I'm walking toward the baseball game, and somehow I get caught up with this big group of people. They're all from the United States, and they're shouting, "USA! USA!" I get right in the middle of them, because I'm figuring I won't stand out so much, and they start yelling, "We're gonna kick ass!" We get up to the field, this crowd of Americans, and some official tells us they've switched the venue.

By now I'd say there's around three hundred people milling around, looking for baseball, so I ask the official where we have to go. He pulls out a map, and it's about twenty-five miles away, and the game is starting in forty-five minutes. Me and this group of people run out to catch a bus, but there's a huge crowd and a line, so we get back on the subway, and it takes us about forty-five minutes to get to the right baseball field. We had to walk a mile from the subway to get there, and my back started hurting, but I didn't care. I was having fun. The U.S. was playing Japan that day, and it was absolutely fantastic. It was a beautiful day, and me and my new friends I met on the subway took turns going to the concession stands to get beers. I hadn't enjoyed myself like that in a long time. The truth is, I've always loved baseball. When I played for the Celtics I went to Fenway Park a couple of times to watch the Red Sox, but I stopped going, because I spent the whole time signing autographs, and I didn't get to watch any of the games. I always felt that was too bad, because our house in Brookline was so close to Fenway.

Anyhow, I had such a great time at that baseball game, when I left the guys asked me if I'd be back, and I said, "Sure. See you tomorrow." The Dream Team never had any practice, because we really didn't need it, and the next game didn't start until midnight the next night, so the next morning I got up and said to Dinah, "C'mon, you've got to go with me to this game. It's absolutely wild. You'll love it." So off we go, through the side door, and when we get to the baseball stadium the same group of guys I hung out with the day before are there, taking turns with the beers. I went to more games, and every time I went I brought more and more people with me. By then the U.S. team had found out I was watching all their games, so one of the team officials asked if I would go down on the field after the game and say hello. I said I'd be glad to do that. I went down there and met some of the players, and found out later the U.S. was fined because someone other than a team official or player had been on the field.

I loved those baseball games, and I loved the freedom that side door had given me. One time when I was in the lobby I watched Magic getting ready to go out. I was thinking about telling him about the side door, and then I realized he wasn't interested in that. Magic would never go out a side door. The whole time in Barcelona, every time he went somewhere he'd bring along four guys with machine guns and walk right out front. That draws even more attention, but that's how Magic liked it. That's the difference between him and me. He would march out there and people would go crazy, and he would love it. Me? I was just happy nobody found out my little secret escape.

It was a little strange being there in Barcelona, know-

ing it was the last time I would ever play basketball. I'm
sure there were plenty of people that suspected it was true,
but the only one I had really told at that point was Dan
Dyrek. I didn't say anything to Michael or Magic or Patrick
about it. I do remember warming up for the gold medal
game, and we were doing a layup line, and I said to myself, "Well, this is it. This is gonna be my last game ever.
I think I'll dunk one of these layups." So I go in and come
up under the basket to dunk it, and Jordan was coming
from the other side of the line to get the rebound. I knew
right away I wasn't high enough up. Michael kind of
laughed and said, "Hey, leave that part of it to me." We
switched over to the other side, and I went up again, and
I dunked one. It was just one of those crazy things. I was
warming up for that game, and I just got it in my head,
"You know, I should dunk this ball."

I don't know why things like that pop into my head. It
used to happen all the time when I was playing. I'd be in
the middle of a big game, running down the court, and then
I'd start thinking, "I wonder if Granny is watching today."
I'd always catch myself and say, "Stop that. Think about
what you're doing," but every once in a while I'd be running out there and start thinking, "I've got to remember to
water my lawn tomorrow," or, "Oh, wow, I forgot. I've got
to meet those people after the game."

I don't have too many vivid memories of the actual
gold medal game. It was such a foregone conclusion we
were going to win the whole thing that there never was
any real drama to the Olympics, in terms of the competition. I do remember I didn't play at all in the first half.
Dave Gavitt was all upset about that. He said to me afterward, "You deserved to be out there." But honestly, it
didn't really bother me that much. By that point I just

wanted to get out of Barcelona. For me, after playing in
the first game, that was it. That was the biggest thrill—to
say you were an Olympian. When you know all along you
are going to win it, that's a different kind of feeling. I
probably would have cared more if my back felt better,
but I was really hurting, and the game didn't start until
eleven o'clock that night so that everyone back in the
United States could watch it live. We were leaving that
night after the gold medal game, and it was going to be
a long, long flight home, and that was on my mind a little bit.

We were in the locker room at halftime and Chuck Daly
came up to me and said, "Hey, I forgot about you in the
first half." I told him, "Hey, don't worry about me." Of
course you want to get in there for a few minutes in the
gold medal game. But I played more than I ever imagined
I could in the Olympics, more than I should have, actually. I think I averaged around seventeen minutes a night.

The ceremony to receive our gold medals was awesome. Just standing up there and listening to the national
anthem was something I'll never forget the rest of my life.
I swear to God, I always wanted to hear that national anthem, and know how it would feel to have a gold medal
around your neck, and watch them raise the American flag.
It was the greatest feeling ever—the greatest feeling in the
world.

I don't remember exactly where I was standing, but I
had to be standing next to Patrick Ewing. Patrick and I
became good friends during the Olympics. I had no relationship with him before that, but I always appreciated
that he was tough and he played hard and he wasn't interested in second place. He wanted to win it all, just like
I always did. I always hoped Ewing would win a cham-

pionship. I still hope that, as long as Indiana isn't playing the Knicks along the way.

I don't think Patrick liked me very much before the Olympics, which is good. He was a Knick and I was a Celtic, and that's how it should have been. He was never the kind of guy who would initiate a conversation with you, but he's a lot different than most people think. He's a big, imposing guy, but he's really pretty softhearted. I first got friendly with Patrick in Portland, just from trading wisecracks, really. We went out to eat a couple times, and like so many of these guys, we realized we had a few things in common. He had a buddy of his whose nickname was Baby, who I thought was just the greatest guy. He was one big teddy bear, and he was a blast to be around. I still don't know his real name. I got the biggest kick out of him, so me and Baby and Patrick were always together in Portland.

We started calling Patrick "Harry," after this character in a movie called *Harry and the Hendersons*. Patrick had dislocated his thumb and he wasn't playing, and neither was I because of my back, so the guys started ragging on us, calling us "Harry and Larry." The team trainer, Ed Lacerte, had these T-shirts made up that read, THE HARRY AND LARRY SHOW . . . TO BE CONTINUED IN BARCELONA.

Then, when our training camp switched to Monte Carlo, me and Patrick used to meet up at the pool every day. The girls up there were all topless. Our wives and kids were with us and everything, but Patrick would get up there and put on a pair of dark sunglasses, and we'd be laughing about the whole thing.

So the first day I'm up at the pool, my friend Quinn Buckner is with me, and Dinah was there, and some other people, and we're all hanging out on one side of the pool, and there's Patrick on the other side, lying in the shade. He hollers out something to me, and I say, "Hey Patrick, buy me a beer!" because the beers in Monte Carlo were something like eight bucks, and I was having a hard time justifying paying that much. I was just kidding Patrick, of course, but about two or three minutes later a waitress comes over and says, "That man over there would like to buy all of you a beer." We say, "Okay, great," but by this time some of our other friends have come up, and it's getting to be a crowd. A little while later the lady comes back and says, "Would you like something else?" and I say, "No, no, this is fine." She's still standing there, and she says, "He says to order anything you want." So we sat there and we drank some beer, and there were six or eight people. The next time I see Patrick I said, "Geez, I bet that beer bill was pretty steep." He said, "I don't know, I just signed it, I didn't really look at it." It had to be at least a couple hundred dollars, but he was waving it off like nothing. I said to him, "Do you know how much those beers cost?" He said, "No." I said, "They were eight bucks apiece." Patrick looks at me and says, "Yep." I told him, "Eight bucks apiece, Patrick." He says, "So what do they usually go for?" I tell him, "Back in the States you pay a buck and a half for a beer." He says, "Oh, okay." But to him it was nothing. Here I was dying, all day at the pool, worrying about this bill we were running up, and he could have cared less. That's when I put my arm around him and said, "Patrick, you can hang around me the rest of the trip."

Whenever I see Patrick now, I smile and I think about those eight-dollar beers. They were some of the best beers I've ever tasted.

CHAPTER 3

On My Time
in the Front Office

When I retired and took Dave Gavitt up on his offer to work in Boston's front office, it was an easy decision. I couldn't imagine working for any other team. But over time that changed.

I knew my days with the Celtics were over when I told our owner that Sherman Douglas was the most valuable guy on our team, and then he traded him a month later.

That was in October of 1995. I had been working in Boston's front office for three years at that point, and I was getting more and more frustrated, because Paul Gaston, the owner, and my old teammate M. L. Carr, who was the general manager, would ask my advice about certain personnel moves, then turn around and do whatever they wanted. I mean, why ask my opinion if you don't really care what I think? Paul Gaston always told me I could have any job I wanted in the organization, but the truth was I had very little input. I think Gaston had trouble looking at me as anything except a former superstar, like some kind of figurehead. In a way I can understand that, because the first couple of years after I retired I wasn't around much, but whenever I did come to town everyone wanted to know what I thought about this player or that player. There's no question I had achieved a level of respect in Boston, but I spent a lot of years earning that respect. I think it was hard for Gaston to have me around sometimes, because it seemed like no matter what he did he took a beating in the press, while in their eyes I could do no wrong.

I was named special assistant to the team's CEO, Dave Gavitt, in 1992, right after I retired. In fact, Dave made the announcement at my final press conference as a player. He told me he was really looking forward to working with me, and talked about how he really thought he could put the Celtics back on top. He had all sorts of great ideas about making the team better. He was also very creative. For example, he was the one that arranged to put all the Celtics legends together for the closing of Boston Garden. He understood about the little stuff too. One of the first things he did when he got hired was have the practice locker room completely done over. All it really meant was a couple of coats of fresh paint, but it meant a lot to the team. Dave Gavitt was a guy who talked to players. He knew which guys needed a little pep talk, and which guys needed a kick in the butt, and he got his message across without seeming like some guy interfering. He was fun to watch. The main reason I was interested in the job at all was because of Dave.

Unfortunately, by the time I was really ready to become a factor in the front office, Dave Gavitt was gone. Officially, he resigned, but the Celtics owners kind of forced him out, which is really too bad, because Dave Gavitt is a genius. He is very straightforward, which I've always liked in a person, and he treated me great. I guess in a way he was sort of a father figure to me. I know he's the one that pushed for me to be part of the Dream Team, which is one of the most memorable experiences I've had. Plus, he understood the game. He never would have traded Sherman Douglas!

When Dave first hired me I would have been more enthusiastic about my contributions if my back wasn't so bad at that time. People kept asking me if I missed playing, but I couldn't have played anymore even if I wanted to. Every time I made any kind of sudden movement, this burning pain would shoot down my leg. I kept thinking that since I was retired, one day I would wake up and the pain would finally be gone, but I was wrong. The doctors were hoping my nerves would calm down, and I tried all sorts of treatments and stretching exercises to make that happen, but I was still miserable.

Finally I called up Dan Dyrek and said, "Dan, I can't handle this pain anymore. Mentally, it's really gotten to me." Dan told me it was time to have fusion surgery. It's a pretty serious operation. In my case, it meant removing pieces of bone on the side of my spine where the nerve exits, which would widen the canal from where the nerve exits to my leg. They were also going to have to put screws into my L-4 and L-5 vertebrae to act as anchors, then attach rods to the anchors to stabilize my back. The danger of an operation like that is suddenly you are asking the segments above the disc area to handle all the motion in your back. That means a significant amount of added stress to that area, and nobody can ever be sure how long it will hold up to that stress. That's why shortly before I had the fusion surgery, Dan told me, "Larry, you better go out and play golf, because you may never play golf again."

I had the surgery, which wasn't scary at all to me, because I just wanted the pain to stop. It took me a good nine months before my body started to feel the same again, but it was worth it. That searing, burning pain is gone. I can jog, play tennis, play golf. I still can't push it, though. If I went out and scrimmaged with my team for twenty minutes, the small of my back would start having spasms. The difference is those spasms are nothing compared to what I had experienced before. But my Indiana players can rest easy. I won't be challenging any of them to a game of one-on-one.

During the time I was recovering from my surgery, I wasn't really doing that much for the Celtics. I'd make an appearance here or there for them, and sometimes I'd scout a player off the television from my home in Naples. I'd show up for the draft and a couple of games a season, but that's all I could handle for a while.

When I felt strong enough to be around more, I started hearing all sorts of rumors from people in the office that Dave was in trouble. I was hoping they weren't true. It wasn't Dave's fault that my back gave out, or that Kevin McHale's foot was never the same. I think one of Dave's biggest problems with the Celtics was that he didn't tell Red Auerbach and the owners every little move he was making. He was his own man, with his own ideas, and that was something new to the Celtics. The old general manager, Jan Volk, never did anything without running it past the owners and Red and the coach and who knows who else. Everything had to be done by committee. When Dave took the job, he was given total control, and that meant he was going to make the final decisions, even if everyone wasn't in total agreement. Back then the team was owned by Alan Cohen, Paul Dupee, and Don Gaston, Paul's father. They were a group with a lot of strong opinions. I think they were also a little impatient about turning things around, and when it didn't happen right away, because of retirement and injuries, they made Dave take the fall for that.

I remember being in the office one day and Dave telling me he had a meeting with Paul Gaston, who was taking over controlling interest of the team. I'm not sure how long that meeting lasted, but when Dave came out I could tell what had happened by the look on his face. Dave was really shocked, and so was I. He shook my hand and said, "They want me gone." It wasn't justified. They hadn't given Dave enough time or support to run the team the way he wanted. I'm still not really sure why everyone changed their minds about Dave, since they all agreed he was a terrific hire when they brought him in. I knew that one of the owners, Alan Cohen, was frustrated with him because he'd make suggestions and Gavitt would end up doing his own thing. With Don Gaston I think it was a matter of being impatient and wanting results more quickly. And there was certainly a split that developed between Dave and Red Auerbach, although I never did find out what that was all about. Red is the one who brought Dave to the Celtics in the first place. But, like I said, Red was used to being in on everything, and that didn't happen with Dave.

Anyway, it put me in a tough position, because everyone knew how I felt about Dave. Not long after that, Paul Gaston asked me if I would be interested in taking on a bigger role and doing something in the front office, but I said no. I was not about to go in there after Dave Gavitt. He was my friend, and I would never do that, not after the way they had treated him.

I wasn't involved in finding a replacement for Dave. I

know at one point they made a call to Frank Layden, who used to coach the Utah Jazz and had a reputation as one of the funnier guys in the game, but he wasn't interested in being their comic relief. He thought they wanted him to crack jokes all season, to keep the fans smiling through what was probably going to be a pretty awful year. For a guy who had coached successfully in the league for years, he found that pretty insulting. Finally, Gaston told me he was thinking of M. L. Carr to take Dave's place. Even though M. L. and I were friends, I had my doubts. I just couldn't see M. L. in that role.

M. L. is a great person. He has lots of energy, and he's great with people. You always wanted him on your side, because he was always getting the crowd riled up—and sometimes the other team too. He was the kind of guy that would back you up out there no matter what, and he was great in the locker room. He always knew how to break up tension and keep everybody loose. People forget M. L. was also a pretty good basketball player. He led the league in steals for Detroit before he came to Boston. He has always been someone I considered a friend, but I just didn't feel he was the right person to run the Celtics franchise. I wasn't convinced he was serious enough about the job to do what needed to be done. To me, a big personality wasn't going to be enough to help Boston win another championship. I wasn't convinced he had thought this decision through, to run an entire basketball team.

Right away I could tell M. L.'s basketball judgment was much different than mine. I would listen to him talk and think, "Did we just watch the same game?"

There were a number of things the Celtics did while M. L. and Paul Gaston were in charge that bothered me, but Sherman was the one that really got to me. He was a tough point guard, only about 5 foot 9, and even though he didn't lead Boston to a championship, at least he was out there every night competing. The only reason the Celtics had a chance in the 1995 first-round playoff series against Orlando (they lost in four games) was because Sherman Douglas almost singlehandedly kept them in it. He wasn't the best player on that team, but he was the leader, the way Mark Jackson has been for the Indiana Pacers.

You'd think a player would be rewarded for that, but instead the Celtics went out and offered Dana Barros, who was a free agent, a huge contract. Paul and M. L. told me about it in a meeting we had up in Boston, and I was sitting there wondering, "Where is Dana going to play?" I told them he wasn't a point guard, and besides, we had Sherman. But they started talking about how Dana was a local kid from Mattapan, Massachusetts, and Boston College, and the fans would love him, and that's when I realized the decision really didn't have very much to do with basketball. I told them Sherman was their MVP, and they nodded their heads, but they weren't listening. They had already made up their minds. So they signed Dana Barros, and Sherman got ticked. He wasn't stupid. He knew they weren't going to bring Barros in there to sit on the bench. This was right at the beginning of the season, and there had been a newspaper article quoting Gaston talking about the business aspect of owning the Celtics that had him saying, "I think I know our team stinks." Gaston said he was misquoted, but Sherman wasn't buying it. When reporters asked Sherman what he thought about Gaston's comments, he said, "I think he stinks too."

They ended up sending Sherman to Milwaukee for Todd Day, who was a shooting guard, and Alton Lister, a center who was around when I was a player. It was a terrible trade. Todd Day was a selfish player who thought about only one thing—how to get himself a shot. Alton Lister was in his late thirties and on the downside of his career. When I heard about the deal, that's the day I made up my mind I wouldn't be in Boston too much longer.

I don't have anything against Dana Barros. He works hard, and he's a nice kid, but Boston paid him half a million more a season than they had to, just to get him. Dana had one great year, in 1994–95 with Philadelphia, when he averaged over 20 points a night, but what the Celtics didn't look at was he played the most minutes of anybody in the league. He had a total green light. Give that kid a green light, and he can score, but look how many games the Sixers won that year. Twenty-four. Is that worth $21 million?

So if I knew I was leaving as early as 1995, why did I wait two years before I actually did go? I probably should have left sooner. We'd have ten guys in a room trying to make a decision on one player, and it drove me crazy. I'm not saying I had all the answers, but the way they tried to do things, it's a wonder they got anything done. As much as that bothered me, I had my reasons for staying. The one thing my doctors told me after my fusion surgery was to be really careful about letting my back heal. They warned me, "Take it slow, or you could have some major problems down the road." My feeling was, the Celtics had such great insurance, why should I have to pay for my care when I got hurt on their job? I stuck around because it made sense from a business perspective.

In the last year or so before I left the Celtics, Dan Dyrek told me about a group that was interested in buying the team. He asked me to meet with one of the guys, who happened to be a friend of his. I talked to him, and I liked him a lot. His group said the only way they'd be interested in buying the team was if I stayed on. At that time it sounded like a great situation, but Paul Gaston didn't want to sell. And I knew as long as Gaston was still there I wouldn't be staying.

It wasn't easy watching what was happening in Boston. There was another move the Celtics made in the summer of '95 that I didn't like: signing Dominique Wilkins as a free agent. Gaston never even bothered to ask me what I thought about that one. The Celtics signed Wilkins without telling me. I heard about it on the news.

It's just as well they never did ask me about Dominique, because I would have told them it was a big mistake. From day one I knew there was no way that one would work out. Dominique was at the end of his career, only he didn't know it. He still had a superstar's mentality. He thought he was good enough to run the show, but his skills had deteriorated and he just didn't have the same mobility or lift that he had in his prime. But what bothered me the most about that signing was that Wilkins wasn't a Celtics kind of player. A true Celtic is a guy that's going to do everything for the team. Dominique was always one of those guys who wanted to do it all himself. You can't win that way.

I had some great battles with Wilkins during the eighties, when he played for Atlanta. He was so good back then. There's no question he's a terrific basketball player, but I always felt we could beat his teams, because one guy can't beat five guys, and Dominique always died trying.

We were involved in a classic playoff series against Atlanta in 1988. The Hawks were a young, up-and-coming team, but even though people considered our "old" Celtics team dead and buried, we knew we still had what it took. The series against Atlanta was in the Eastern Conference semifinals, and Dominique and I got into some major scoring duels. Wilkins was at the top of his game, but even after seeing him score all those points I never doubted that we'd come out winners, because our guys knew how to make the pass to beat them. When the game was on the line, Kevin McHale and Robert Parish and I never worried about who was going to take the shot. We just made sure it was the best possible one we could take. We beat Atlanta in seven games because we played together. After that series the Hawks were never the same. In fact, I think they lost in the first round of the playoffs the following year.

Dominique was a big name, and that's why Boston went for him. You have to understand that at that time the fans were getting antsy. I was retired, and Kevin was retired, and Robert Parish had gone to play for Charlotte. The Celtics felt they needed a draw, and they were convinced Dominique Wilkins was going to do that for them. But they should have listened a little more closely to the people around them who knew basketball. Chris Ford, who was the coach at that time, didn't want the Celtics to sign Dominique either. He was mad at Wilkins from his first day of camp because he showed up out of shape. The whole relationship was doomed from the start. Wilkins had a terrible year in Boston. He was unhappy with his minutes, the way Chris used him, everything. That summer the NBA locked out their players while they negotiated a new collective bargaining agreement, and Dominique used that to escape to Europe. The Celtics were lucky, because by then the fans had turned against Wilkins, and it was getting pretty ugly. I honestly felt sorry for 'Nique. He's not a bad guy at all. He got set up to be some kind of savior, and that was never going to happen.

It must have seemed to Chris Ford that he never got who he wanted. In 1994, when the Celtics had the eighth pick in the draft, he wanted the guard from Temple, Eddie Jones, really bad. I could see why. I liked Eddie Jones too, because he was tough and athletic and played really good defense for a college kid. But the Celtics ended up taking the big center from North Carolina, Eric Montross. Somehow it came out that I was against taking Montross, but that really wasn't true. I wanted to take him, because I knew Parish was going to sign somewhere else as a free agent, and both Red Auerbach and I realized how vital it was to have a center. I figured if it turned out we didn't like Montross, we'd always be able to trade him. I mean, the kid was seven feet tall, and he was a hard worker.

Besides, the Celtics had just signed Dee Brown to a big six-year contract, and he and Eddie Jones played the same position. There's no doubt in my mind that Jones would have come in and beat out Brown for the job, but then what are you going to do? You'd have a veteran sitting on the bench making all that money and being very unhappy. I don't think the Celtics wanted to deal with that. Dee had talent, but Eddie Jones would have beaten him out.

Anyhow, Montross had a really solid rookie season. I thought he might be the best backup center in the league at that time, even though we were asking him to start games. Ever since then, it's been all downhill for him. Part of it was that Chris Ford got fired after Montross's first season, and M. L. Carr took over as coach, and he just didn't use him the right way. The kid lost all his confidence, and then he got traded to Dallas, and has been traded again twice since. I think Montross still could be an effective backup if someone would just spend some time with him and help him get his confidence back.

Of course, the Lakers ended up drafting Eddie Jones with the tenth pick, and he was a steal. He's been to two All-Star games and has proven he can be a big-time scorer as well as a great defender. No wonder Chris Ford wanted him so bad.

Most of the time when the Celtics ignored my advice I didn't really say anything. Hey, it's Gaston's money, it's his team. But there was one time, in 1996, when they were talking about trading their number six pick in the draft plus their first-round pick the following season to Toronto. The idea was to get the Raptors' number two pick in the 1996 draft so the Celtics could take Marcus Camby. For some reason, Gaston and M. L. were really hot on the idea of getting Camby, but I told them I strongly objected to the deal.

They kept talking about how Camby was such a huge star at the University of Massachusetts, and how he would be a big draw, but I couldn't see that. I was really upset about it, because I felt strongly that either Antoine Walker, who was a scoring forward from Kentucky, or Ray Allen, who was a shooting guard from Connecticut, would be much stronger picks, and would be there when we selected sixth. Plus, we knew Boston wasn't going to be that strong in the upcoming season, which meant the draft pick in 1997 had a chance of being a very high pick (number three, as it turns out). Even after I said all this, I could sense they were still going to do it. I was flying back to Indiana that day and I remember after the meeting I told Gaston, "I can't leave town knowing you might make that trade. Tell me you won't make that deal." He never gave me an answer.

Thankfully, they didn't make the trade, and Boston drafted Antoine Walker with the sixth pick. Walker is a terrific talent, a superstar in the making. I love the way he plays. He passes the ball so well for a big man, and he can rebound the ball. He takes a lot of bad shots, but he's still very young, and a good coach will get that straightened out. Camby has talent too, but it's hard to say how good he is, because he's injured so much. Maybe now that he's been traded to New York and will be around all those veterans, his game will blossom.

As it turned out, in the summer of 1997, after Walker's first season in Boston, Gaston came to me and said they were ready to replace M. L. as head coach. He asked me to put a list together of the names I thought would be good choices. I asked him if he had talked to M. L. about it, and he assured me M. L. understood they needed to go in a different direction, and that M. L. was going to be taken care of, with a different job in the organization.

I started quietly making up my list. Not long after that, I noticed M. L. was acting a little funny. Something was definitely wrong, so I went in to talk to him, and he was really hot. He started saying to me, "How could you do this behind my back?" He was really mad. He said he had gotten a call from someone in Cleveland who said I had contacted the Cavaliers to see if the Celtics could get permission to talk to their coach, Mike Fratello, about the coaching opening they would have at the end of the season. M. L. said that was how he found out he was going to be replaced.

The funny thing about that was I never did call Cleveland to ask about Fratello. It's not because I didn't think

Fratello would be good, it's just that I knew he was under contract and doing a good job there, and I didn't expect he'd be available. I was concentrating on finding people who I thought might be ready to move on.

Anyhow, M. L. was really upset. He said to me, "How could you betray me, after all we've been through together?" That's when I told him, "Listen, you better call up your boss, because Gaston told me you knew all about this. He told me you knew everything. You're mad at the wrong guy." I could tell M. L. didn't believe me, so I closed the door and I called up Gaston in New York and got him on the phone. After a minute or so, Gaston admitted, with both of us listening, that he made a mistake by not telling M. L. He told M. L., "I'm sorry. I forgot."

I can understand M. L. being upset, but I wasn't out to hurt him. I thought he had been told he was being replaced. I think M. L. was feeling I might want the Celtics coaching job, and I was going back-door on him to get it, but I had no interest in doing that. I had already made up my mind I was leaving the Celtics as soon as I finished the coaching search. I just hadn't told them yet.

M. L. and I go back a long way. He was one of the best teammates I ever had, but our relationship will never be the same. I hope he understands I was just trying to make the franchise better. I was also following orders.

M. L. wasn't the only one upset about the coaching job. Dennis Johnson, who was an assistant coach with Boston and had played with me on the 1984 and 1986 championship teams with the Celtics, was hurt that his name hadn't appeared on the list of candidates. D. J. and I won a lot of big games together, and I always said he was one of the best clutch players I've ever seen. I think D. J. would make a good coach, but I knew Gaston had someone a lot more high-profile in mind. He had no intention of hiring D. J., that's for sure. My understanding was that D. J. would be kept regardless of who the head coach was. That turned out not to be the case. He was fired later that year. By then, I was in the middle of negotiations with the Pacers, and talking about putting together my own coaching staff. I found out later that D. J. was upset because I didn't offer him an assistant's job in Indiana, but I thought he was set in Boston. I also thought he wanted to be a head coach. Besides, I had already made up my mind that I was going to use two assistants, not three.

It was clear to me that Paul Gaston wanted Rick Pitino to be his coach, so I called up Pitino and asked him if he was interested. He said he liked his situation in Kentucky, but he asked me a lot of questions. I probably talked to him two or three times, and it was always the same: he said he wasn't interested, then would pump me for more information. He'd ask me things like, "So what are the Celtics going to do with M. L.?" Later on, he started asking me about Red and his role in the organization. Every time we talked, I sensed he was getting closer and closer to taking it, even though he kept insisting he didn't want it.

Until those phone calls, I had no past history with Rick Pitino. I scouted his Kentucky teams for the Celtics, and I was impressed with the way they trapped and applied defensive pressure—it was hard not to be, really—but I had no relationship with him at all. I have very few memories of him as coach of the Knicks, other than that those teams always played hard and gave us trouble. But in terms of having a personal opinion about him, I didn't. I had no feelings for him one way or the other.

Even though I felt from the beginning that Pitino would

end up with the job, my first choice would have been Kansas coach Roy Williams. I thought he was a perfect fit for the Celtics. His system would be great in the pros. His teams run, but they can slow it up. And his style is right to the point. That's what I like. His players always seemed disciplined, and fundamentally sound too.

Williams sounded really flattered when I called. He said the pros might be something that would interest him someday, but he was happy with his job and wasn't ready to make a move. At that time Kansas had a lot of talent, with Raef LaFrentz and Paul Pierce, and he said the timing just wasn't right. I could tell he was being sincere, not using it as leverage, and I appreciated that. So I crossed him off the list.

The other name I gave Paul Gaston was Bob Hill. I always felt he had done a good job as head coach of the Knicks and the Pacers. I liked him because he's firm and he knows the game, and I felt he'd have the respect of the team. But when I brought up his name to Gaston, I could tell it wasn't going to happen. Bob Hill might be a good coach, but he wasn't a big enough name for the Celtics.

Larry Brown was a big enough name, and everyone knew he was unhappy in Indiana and looking to make a move. I checked with some of my contacts, and they all said there was no way he'd be back with the Pacers next year, so I called the Pacers and asked permission to talk to him about the Celtics job. They said yes. By this time Pitino had told the media he was not leaving Kentucky. I remember being surprised when I heard that, because I really thought he was ready to come to Boston, in spite of all his denials. Gaston told me to call Bob Hill and tell him they had decided not to interview him, and I felt bad about that, because I figured they could at least talk to

him. But the feeling I was getting was that Larry Brown
was now their man, and I was very happy about that. He
is the perfect coach to bring in when you want to turn
something around. He runs a great practice, he's a per-
fectionist, and he lives for basketball. If Larry Brown ended
up as the Celtics coach, there was no doubt in my mind
he'd get them back on track. He seemed like he was the
front-runner, but I was guessing. Once I gave the Celtics
my list of coaches, I was frozen out. The Celtics weren't
telling me anything.

Brown interviewed with the Celtics and called me afterward. He sounded excited. He told me, "I think I've
got the job." He said Gaston told him he needed just a
couple more days, and he'd get back to him with the details. I congratulated him and wished him luck.

Next thing you know—BOOM!—Larry Brown is *not*
the next coach of the Celtics. A couple of days turned into
a week, and suddenly Pitino was back in it. I don't know
how it all happened, because I was out in the cold at that
point, but various newspapers later reported that Larry
Brown and Rick Pitino were playing in a golf tournament
in California and Larry told Rick he thought he had the
Boston job and he was just waiting for the owner to wrap
everything up. The next thing you know, Rick is back into
the picture and Larry Brown is out of a job.

When I heard what happened, I was sick about it. Larry
called me up and said, "What is going on?" I couldn't
give him an answer. The truth was, I had no idea what
was happening. I called up Gaston and said, "What are
you doing? You've got this guy sitting over here wanting
the job and you're messing around with him. You're leaving him hanging. Do you want him or not?" But Gaston

wouldn't really tell me. He said if Larry Brown wants to get another job, then he should do that.

That's when I knew Pitino was in and Larry Brown was out, and it really ticked me off. It was done all wrong. I had no problem with Rick Pitino being the coach—it was the way it was handled that bothered me. Larry Brown should have been treated with far more respect throughout the process, and Paul Gaston should have been more straightforward with me. But neither one of those things happened. In the end, all I could do was call Larry and apologize and tell him I was sorry. Soon after that, the Sixers hired Larry Brown. I bet the first thing he did was circle all the dates on his schedule when his team played Boston.

I knew what was coming next. Pitino officially accepted the job as coach of the Celtics and fired a whole bunch of people who had been with the team for years, which is what I would have done too, if I had taken over some management role in that organization. There's no question that a fresh start was the best way to go with the Celtics. Actually, Pitino was smart enough to have Gaston fire all those people before he came on board, but everybody knew who was calling the shots. Pitino didn't fire Red Auerbach, but he changed his title of president to vice chairman of the board.

I felt really bad for Red, because he's the reason the Boston Celtics were the best organization in basketball. As far as I'm concerned, he saved the NBA, not just the Celtics, by the way he coached and won championships. From what I understand, Red was pretty upset about it, but he wasn't too happy with me either. During the process of finding a coach I did an interview with the *Boston Globe,* and in the story I said I could never be coach of the Celtics because I would have to make some tough changes, including firing people I really liked. I said there were too many people trying to make decisions for the team, and then I made a comment about how I hardly ever agreed with Red on anything, so how could I coach his team? It was a joke, but I guess Red didn't find it very funny. The thing is, he took it the wrong way. I'm telling you right now: if I ever had taken the coaching job or general manager's job for the Celtics, I would have had Red right there beside me. He would have been president forever if I had any say in it. I have the highest regard for him, and I always will.

I don't understand exactly what happened between me and Red, but I'm just as stubborn as he is. If Red's ticked off with me, that's fine. I always say if you don't like somebody, then don't be around them. But I think there's mutual respect there, even if we never talk again the rest of our lives.

I did call him after the article, because I heard he was steaming about it. I said, "Red, I understand you are upset about some things I said." He told me, "No, Larry, that's a bunch of bull. We're fine. Larry, you were always one of my favorites." I told him, "I don't really care whether you like me or not, Red, just as long as your wife, Dot, still does."

By the time we hung up, I figured everything was fine. But then about two weeks later a friend of mine called me up and said, "I talked to Red today, and he was killing you. He's really mad at you for saying that stuff." So I guess we've got a problem. All I can tell you is that it hasn't changed my feelings for the man.

It's too bad my time with the Celtics ended that way. I had some great years in Boston, and I still love it out there. I'd love to go back someday, but things have changed, and that whole organization is completely different than it was. There's nothing for me there now.

It's disappointing that so many relationships I had with people fell apart. But I would feel a lot worse about it if I thought I had done something wrong. I'm not wrong. I'm sorry M. L. didn't like it that he lost the coaching job, but it wasn't my decision. And I never would have purposely kept it from him about looking for a new coach. I thought he knew. And I feel badly that Dennis Johnson was frustrated. He, like everyone else, probably thinks I should just stop everything and tell the Pacers to hire him, but I can't do that. I don't believe that should end our friendship.

In the end it all comes down to one thing: sports is a business. I'm sure Pitino would tell you the same thing. The one thing I did find unbelievable was how Pitino kept telling the media the only way he'd take the job is if I stayed on with the Celtics. He knew that was never going to happen, because I told him that. He made it sound like he wanted me to be the general manager or something, which I never would have agreed to anyway, but you know what he offered me? An assistant coach's job. I told him the best thing that could possibly happen was for me to move on, so he wouldn't have to look over his shoulder all the time.

That's when I resigned from the Celtics. I have never looked back.

CHAPTER 4

On Joining the Pacers

When I was a player, people asked me if I'd ever consider coaching. I told them to forget it. I couldn't picture myself in that role, and I had no interest in doing it. For one thing, I didn't want to wear a suit. I said the same thing again when I retired in 1992. Right away, a couple of teams called me up and asked me to consider working for them, but that was before I had fusion surgery on my back, and there was no way I could physically do it even if I wanted to. I was still in terrible pain. I couldn't even walk without trouble. At that time, teams still flew on commercial flights instead of the private jets most teams use now, and I knew my back could never hold up through the grind of all that traveling. Airplanes were not made for people my size.

Besides, I wanted to take some time off and to be with my family. For thirteen years I had been flying all over the country, playing basketball, and I promised my wife, Dinah, I would take a break from that. Our son, Conner, was growing up real fast, and I liked the idea of spending time with him, teaching him how to swim, going fishing, or even just hanging around the house. We also had a new addition to our family—our daughter, Mariah—and I was looking forward to watching her grow up too. Coaching wasn't going to allow me to do that. There wasn't anything about it that was appealing to me.

I can't tell you exactly when I changed my mind, but it was probably after a couple of years, when my back started feeling better. We were living in Naples, Florida, which is the greatest place in the world to live, but there's only so much to do.

At first I really loved being down there. People would know who I was, but there weren't a lot of them looking for autographs. They seemed happy enough just to wave or say hello. That part of my life had really quieted down, and I was glad about it. It was nice to move around Naples without worrying that a mob of people would be following you. I've never been comfortable with people recognizing me and making a big deal of it, and there were times when it could make you a prisoner in your own house. When I played for the Celtics it was hard for me to move around Boston without people finding me. The Celtics fans were great, don't get me wrong, but you couldn't just show up at a seven o'clock movie, or go to the mall, and expect people to leave you alone. It just wasn't going to happen. I never had any problems with one or two people coming up and looking for a picture or an autograph, but when a whole crowd of people start coming at you when you're not expecting it, that's when I get very uncomfortable. Sometimes it can even be a little scary, with so many bodies all swarming at you like that. When that happens, I tend to get pretty anxious, and the last thing I feel like doing is signing something. I just want to get out of there.

I had a pretty easy time of it once I retired. I could play golf whenever I wanted to. But after a while I got tired of golf. Then I got tired of fishing. I was bored. So I'd be in and out of Naples a lot. At least every week Dinah and I and the kids would take off and go somewhere, but it wasn't enough. I didn't feel like I was getting anything accomplished. I knew I was too young to stop working. One thing I was sure about: I didn't want to spend the next twenty or thirty years of my life doing nothing. I needed some kind of challenge, and during the five years I was retired, that challenge was definitely missing.

Dinah knows me inside out, and she could tell I was getting restless. One of the greatest things about Dinah is she doesn't care what I do—she'll be there to support me. She is ready to try new things, ready to go anywhere. I could tell her tonight we are packing up and moving to Los Angeles and she'd say, "Really? Okay." I know I'm really lucky she's that way, but it's how we've been for as long as we've been together.

Before we had the kids, we'd be sitting in French Lick and I'd say, "You want to go to Terre Haute?" She'd tell me, "Give me five minutes." She'd throw some stuff in a bag, and we'd be gone. Then we'd get to Terre Haute and I'd say, "Let's go to Vegas and visit our friends for a couple of days." Dinah would call them up, throw some more stuff in a bag and—boom!—we'd be gone. It was just the way we lived. We never really had one place that we settled in. It's crazy, really, when you think about it. We had all these houses—one in Indiana, one in Naples, one in Boston—but we never really had a home.

I don't know why it was like that. Maybe because when I was young we moved all the time. My parents didn't have a whole lot of money, and it seemed like we never really knew what we were going to do from day to day. I think we moved about fifteen times by the time I finished high school. But it never really bothered me much as a kid. As long as we were together, I didn't care where we lived.

Now we have Conner and Mariah, and they are terrific kids. They are a handful sometimes, but Dinah and I don't mind. When Conner was a baby he went with us to Barcelona when I played on the 1992 Olympic Dream Team. He kept us up all night, because he was so confused with the time difference, but I didn't care. I was just happy he was there with us. When we started talking about a second child, Dinah said she wasn't sure. She said, "I don't know. I don't think I could ever love another baby like the way I love Conner." But let me tell you: Dinah and our little girl are ridiculous together. They are inseparable. I know Dinah meant it when she said she could never love another child as much, but about three minutes after she was holding that little girl, that took care of that. Same with me.

As Conner and Mariah got older, they started hearing a little more about their dad and how he used to be a pro basketball player. Conner started getting a little curious about it. He'd ask me questions like "Were you good?" or "Did you have to practice a lot?" (The answer to both is yes.) One day he came home and asked me if I knew Michael Jordan, and if I did, could I please have him come over to the house so he could meet him? I told Conner he had already met Michael Jordan in Barcelona when he was little, and that he played with Jordan's kids during the Olympics. He was satisfied with that answer, and I didn't hear much about Michael Jordan for a while.

Then Conner came home from school one day and said,

"Now what is it you do again, Daddy?" I didn't know what to tell him. At that time, in 1997, I was supposed to be working for the Celtics in their front office, but I wasn't doing much at all for them, and I knew I wanted to get out of there. That's when I realized, "Maybe it's time to go back to work." I didn't want my kids growing up thinking all their daddy did was play golf all day.

At least three different teams had offered me head coaching jobs over the years. Two asked me to keep our conversations private, and since I gave them my word, I won't say who they are. I will tell you that the Pacers were one of the teams that approached me in 1993, the year they eventually hired Larry Brown. But the timing wasn't right, again because of my back. I was still in such a bad way that I never considered it.

When my back got stronger, I didn't miss playing, but I started to miss the competition. I used to turn on the Miami Heat games, but I hardly ever followed the players. I was watching their coach, Pat Riley. Mostly I just watched the decisions he made during the course of the game. He was so excellent at motivating his guys, and it fascinated me. No matter what Miami game you were watching, it seemed like their players were always at the right spot. He spread the court very well, and guys played very hard for him. Even when his players went down with injuries, he always seemed to find ways to win. To me, that's unbelievable. I found myself keeping track of Miami's schedule so I could watch all their games.

Pat Riley was, without question, the toughest coach I ever played against. We had some great battles with the Lakers in the eighties, and Riley was one of the big reasons L.A. gave us so much trouble. He really hated the Celtics, and it showed. He was always talking about how much he disliked Boston Garden, because of the dead spots on the floor, or because the locker rooms were too small, or how there was no air-conditioning, and the hot water didn't work (he used to blame Red Auerbach for that). It seemed like he always had something to say, but you can be sure none of it was by accident. He always had his reasons. He knew how to work the media, the referees, and his opponents.

Of course at the time I would never have admitted that. As a player, I totally dismissed Riley to the media. I never had anything good to say about him, even though in my heart I knew he was a very real threat to our championship hopes. He was one of the few coaches who could actually force me to alter my game.

It seemed like Riley was always making some kind of adjustment to slow me down. I'd score six or eight straight points, he'd call a time-out, and then they'd come out with a different look, hoping to knock me out of my rhythm. Riley gave me all sorts of problems back then, but I never said so. I would never let him know. It was so important during the Finals not to give the Lakers even the slightest edge, so whenever someone asked me about Riley, I'd shrug it off. He was a Laker! There was no way I was going to admit to anyone that he was giving me fits!

Sometimes he'd come out of the time-out and have his guys double-team me all the way down the court. When the game got really tight, Riley would bring Magic Johnson down to double me. It's one thing having Norm Nixon, who was one of their guards, doubling me. Smaller guys never bothered me, because I could always pass over them. But when Riley sent Magic, who was about 6 foot 9, down there, he was bigger, with longer arms, and it made it tougher for me to see the floor.

Another trick Riley used was to instruct his guys to make me overextend to receive a pass, thinking it would keep me off balance, or away from a more comfortable passing position. Sometimes it was something as simple as pushing me out a little farther away from the basket, or preventing me from operating on one side of the floor. The Lakers were always using someone different on me too. People have told me that it was Riley who got his defensive forward, Michael Cooper, to become totally focused on guarding me. He convinced Cooper that he could make a career out of it, and he was right. Cooper was one of the tougher guys I went up against. I read a story once where Cooper said he used to watch films of me while he was lying in bed with his wife. I believe it. That is the kind of dedication, I'm sure, that Riley demanded of his players.

All I know is Riley's Lakers teams always had something ready to throw you off. They were constantly changing up. I knew even back then Riley was different.

Then he left L.A., took over with the New York Knicks, and changed styles completely. It's amazing how everyone thought Pat Riley could only play one way, as a wide-open, run-and-gun type of coach, because the Lakers played that way, and if you got physical with them, they didn't like that. But once Riley got to New York, he changed. All of a sudden he was the aggressor. He got those guys to play really tough, just like he's done with the team he has now in Miami. Those guys will go after you, they'll bump you. It's a battle every night. It's a sign of a good coach when you play both ways, both the finesse and the physical game. That's what I made up my mind I wanted to do if I did get into coaching.

I found myself thinking about coaching more and more.

It would have to be the right situation, I was set on that, and the more I thought about it, the more Indiana made sense. It's not like I grew up a Pacers fan my whole life, because the truth was I didn't follow pro basketball at all very much as a kid. I was more interested in pro baseball (I was a St. Louis Cardinals and Chicago Cubs fan). In a lot of ways, Indianapolis was a million miles away from French Lick and West Baden, where I grew up. We hardly ever went up there—Indianapolis might as well have been a foreign country. Even when I started playing for the Celtics, I didn't get to know Indianapolis at all, except for the hotels we'd stay in. I always had a lot of people visiting me when we played the Pacers, like my mom, my brothers and my sister, and my friends from home, but it wasn't like we all went out to dinner or anything. I had a game to play, and they understood that. Sometimes after the game a few of my buddies and me would go to the hotel lobby for a couple of beers, but that was about the extent of it.

There was a time when I thought I might play for the Indiana Pacers, because they had the number one pick in the 1978 draft. I was a junior at Indiana State at the time, and I was eligible for the draft, but my plans all along were to go back to school for my senior year. I got a call from my friend Ed Jukes, who ended up being my financial adviser during my career, and he said he had gotten a call from the Pacers general manager, Bob Leonard, who said Indiana had the number one pick and would like to use it to take me in the draft. Ed told him, "I don't know, you better talk to Larry about it." So Leonard, who everyone called Slick, says, "Well, I'd like to sit down with Larry." So Ed and I drive to Indianapolis and we meet Slick at a hotel room in the Hyatt Regency.

Actually it was a suite, so I guess they were trying to impress us, especially since at that time the Pacers really didn't have any money. They had paid millions of dollars to come into the NBA from the ABA, and they had no television rights or anything, and I think they only had about twelve people running the whole franchise. In fact, Slick told me up front the Pacers really wanted me to play for them, but they couldn't pay me very much.

We had been talking a little bit when Slick asked me, "Would you like something to drink?" I asked them what they had, and he said, "We've got beer, sodas, whatever you want." So I said beer. He asked me what kind I wanted and I said, "Heineken!" In college I'd drink all this other stuff, the cheaper the better. I don't think I had ever had a Heineken in my life. But I figured, hey, why not? They said I could have anything.

It's funny how things work out, because more than twenty years later, Slick Leonard and I have become good friends. He does the radio for all the Pacers games, so he travels with the team, and nine times out of ten he ends up in my room having a beer with me after the game. Every time I see Slick he starts teasing me. He says, "Some old hillbilly you turned out to be. You came up here and ordered a two-dollar bottle of beer back when just about everything else cost fifty cents." Slick has a long memory, just like me.

The Pacers never did draft me in 1978, because I told them I had promised my mom I would go back to college for my senior year and graduate. Indiana was in a position at that time where it needed to do something right away. The Pacers couldn't afford to wait a whole year to get me. And at the same time they were talking to me, they were trying to re-sign one of their free agents, Dan

Roundfield. It turns out Slick offered Roundfield $200,000, which was $200,000 more than the Pacers actually had, but Roundfield ended up signing with Atlanta for $420,000.

Having lost Roundfield, and knowing they had no chance of getting me for at least a year, the Pacers ended up trading the number one pick to Portland for some players and the number three pick. They ended up taking Rick Robey, a big center from Kentucky, with the third pick. In fact, the day I went into my interview with Slick he asked me about Robey, who I had played against in some All-Star games, and I told him I thought he'd be a solid NBA player. As it turns out, Robey and I became teammates for four years with the Celtics, and he became one of my best friends. We had a lot of fun running around town together and drinking beers. The year after Robey got traded from Boston to Phoenix, 1984, was the first time I won the MVP. Robey always says I should have given him the trophy, because if he was still in town I never would have won it, and I have to agree with him. I loved Robey, but he wasn't good for my career.

I was taken in the 1978 draft by the Boston Celtics, with the sixth pick. They knew I planned on finishing my senior year at Indiana State, but they were willing to wait. The Pacers weren't, and I figured any chance I had of being part of their franchise was gone.

Over the years, Indiana tried to trade for me many times. They approached me about various jobs when I retired. But for whatever reason, nothing ever came of it. But that changed in the spring of 1997, when the Celtics had put me in charge of their coaching search. I called and asked permission from the Pacers to talk to Larry Brown about the opening Boston was going to have at the end of the season. Their president, Donnie Walsh, said yes, then asked me if I would be interested in talking to them about their coaching vacancy if Larry Brown did in fact move on. I told him I'd be willing to listen. The next day Donnie Walsh called the Celtics and asked permission to speak with me. Since I was going to Indianapolis to scout the Final Four for the Celtics, I agreed to sit down with Donnie while I was there to discuss any possible future I might have with them.

I wasn't really sure what to expect. The Pacers are owned by two brothers, Herb and Mel Simon. I had known Mel for years because he used to rent office space to a friend of mine, Lu Meis. I always liked Mel a lot. He's a happy-go-lucky guy, and a huge basketball fan. We used to play golf together once in a while. I don't think he pays much attention to the finances of the team. I think he leaves that up to Herb.

By the time I went to Indianapolis, I had been hearing from a number of my contacts that Donnie wanted me really bad, and he'd do whatever he could to get me. So the first thing I had to figure out was could I work for Donnie Walsh? I didn't have any strong feelings about Donnie one way or the other before then, so I did one of my background checks on him.

I do background checks on people whenever I might be entering some kind of business relationship with them. Nothing too scientific—I just talk to a bunch of different people, listen to their thoughts. I usually go to a guy who's ticked off at the world for his opinion. If he says something good about the person and has nothing but bad things to say about everyone else, then you'd better pay attention.

Whenever I asked someone about Donnie Walsh, the same thing kept coming back to me. All I heard was that

Donnie was just like me, that he would put everything out there, and he wouldn't pull any punches. And you know what? That's exactly the way it has been. Donnie has never lied to me, and he's never going to. I knew that two days after I met him. You don't find that very often, especially in this business.

I felt my meeting with Donnie went pretty well. I laid it out for him right then and there how I would handle the team. I told him I would stress conditioning, and being on time. I told him I thought they had a real chance to win the championship if they could get their players to believe they could beat Michael Jordan. To me, that was going to be one of the biggest problems. Jordan had become bigger than life. Everyone in the league seemed to be afraid of him, or intimidated by him. Even the referees! Somehow the Pacers needed a new mindset, one that would convince them Jordan was human and Chicago was not untouchable.

I had some other ideas I told him about that day. I told him I would want two assistants: a young guy with ideas, and a veteran who has been around. I knew that wasn't going to go over too big in the coaching fraternity, because most teams hired three assistants, and in some cases four, but I knew what I wanted. I wanted to keep things simple, and for all of us to be focused on the same issues. To me, three coaches was more than enough to run a team that had only twelve guys. Sure enough, after my coaching staff had been announced, there was a lot of grumbling that went on among the other coaches. I guess some coaches felt I was setting a bad trend, and they were worried that if our staff succeeded, it might convince other teams to downsize the number of coaches. Hey, the last thing I wanted to do was cost anybody a job, but my feeling is that if you are good enough, somebody will hire you. I wasn't going to hire three coaches just because somebody decided that was what you were supposed to do.

I wasn't going to waste a lot of time worrying about whether I fit in with the other coaches or not. I knew there were plenty of them who were ticked off that I was handed a head coaching job without any previous experience, but my feeling was, why not wait and see what I can do before you criticize me? I also knew there were plenty of coaches out there rooting against me in my first season. That's fine. They can do what they want. Actually it made it easier for me, because I had already decided there wasn't going to be a whole lot of handshaking and chatting going on between me and somebody I wanted to beat that night. I prefer to take the floor, play the game, and get off without talking to anybody from the other team, whether it's a player, coach, or general manager. I never liked it as a player when guys socialized with the opponent. When the Lakers played Detroit, Magic Johnson used to kiss his friend Isiah Thomas, who played for the Pistons, before the game. I couldn't believe it. I hated that. That's against everything I believe in. I tell my guys, "Hey, this is a game. If you want to hug and kiss those guys, you do it afterwards."

There was one more point I wanted to make to Donnie Walsh at our meeting in Indianapolis. I told him that I wanted the players, not me, to be the focal point of the team. Coaches don't score a single point out there. They don't play hurt, or take a charge. In the end, the players determine who wins and who loses, and the last thing I wanted was a situation where I was expected to be an attraction. There was no way I would ever take a job if that was the case.

That's when Donnie assured me he wanted me to coach because he believed I could handle the job, not because it would help put fans in the seats or because it would help the construction of their new arena. I knew that if I took the job some people would think that's why the Pacers hired me, but I took Donnie at his word. I knew I could be a lot more than some kind of marketing tool.

I went back to Naples and started looking at the bios of the Pacers players and their stats for the last four or five years. Anyone can get that kind of information. Most of it is on the Internet. I also called a few contacts I had around the league, people I trust, to ask them what they thought about the Pacers players, the front office, the city in general. That's right—another background check. It wasn't hard for the people I called to figure out why I was asking, and I think most of them, even though they were good friends, were shocked that I was considering going into coaching. Many of them told me it would be a mistake. Some of them, I think, felt I was risking ruining the so-called image I had built up over the years in the NBA, but I didn't care at all about that. I wasn't worried about whether I would succeed. I knew I'd work hard enough to be good at it.

But I still wasn't sure this is what I wanted. I wasn't sure I wanted to get myself and my family back into the spotlight, and move them back to Indiana. We had the house in French Lick, but that was more than two hours away, and if I was going to coach the Pacers I knew I'd have to buy something closer to Indianapolis. It was going to mean some big changes. No more golf or fishing. Instead, I'd be traveling, dealing with the media, staying up late agonizing over a loss. There would be renewed interest in my career, which I knew meant a renewed loss

of privacy, but the one thing I felt good about was that I
know what kind of people live in the state of Indiana, and
for the most part they are decent, hardworking people. I
always felt a little more comfortable when I went back
home, because it seemed like everyone was the same: con-
siderate, friendly, neighborly.

When I said the Pacers job was the only coaching job
I would have taken, I was being truthful, but it wasn't because the Pacers were in Indiana. I was glad to be back
in my home state, where I was born and raised, no question about that, but that really didn't have anything to do
with my final decision. The truth was I wanted to coach
a veteran team that had a chance to win it all.

If Portland had the same roster as the Pacers, I would
be in Portland right now. It was never, "The only place
I'll coach is Indiana." I do love Indiana, but too much was
made of that. It seemed like every story that was written
talked about me coming home, and how that's why I took
this job. I could have said something then, but Indiana is
a small market, and that kind of publicity was good for
the team and the state, so I just sort of rolled with it. But
my friends knew the real reason I was attracted to Indiana was because they had a Pacers team who knew what
it was like to win, who had been moments away from the
NBA Finals, and who were hungry to get back there—and
who, I hoped, would listen to me when I tried to help get
them there.

The thing was, I had always watched the Pacers games.
The one thing that caught my eye with those guys was
that I always felt if they could have gotten to the Finals
that one year, in 1994, when they lost to the Knicks in
seven games in the Eastern Conference Finals, they would
have won the championship. I truly believe Indiana

matched up with Houston well enough that year to have beaten them.

I always said that if they could have won that one game, Game 6 in Market Square Arena (which they lost, 98–91), they would have been world champions. I watched that whole game, and it made me sick, because I knew they could beat New York, but there were a few key moments in the game where they lost their edge. It looked like they didn't believe they could win. There were a couple of little breakdowns defensively, a missed rebound, and those were the difference in the series. When I met with Donnie Walsh in Indianapolis I reminded him of that game, and told him it cost them a ring.

After I retired, I used to root for the Pacers, as long as they weren't playing the Celtics. I liked the guys on their team. I always felt Reggie Miller was one of those rare guys who can hit the big shot, and who wanted the chance to do it. I enjoyed watching Mark Jackson play, because even though he didn't have the most quickness of the point guards, he found a way to make things happen. And the center, Rik Smits, played very well every time I saw him. They had a nucleus of a team that I always thought I could get something out of.

But I knew I needed help. With no coaching experience at all, I needed an assistant I could count on for everything, and I knew who I wanted: Rick Carlisle. Rick was one of my closest friends. He was an assistant coach in Portland when I called him and told him I was thinking of coaching.

He tried to talk me out of it right from the start. He kept saying, "Larry, you don't want to do this. You have no idea how much work it is, and how hard it is." He sent me his entire playbook from Portland, just to give me an idea of what it entailed. He had defensive plays, offensive diagrams, stats, workout plans, everything. It was a big, thick packet, and I bet he was thinking I wouldn't bother to go over it, but I went through all of it—every page—and all it did was get me more interested in coaching.

I said, "Rick, if I decide to do this, are you coming with me?" Because I really didn't want to do it unless he was going to be part of it. Rick Carlisle is one of the most dedicated coaches in the league, and I needed his experience, his instincts. We had been friends so long I knew we'd have no problem working together. I knew in my first year I was going to have to really rely on someone, and Rick was the only one that made sense to me.

I first met Rick Carlisle when he came to the Celtics camp as a rookie in 1984. He was a third-round draft pick out of Virginia, and he didn't have all the talent in the world, but right away, even as a rookie, he knew he shouldn't come in and try to beat people out, but try and come in and make the people who were already there better. That's a big difference. The Celtics were a veteran team coming off winning a championship, and the truth was we didn't need much help. Our first-round pick that year, a kid named Michael Young from Houston, didn't even make the team. But Rick Carlisle did, mostly because of his smarts and his understanding and willingness to push us in practice.

Carlisle was always on the verge of being cut, and in his second year, the 1985–86 season, the guy he was up against for the final spot on the team was Carlos Clark. Clark had played with us the previous season, and felt he should be playing more. He spent most of preseason trying to steal everybody's job. If something didn't go right for Carlos, you could see it by the way he reacted in practice. Meanwhile, Rick was fighting every day, tooth and nail, trying to help all of us improve. He reminded me of another old teammate of mine, Chris Ford, because he got the absolute most out of his talent. I knew Rick would be around basketball a long time, because he was very organized, he loved the game, and everything he did was for a reason. That's why Rick hardly ever made any mistakes, and that's why he got the final 1985–86 roster spot, not Carlos Clark. He also got himself a ring, because we won a championship that June.

Anyhow, Rick and I became friends. In the summer he'd come out to French Lick for a couple weeks at a time and work out with me. Then we'd go fishing, or head down to Jubil's, a local bar in town, and have a couple beers, or sometimes we'd just go up to my friend's filling station, called Brownie's, and hang out. But mostly we used that time to really push each other on the court. That's the other thing about Rick. There weren't too many guys who worked harder at it. He only stayed in the NBA about five years, but nobody was surprised that he went into coaching. He was a natural.

I couldn't imagine having my first coaching job without Rick beside me, but weeks went by and he wouldn't give me an answer. I suppose he had doubts about a team that had only won 39 games the year before, a team that was definitely getting older. He had been in this business long enough to know that if I came in and things went real bad, it would reflect on him too, and he was really close to getting his own chance at a head job.

There was another problem: there were rumors that head coach P. J. Carlesimo was going to be fired in Portland, which meant Rick's own future was up in the air.

He wasn't sure he could stay in Portland, or whether he would want to stay. He was talking to Danny Ainge about an assistant's job in Phoenix, and to Chuck Daly about an opening he had in Orlando. I knew Rick would rather live in Phoenix or Orlando than Indianapolis, but what I was hoping it would boil down to was loyalty to me. I really believe he didn't want to see me fail, and my gut feeling was he was going to sign on with me, but I also knew he really respected Chuck Daly, because he had worked for him before in New Jersey. But I kept telling Rick that Chuck already had his number one guy, Brendan Suhr, who had been with Daly forever, and that Rick would always be under Suhr.

Rick was having trouble deciding. Finally, one night in May of 1997 I told him I needed to know if he was coming to Indiana or not, and he needed to call me that night. He got mad and hung up. I never did hear from him. He called Donnie instead and told him he was coming.

Once Rick was all set, we started talking about who I should hire as the veteran assistant. Since drawing up offensive plays was Rick's strength, I wanted someone who was defensive minded. My first choice was Jimmy Rodgers, whom I had played for in Boston, and who I thought knew the game as well as anyone. Also, since I knew Jimmy and had a history with him, I figured there would be no problem in terms of trust and understanding each other. So I called the Bulls, where Jimmy was an assistant under Phil Jackson, and asked for permission to talk with him. At the time Chicago was in the middle of the playoffs, and they said I would have to wait until their season was over before I could talk to Jimmy.

Both Rick and I felt we couldn't wait. We were going to have a new coaching staff and we needed to get going.

Rick said he knew the perfect guy for the job: his fellow assistant in Portland, Dick Harter. I didn't know Dick Harter at all. I had heard of him, because he had been around a long time, and he was the head coach of the Charlotte Hornets when I was a player, so I started doing a little checking on him. Everybody agreed Harter was an excellent coach who knew the game, but there was talk that some of the negative experiences he had had in recent years had soured him.

All I know is I talked to Dick for five minutes and it was obvious to me he loved basketball. His defensive philosophy sounded like exactly what I had in mind, and Rick assured me he was the kind of person I would really grow to appreciate. He was right. I learned so much from Dick and Rick in that first season. We could never have made it to the Eastern Conference Finals without their input and their guidance. When I won the Coach of the Year award, I felt like giving Dick and Rick the trophy instead. They deserved it a lot more than I did.

When I settled on a staff of Rick Carlisle and Dick Harter, I knew that would cause people to talk, because I hadn't hired a minority. I wanted to make sure this wasn't going to become an issue, so I called up two of my players, Mark Jackson and Reggie Miller, who are black, and asked them if they minded that I had hired two white coaches. I explained to them that I didn't care what color they were, I felt they were the best two people to help us win. Both Reggie and Mark said they were fine with it, and that's all I needed to hear. I didn't care what anyone else thought, as long as everyone on the Indiana Pacers was thinking the same way.

To me, coaching is a "we" thing. It shouldn't be the head coach running the whole show himself. Rick and

Dick and I split up responsibilities, and we all did what we were supposed to be doing, and it worked. If some people don't like it, too bad. All I know is that one of Dick's friends told me our first season together in Indiana was the most fun Dick had in over forty years of coaching. That made me feel great, because Dick helped me so much.

Looking back, Dick Harter is one of the best things that happened to me in my first season. I absolutely love being around him. He's not going to change for anybody. When we're at some league event, he doesn't want to go over and schmooze with all the other coaches. Everybody in this league is trying to set themselves up for their next job—everybody but Dick. He's too honest for all that. We were at the Chicago predraft camp in June of 1998, just after we had lost to the Bulls in seven games in the Eastern Conference Finals. Everybody was gossiping and whispering in the stands. Dick turned to me and said, "C'mon, let's get out of here so we don't have to go out there and shake hands and kiss everyone's butt."

That's my kind of guy.

CHAPTER 5

On Private Matters

Before I took the Pacers job, I felt there was one thing I needed to share with Donnie, and that was that I had been diagnosed with a heart condition. It wasn't anything life-threatening, but I was on medication for it, and I thought I should tell him about it before we got too far along.

We were driving around, killing some time before we went to a restaurant where we had planned to eat. I explained to Donnie that I had an arrhythmia, which caused my heart to kick out of rhythm once in a while. He listened closely, but I could tell he wasn't too concerned. I wasn't either. There was no reason to be. We thought we were going to have a private meeting at this restaurant, but as soon as we were done eating and had walked out the door, there was a television crew there waiting for us, shining lights in our faces. So much for privacy. I'm just glad they couldn't hear our conversation, because the last thing I wanted was for the media to start speculating about my health.

I always knew there was something funny about my

heart. Back when I was playing for the Celtics, I'd have these episodes. They would only happen once a summer, usually after I had just finished working out really hard, and I'd think to myself, "Oh boy, you overdid it that time." All of a sudden I'd get this rush of feeling really tired, and I'd start feeling my heart jumping around. I never went to the doctor for it. I just thought I was dehydrated, or I had been going too hard, with all the workouts and traveling and everything else I was doing. If I couldn't make it stop, then I might have been more concerned, but I'd walk a hundred yards, then stand and rest. I never quite understood what it was, but I always knew I'd better lie down. I'd close my eyes and take a nap for three or four hours, and I'd wake up and feel fine. It wasn't that unusual for me to take a big, long nap like that. So I would forget all about it, until it happened again the next summer.

After I retired and started working for the Celtics in their front office, it was happening more frequently. I remember it happened once when I was down in North Carolina with our team during training camp. My heart kicked out of rhythm, but it wasn't like before. For one thing, I hadn't just worked out for two or three hours. I mentioned something to the team doctor, Arnie Scheller, and he suggested I go to Boston and get checked out. When I got back to Boston I mentioned it to Dan Dyrek too. I told him that most of the time it wasn't a problem, but once in a while my heart felt like it was racing out of control. I wasn't too pleased with myself at that point. Dan looked at me kind of funny and said, "I'm making a call and having you go see someone right now. You know, Larry, this isn't something to fool around with."

By then, Arnie had already arranged for me to see this

specialist over at New England Baptist Hospital. The doctor checked my heart, but at that time I was in normal rhythm. He said, "Your heart is great. Everything seems fine," so I said, "Well, it is now, but every once in a while it starts going crazy on me." So that's when they started checking me out. They had me do a standard stress test, and they did an EKG. They had me put this little computer chip on my chest so that anytime my heart kicked out of rhythm they could pick up the patterns of my heartbeat. I got a doctor in Naples to check me out too, since I was still spending a lot of time there.

They told me I had an arrhythmia—something called atrial fibrillation—which means the arrhythmia occurs sporadically instead of consistently. Basically, when my heart starts fibrillating, or twitching uncontrollably, the blood flow to my body is affected, and it makes me weak, tired, and lightheaded. There's another kind of condition called ventrical fibrillation, which is a lot more serious and can cause a catastrophic episode within a matter of minutes, or even seconds. I'm lucky not to have to deal with that.

Anyhow, one of the things all the doctors told me was that I needed to cut back on my lifestyle a little bit. I have to do everything in moderation now. I have to watch my diet, how much I exercise, and tone down my alcohol consumption. I also have to make sure I take my medicine regularly.

I've had this for so long now that I can almost predict when it's going to go out. I know when it's happening in a second. I also know it eventually goes away. I remember there was one time it went out on me in Naples, and it was going really bad for some reason. I was real short of breath, and I felt like I needed to see my doctor. I called him, and he told me he wasn't going to be around, but there would be another guy there to take a look at me. So I went in to see this other doctor, and he checked my heartbeat and said, "We're going to admit you." I'm thinking, "Hmmm." Because that wasn't ever necessary before. But this guy was just covering himself. I don't think he wanted to be the guy that let Larry Bird go home with his heart going crazy. Meanwhile, all I wanted to do was go to bed. So I go down to talk to some more doctors, and they all want to keep me overnight. I'm saying, "Look, this has happened a number of times. I just need to go home and get some rest." Finally, they let me go. The only thing they did was put an IV in me and put me on a heart monitor. They thought this thing might be flashing in and out all the time, but I knew better. I told them, "Trust me. I know when it happens, and it's not going on all the time."

There was a period of time when I was only having a few episodes here and there. But when I started talking to the Pacers in the spring of 1997 about coaching, my heart kicked out of rhythm again, only this time it was kicking in and out for almost three months. I kept trying to work out, but I couldn't do it. After I tried any kind of exercise, I would walk ten feet to the bathroom and my heart felt like it was jumping out of my chest. I got a little scared, because it didn't seem like it was going away. I went to Donnie Walsh and told him about it, and he got me an appointment with the team cardiologist, Dr. King Yee.

I went to Methodist Hospital in Indianapolis and told them what would happen to my heart, but it never seemed to happen when I was around their doctors. Finally they put me on this treadmill, and I was working real hard, sweating like crazy and feeling about ready to die, when all of a sudden it kicked out again. That's when they were able to monitor the arrhythmia and start me on medication that was specific to the kind of problem I had.

I was on the medication for probably three weeks. Dr. Yee would continue to put me on the treadmill, to see if the medication would hold up under stressful situations. But even with the medicine, my heart was still knocking out of rhythm. At that point I was thinking to myself, "God, this is getting bad. It's been too long." For the first time, I was really getting concerned. Dr. Yee said my heart needed to be jolted back into its normal rhythm, so he decided to give me an electric shock treatment.

It sounds a lot worse than it actually is. In fact, it's a pretty common procedure for restoring a normal heartbeat. I don't even remember it happening, because they sedated me, then put me on a table and administered a little current of electricity across my chest with defibrillator paddles, just like the kind you see on any medical show on television. The electrical current jump-starts the heart back to its normal rhythm. I didn't feel a thing. They got me up, I left the hospital, I slept all the way to French Lick, and I was fine again.

Before I left, Dr. Yee stressed how important it was to take my medication. I don't really like to take medicine, and I knew I should have been more careful about it, but sometimes I'd forget. A couple of things Dr. Yee warned me about were to be careful around the stress of really hot weather, like we get in Naples sometimes, and to be leery about high altitudes, where there is less oxygen. Sure enough, on one of our early road trips to Denver my heart went out. It was the first time our trainer, David Craig, had to deal with it, so he was a little frantic. He called Dr. Yee back in Indianapolis. I admitted to him I had forgotten my medicine, and he arranged for David to get me some more. After that, Dr. Yee decided I needed a watchdog. From that day on, it was David Craig's job to make sure I was taking my medicine when I was supposed to be taking it. Like Dr. Yee told me, "You know, Larry, you're not the most compliant guy in the world." I got the message. After that, I made sure I took my medicine when I was supposed to take it.

Even so, I didn't want to make a big deal of it. I was the same way when I had an injury as a player. I didn't like talking about it. The last thing I wanted was for Donnie and everyone else to be thinking about my heart. I didn't tell the players about it. I didn't see any reason for them to know. Of course I told Dick and Rick, but I regretted that as soon as I did it. Every time we were out after a game, one of them was saying, "Larry, are you sure you should have another beer? You know, Larry, you've got to watch yourself . . ."

For most of the season my heart condition really wasn't an issue. But on March 17, 1998, when we were playing Chicago at home, I had it kick out on me. What happens is, my heart, when it is at rest, beats around 52 times a minute. But when it gets out of rhythm it shoots up to 102, 104 beats a minute, so it's going twice as fast, and it feels like your heart is jumping all around, and you can't breathe very well. It's not like you are gasping for air, but you feel uncomfortable all the time. We're in the middle of this big game against Chicago, and the score is really close. I really wanted us to beat them, because I had a feeling we would meet them again in the playoffs, and I wanted my guys to believe we could play with the Bulls. So I'm all caught up in the excitement of the game, and it starts happening. My heart starts fluttering, and then it starts banging around in my chest. I started sweating like crazy. I remember I kept turning to Dick and Rick and saying, "Is it really hot in here or what?" They were into the game, so I don't think they noticed that I didn't look so good. Dick just said, "Yeah, Larry, it is hot in here. Real hot." The game was going on, and I don't really remember what play was being run. I was standing on the sideline and hoping for a television time-out, because I felt like I was gonna pass out. Finally, the ref whistled time. Whenever we have a time-out, they always put a chair on the court for me so I can sit down and talk to the guys. This time I fell into that chair, because I was going out. The sweat was just pouring off me. Whenever my heart kicks out like that, I sweat really bad. I don't know what I would have done if I had passed out on the floor. You just hope you don't do a Jerry Reynolds and go out in front of everyone. Jerry was the coach for the Sacramento Kings, and he fainted dead away on the court once. It was a scary thing, although he's just fine now.

By the end of the game everything had calmed down. I saw my friend Joe Kleine, who was on the Bulls. He came over to say hello, and I said to him, "Hey Joe. You got to get into these games. Tell Phil I think you should be playing more." He just laughed. I'm sure he didn't notice a thing.

I didn't tell my players anything was wrong that night. I didn't tell Dick or Rick either. The only one I really did tell was David Craig, because I had promised Donnie I would keep David informed about any problems I had. Craig told Dr. Yee, and I heard from him the next day. He reminded me that I needed to take my medicine, and that I needed to see him at least twice a year. Then he gave me a little lecture about how I had to take this condition seriously. If you let atrial fibrillation go unchecked and you don't take your medicine, your heart won't pump efficiently, and you could develop little blood clots, which could lead to a stroke. That's an unlikely scenario for me, because I'm also on blood thinners. But Dr. Yee wanted me to realize the dangers. I guess Dr. Yee was trying to scare me. I'm not going to be stupid about this heart condition, but I'm not going to live my whole life in fear of this thing either. If it goes, it goes.

My mom had something like it. You'd be sitting with her, and then all of a sudden you could hear her breathing a lot harder. She'd say, "There goes my irregular heartbeat." She'd sit there for a minute, then say, "I can't go up the stairs right now." I'd say, "Aw, c'mon, Mom, what are you talking about?" But when I started getting it, I started thinking to myself, "Holy cow!" Mom said it was hereditary, but all my doctors say it's not.

Dr. Yee should be really happy with me, because I'm paying attention to everything he asked me to. I take my medicine, and I haven't had my heart go out for almost seven months. According to Dr. Yee, as long as my arrhythmia is sporadic like it has been, there's no major cause for concern. I exercise every day like I always have, and I'm feeling great.

Donnie wanted to make sure we have a defibrillator courtside, but that's for the players as much as for me. The NBA has been a lot more focused on heart ailments since Hank Gathers died. NBA player Monty Williams also has a heart condition. So I think all the teams became more aware, and figure a defibrillator makes sense. The last thing anyone wants is for something to happen like it did to poor Reggie Lewis, the Celtics star who died of heart failure while he was shooting baskets. I don't know exactly what happened to him, or why, but I still can't believe it happened at all. It's just a complete shock when somebody that young is gone all of a sudden, just like that.

I was in Florida when it happened. I heard a news flash on television, and I almost fell over. I called Dave Gavitt right away, and he told me it was true. It was a sad, sad day. I felt so awful for his family. I was never really close with his wife, Donna, but I know her and like her. She tells it like she sees it, and I respect that about her.

I wasn't in Boston when all of Reggie's care and treatment had been going on. I knew that the Celtics doctor, Arnie Scheller, had put together a top team of cardiologists so Reggie could get the best care he could possibly get. Next thing you know, the *Boston Globe* had a story about how Reggie and Donna switched hospitals in the middle of the night, and that got me worried. I don't know why that happened, but I'm sure Donna and Reggie had their reasons.

I guess the part that gnaws at me the most is wondering if it had to happen. I know it would have been really tough for Reggie to give up basketball—he loved it so much—but he had a little boy and a little girl on the way when he died, and now they don't have a daddy.

When Reggie died, I think we all had the same thought: you never know what's going to happen. I just wish he was around. Reggie was a great kid. When he was a rookie and wasn't playing very much, he used to come in for me at the end of a game and he'd shoot every time he got the ball. What was so exciting was to watch him develop into the kind of player he became. He worked very hard to improve his ballhandling, his defense, and his shot selection. He could always shoot the ball, and when he finally got to where he was the guy the team counted on, the heart problems happened. It doesn't seem fair.

I'm sure it made it harder for Donna and Reggie that it was all so public. That's one of the worst things about being a professional athlete. People think everything that happens to you is their business too. Like when I went to Indianapolis to get my shock treatment. I wanted to make sure nobody knew about it, so we scheduled it for real early in the morning. I made sure I went in a side door and that as few people as possible saw me. The good thing was it didn't take very long, and by the time word got out that I was at the hospital, I was already long gone.

It's mind-boggling sometimes, what you have to go through to guarantee your privacy. But we're used to it. This is the part of my career that I have never liked.

When I was playing, some guys used to use aliases when we checked into hotels on the road, but I never did that. I just blocked off my phone. Of course, that was after being around the league a couple of years. I remember during my rookie year we played an exhibition game in New York City. I was rooming with Tiny Archibald, and the phone rang and I picked it up, and somebody was on the other end telling me they were going to kill me. I hung up, and Tiny said, "Who was that?" I told him, "Some guy that's going to kill me." The phone rang again, and this time Tiny picked it up. He chewed that guy out for a good ten minutes, but I really wasn't upset about it. I just went on. I knew the guy wasn't really going to kill me. You have to get used to that kind of thing when you are in the public eye. I've received so many death threats, I've lost count. But I understand everyone deals with it differently. I read that Karl Malone decided he needed to start carrying a gun after he received threats.

The best threat I got was during the 1984 Finals in Los Angeles. We were warming up for the second half against the Lakers and my coach, K. C. Jones, called me over. He said, "Larry, I've just been told there's been a threat made on your life. You can handle this however you want. See those men all around the rim of this arena? They're security personnel. They can escort you to the locker room, and you can watch the rest of the game there. You can leave the building if you want. Or you can keep playing. It's totally up to you." I said, "Okay, K. C.," and I went back into the layup line. After a minute or so, K. C. says to me, "Larry, I see you're still out here." I said, "K. C., of course I'm still out there. It's the Finals! We're playing the Lakers!" K. C. said, "Great, great. But Larry, do me a favor, will you? When we come back in the huddle to start the second half, can you stay at center court? I'm afraid this guy might be a bad shot." K. C. said it with a totally straight face, but I knew it was his way of trying to defuse the situation. He was trying to get me to relax. He was the best at that. Anyhow, when my team gathered in the huddle to start the second half, I ran to the middle of the group and draped my arm over K. C.'s shoulder.

You've got to understand that a lot of these threats are just kids, or people who are frustrated because you are beating the hell out of their team. I know Michael gets his share of it. Magic did too. That's the way it goes. Get on with life.

The truth is, I've never cared so much about someone that I would be that intensely involved with them. I can't believe anyone would walk across the street to meet me, because the truth is I wouldn't walk across the street to meet anybody else. If somebody told me Miss America was outside the door, I'd wish her all the luck in the world, but I'm just not into that stuff.

When I was a kid we never went to any pro games, but one time our coach took us to Louisville, Kentucky, to see an ABA game. We were all seventh-graders, and my buddies were saying, "Hey, let's get some autographs." I said, "What do you want those for?" They said, "It's fun. C'mon, we'll show you." So they give me a piece of paper, and Dan Issel is walking off the court. My buddies are hollering at him, and I'm kind of standing back with them, and Issel says, "No, no, not now," or something like that. We got turned down. That was exactly what I was afraid of before I went down there. So I never asked anyone after that.

I understand exactly what position Dan Issel was in. I did then and I do now. I can honestly say I've signed as many autographs as probably anyone else in the world my age, but I can just do so many. I know every time you turn one more guy down, it could be Larry Bird left standing there, but it's impossible to please everyone. Autographs are tricky, because so many people are into reselling them. You wish it was all little kids who want to take it home and put it in their scrapbooks, but it isn't.

During the All-Star game a few years ago, when they announced the fifty greatest players of all time, the league wanted us to sign these commemorative lithographs. David Stern told me I had to sign these things, and I told him I'd sign when I had time and when I wanted to do it. They kept hassling me about signing, to the point where I almost didn't do it. Finally I told them I'd do it before the game. So I go to sign the things, and come to find out Shaq didn't sign, because he wasn't even there, and neither did Jerry West, because he wasn't there. They made this big stink about me not signing, but it was okay for these other guys to skip out? They made me out to be the bad guy, and that's fine. I don't really care.

I know some people feel I'm unapproachable, but the one thing they don't understand is that I get very uncomfortable around crowds. I always try to stay away from situations where I might run into a group of people. What I never liked was when I'd go somewhere thinking there wouldn't be much of a fuss, and then all of a sudden there's a hundred kids all around you, pressing toward you. That's when I become jittery. Unfortunately, that happened all the time when I was playing.

One thing I always hated when I was with the Celtics was trying to get home after the game. The way I would get out of Boston Garden was to walk down a ramp and out through the back of the building. I'd always peek out, and I wouldn't see that many people, but the minute I stepped into view all these people who were sitting waiting in their cars would jump out and start running at me. I never did like that. So I started hanging around late after the games, having a soda in the locker room, waiting for the people to go home. Sometimes I'd even order out for a pizza. After a while, the Garden security figured out a way to get my car for me, pull it around back, and sneak me out a door right next to the train station. Even so, there was always somebody there who would figure out it was me. Sometimes they'd even follow me home.

People in Boston really did amaze me sometimes. I lived in a house in Brookline, which is a suburb of Boston, and my street was a shortcut through to the interstate. The first few years of my career I mowed my own lawn, and I'd always be able to get the back and the sides done pretty good, but whenever I tried to finish the front, people always stopped. One after another, they'd see me and put on the brakes, right in the middle of the street sometimes, and come over and try to strike up a conversation. After a while, I realized I couldn't mow my lawn anymore. It wasn't safe! For the most part, the people were pretty respectful. Most of 'em would drive by and honk the horn, and Dinah would say, "There go the fans." Once in a while someone would run up and ring the doorbell after we went to bed. Dinah and I got used to spending most of our time in the back of the house. We had a screened porch, and it was nice and quiet, and sometimes it felt like we lived in the country. Our neighbors weren't much of a problem either. Bob Woolf, who handled my first contract with Boston, lived right near us, and then on the other side there was an older couple. We didn't hear much from them at all, except one day the guy came over and complained about one of our tree branches sticking out on his property.

I can pinpoint the day I lost my privacy forever: when *Sports Illustrated* put me on the cover of their magazine and called me college basketball's best-kept secret. At the time, our Indiana State team was surprising everyone. I was a junior, I had never felt better about my game, and it should have been an exciting time. But that cover took care of that. My life was never the same. Within days, the phone at the school was ringing off the hook. Everyone in America wanted an interview. Back then I was sort of self-conscious, and I really didn't want to talk to anybody. The other thing I couldn't believe was how long it took for those photographers to get the shot they wanted for the magazine. We were there for ten hours with *Sports Illustrated.* I don't know why anyone would need so many pictures. They kept taking them and taking them. The one they decided on for the cover was me standing in my uniform, surrounded by these cheerleaders who were saying, "Ssshh," because I was this secret weapon. But they took pictures of me in a lot of different poses. In one of them they had me run through a hoop. I was so fed up. I told our sports information director I would never pose for another magazine cover—ever! When I got to the pros, my rule was, "One hour. If you can't get what you need by then, you're out of luck."

About the time of the first *Sports Illustrated* cover, the media and other people started calling me the Great White Hope. It seemed like a silly thing to me, but I just never thought about it that much. I wasn't going to get caught up in it. Once in a while some guy on another team might make a crack about it, but for the most part I ignored it.

When I got to Boston I started hearing about it again. I had never been there before I got drafted by the Celtics, and I didn't know much about the place, but I knew the Celtics and the people in the city were following me after I got drafted by them. I knew there was talk about me going to Boston and doing this and doing that, but I had no idea how high the expectations were and how that would affect my new teammates.

So I walk into camp, and it's my first day, and there's Sidney Wicks and Curtis Rowe waiting for me. Cedric Maxwell, who was sitting with those guys, says, "Here comes the Great White Hope." I'm standing there thinking, "Oh no, not this stuff again." Luckily it didn't last long. Once I started playing and proving to them I belonged, I didn't hear anything about the Great White Hope anymore. That was true all through my first NBA season. Once I got on the court, I took care of the stereotypes. I was a basketball player. Period.

I never understood why people made so much of race. I remember when I first got to Indiana State. I had to sit out a year to regain my eligibility, but I would go up to the gym all the time and work out. Every day around two o'clock during the off season, a group of guys would meet at the gym and play pickup games. They were all black. I was always up at the gym shooting around during that time of day. One afternoon, one of my teammates said, "Hey, why don't you come over here and play some games with us?" I could tell the other guys didn't want me to play. They had never really heard of me at that point, and they were really good players. So I waited my turn and got into a couple of games, and after about three days kicking butt out there I was in charge of the whole thing. That was the only way to do it—to go in there and show them what you got. Now all of a sudden these guys are asking me, "Can we have the next game, Larry?" Those guys were good. They could get up and down, and make passes. They didn't care what color you were—as long as you could play.

But I found that out a lot earlier than in college. Back when I was in the eighth grade in French Lick, I used to get on a bus after school and go to the West Baden courts, because all the guys that worked over at the hotel played there on their breaks. They always let me play. They were big guys, in their twenties, most of them, and they were all waiters. They let me play because I was good enough, even though I wasn't as big as them. Getting on that bus was a total joy for me. It was pure enjoyment. I couldn't wait to get over there. As soon as I got off the bus, these guys would say, "Hey Larry, hurry up, come on over here, you're on our team." That was the first time I ever really played with any black players. It wasn't even an issue to me at all, really, because all I knew was these guys were big and strong, and I could learn from them, so I wanted to be around them.

I'm not naive. I know some fans loved me even more because of the color of my skin. They can think what they want. My main concern was to make sure it was never an issue with my teammates, and as far as I can tell, it never was. We never had one problem like that in our locker room during the thirteen years I was with the Celtics.

As much as I loved Boston, I know it could be a tough place for black players. Robert Parish and D. J. and those guys would never say anything to me directly, but you could hear them talking in the locker room once in a while. They'd be talking about how they were stopped by the police for no reason, or how they'd be walking through the North End after having dinner and they'd hear comments. I remember Ed Pinckney coming in all upset once. Ed is one of the greatest guys you'll ever meet, and he had been stopped by the police, with his kids in the car. That kind of stuff is horrible. I really felt for those guys. It makes you sick.

When I came to Boston to play for the Celtics, I called myself the Hick from French Lick. It's just something I said, but before I knew it, that's who people wanted me to be. The reason I said that was I was coming from the country, and I had never lived in a big city, and I felt out of place at first. I was wondering about it the whole time I drove from French Lick to Boston. I had no idea what to expect, and it made me uncomfortable. I wasn't worried about the basketball. I was worried about everything else.

But once I got there it was fine. I lived on the outskirts of the city, which I think was a good idea, so I didn't have to deal with the everyday hustle and bustle. Before long I was finding my way around and getting more familiar with the roads and stuff. It certainly helped that everyone was so excited about the Celtics. People made me feel welcome right away. The Boston fans were the best. Maybe that's because we were winning.

After being in Boston a couple of years, we had already won a championship, and I was getting my fair share of attention. The only problem with that was they forgot you were human after a while. They expected you to be perfect every night, and that's hard to do. That's the one thing I didn't like as a player. Sometimes I'd get off to a slow start, and the fans would get impatient. They expect greatness all the time. I expect it too, but some nights it's slow developing, and some nights it's not there at all. On those nights, you know what's coming. You know they're going to get on your case and tell you, "Wake up!" or "Hey Larry, get moving!" It's the nature of the business.

The other thing I always thought was kind of funny is how people think that just because you are famous you must know everyone else who is famous. That's ridiculous when you think about it, but somehow that's how it turns out. I'll never forget the time John Cougar Mellencamp came to Boston for a concert. I love his music—he's an Indiana guy, and everyone from Indiana loves him—so I told the guys on the team I was going to the concert. My teammate Jerry Sichting, who is also from Indiana, went to the show too. The next day we were talking about how great Mellencamp was, and Jerry said to me, "He stayed at your house, didn't he?" That wasn't true at all, but I couldn't resist. I told him, "Yeah, Jerry, you found out. He stayed with me." Next thing you know, Jerry told the whole team. He must have told some reporters too, because it was in the paper a couple of days later. Amazing.

When I do have some free time, one of the things I enjoy most is fishing. I love to fish for bass. I prefer freshwater fishing, because I have problems when I go out into the Gulf and the water gets rough. I've never been able to handle it. I get seasick when I'm out there—probably half the time. It's just a bad feeling. I've always been a little leery of water anyway, especially out in the Gulf, or in the Atlantic, because storms can blow up so fast, and you wouldn't believe it if you were ever in one, how dangerous it can be. You just get this feeling that there's no way you are ever going to make it. The farthest Conner and I have ever been is twenty miles out, and I don't even like that. I have a real fast boat, but if we go out in the Gulf we'll go in something bigger, like a Boston Whaler.

When I was a kid we used to fish in little rivers or streams, or in the little ponds around town. We used to get up real early, because someone told us once that's when the fish are biting, but as I got older I realized it doesn't make any difference. What matters is you find a little peace and quiet.

I don't have stuffed fish hanging on my walls. I've never caught anything all that big, and besides, it's not really my style. I don't have my basketball trophies all over the house either. They're nice, and I'm glad I have them, but that was never what was important to me.

Let me tell you a story about when I played in the World University Games in the summer of 1977. It was a great experience. The team was made up of guys like Jeff Judkins, who played for the University of Utah and then went on to play a couple years with the Celtics; Dave Corzine, the center from DePaul who played for the Bulls in the pros; Darrell Griffith, who played his college ball for Louisville and went on to be a star for the Utah Jazz; and Sid Moncrief, who starred for Arkansas and later Milwaukee in the NBA. I had just finished my sophomore year at Indiana State, and we went down to Louisville to try out for two weeks. Denny Crum was the coach, and if he put your name up on the board, you made the team and got to go to Europe for a month. I made the team, and we played all over the place—Italy, Yugoslavia, Bulgaria. We traveled all over the countryside in a bus, and there were crowds everywhere we went. Everyone wanted to see the Americans play. Darrell Griffith and Freeman Williams were two of the bigger names on that team, as well as James Bailey, who was a big scorer from Rutgers. I hung around a lot with Jeff Judkins. He was my roommate, a real friendly guy, and we hit it off right away. After a couple of weeks of training, Jeff said to me, "Hey, you're the best player I've ever seen. You are so much better than all these other guys with the bigger names." I just said, "Yeah, yeah, Jeff, right." So we get on the bus a couple of days later, and everyone is talking about college players and who thinks who is the best, and Jeff says, "Hey, Larry is the best player in college right now." The other guys start saying, "C'mon, Jeff, you're just saying that because he's your roommate." Now Jeff is all fired up. He's really getting into it. He said, "I guarantee you one thing. If you play team ball in these tournaments, Larry will be the MVP in every game. He's just better than all of you." I'm sitting on the bus, ready to die. Talk about pressure!

We get to our first pre-tournament venue, and it was absolutely fantastic. It was in Palermo, Italy, and it was an outdoor basketball court, a wooden court with glass backboards. When you walk in, there's a big concrete wall around the court, and they had armed guards standing up against the wall. They had about 10,000 people in the bleachers, and it was as calm as could be outside. The wall was about eight feet high, with apartment buildings all around it. It was unbelievable. People were hanging out their windows, or sitting on their balconies, watching us play. It was one of the greatest places I've ever seen for a basketball game.

It was a round robin tournament, with four teams. We won all four games, and I was named MVP. The next tournament I was MVP again. At this point, we're traveling all through Europe by bus, train, plane, and boat, and I'm carrying these trophies along with my luggage. I never knew how to pack, so I just took everything, and it was getting hard to lug all this stuff around. The trophies were just so darn big. One of them looked like an ashtray with some kind of strobe sticking out. We got to yet another train station, and I turned to Jeff and said, "You know what? I've carried these things for two weeks. I've had enough." So I told Jeff, "Watch this." I opened the lid of a trash can and threw the trophies in there. I said, "I'm not carrying these things anymore." Then I got on the train. A few hours later we got to our next city, and the team is doing a head count, and they're looking for Judkins. He shouts out, "Here I am!" I turn around, and he's staggering off the train with the trophies. He looked like a pack mule. He came up to me and said, "I'll carry these the rest of the way for you. You gotta take them home. They'll mean something to you someday." Every time I look at those trophies, I just start laughing, and think about how Jeff Judkins carried those things all over Europe.

Back then I was still someone who could get around

without being noticed all the time. Those days are long gone. I guess I won't ever quite get used to people looking at me all the time, watching every move I make. I knew it would happen when I was a player, but I'm surprised that some of it has carried over to the coaching. Like the first real game I coached, at the Atlanta summer league in July of 1997. I walked out there for the first time and I could feel all the eyes on me. It's uncomfortable for me. Always has been.

But the one thing I noticed in my first coaching season—and it's completely different than what I expected— is how fans treat you differently than when you were playing. They actually holler and say hi. When I was playing, I never had a guy from Philadelphia saying, "Hey Larry, how are you doing?" But now it happens. I was expecting all the usual, the wisecracking and the smart-mouth stuff, but it really hasn't turned out that way. The only thing I hear is, "Hey Larry, you better take off your suit and get in the game." I'm not sure why they laid off me. Maybe it's some form of respect. I know they give other coaches hell, because I can hear them.

I do sometimes wonder what it would be like to be just another person. Most of my close friends aren't famous at all. They're working people, and they enjoy life as much as I do. There's a part of me that wishes I never became famous. Maybe that's why I enjoy the private time I have.

I've got this idea in my head now that I want to move to Montana. I've never been there. I don't like horses, and I don't do any hiking. I'd just like to have a thousand acres with a cabin on it. But it's got to be a cabin with a garage. That way I can go down to the garage and sit there all day and think about nothing.

Sounds perfect to me.

CHAPTER 6

On My First Year As Coach

Once I took the Pacers job, I couldn't wait to get going. But there were a few things I needed to figure out. My first day of work, I showed up at the office before eight o'clock in the morning and the doors were locked. I had to hang around for almost an hour before anyone showed up. That afternoon I asked Donnie Walsh for my own set of keys. My second problem was I didn't have my assistants yet. Both Dick and Rick had said yes, but they had things to finish up in Portland, and I was on my own. I'd come in, and I used to go right to Donnie's office. After about three weeks I said, "Maybe this guy has other things to do besides having me sitting here looking at him." I asked him, "Donnie, when are you going to show me the coaches' office?" He said, "We don't have a coaches' office." I said, "Why not?" He said, "We never had coaches that ever came in the office." I said, "You've got to be kidding me. I know when Dick and Rick get here, we're gonna need an office." Donnie thought about it for a minute, then he took me to this room that had all sorts of equipment and papers and stuff in it. It's where the Pacers put all their interns. "How big do you want this office of yours?" Donnie asked me. I said, "This is plenty big enough."

I couldn't wait until Dick and Rick showed up. I was really chomping at the bit to get started. If there was one thing I was concerned about with my coaching, it was drawing up plays. For one thing, I didn't like to draw, so I knew that would be a problem. But I don't worry about it at all anymore, because I've got the guy that's the best I've ever seen. We were sitting in our new office before the season, and Rick was showing me how to draw up these plays when I said, "Listen, you're really good at this. You should do this for our team." I could tell Rick wasn't sure if I was serious or not. I told him, "Look, I'll do it, but I don't have a problem if you do. If you think it will hurt you, by people asking, 'Why is Rick drawing all the plays,' guess what? I don't care. My main goal is to get this team to win. I want to win this whole thing." The only other worry we had, I guess, was how the players would react to it. As far as I knew, there was no other assistant coach in the league drawing up the plays in the huddle. But why would I insist on doing it when I knew someone else right next to me who was better at it? The players understood that. They didn't care.

I knew I was giving my assistants more authority than anyone else in the league, but I was proud of that. Dick and Rick were two intelligent guys who lived for the game of basketball. Why wouldn't I give them input? That's not to say we didn't have a difference of opinion now and then. A lot of those differences would present themselves in the middle of a game. For instance, if a defensive player had three fouls on him, Dick was always saying, "Hey, he's got three. Let's go right at him. We've got to run a play." You can run one at him, but if you don't score, why keep hammering away at it? I think it makes your offense get out of sync if you do that. The truth is, most fouls are picked up off the ball anyway, or from a guy coming over to help out. In that situation, I have to make a quick decision on how I want to go for that particular moment, in that particular game, but then it's something that Dick and I will go back and talk about later.

Naturally, when you have three guys having a lot of input, they aren't all going to agree. Early in the year I know I was doing some strange substitutions that had Dick and Rick scratching their heads. One day Rick said to me, "Larry, we've got to talk about these substitutions." But that was one thing I felt strongly about. I knew I was playing too many guys, but it wasn't hurting our team at that point, and I wanted every guy that had worked his butt off to feel like it was worth it. I also knew I saw things in a guy like, say, Fred Hoiberg, that maybe others didn't see.

The other thing I had a little disagreement with Rick and Dick about was time-outs. There were stretches when our guys were playing really bad and it would seem sensible to call a time-out and let them have it, but my urge was often to let them play through it. The upshot of it was I wasn't calling very many time-outs. Dick and Rick weren't the only ones who noticed. Reporters were asking me about it all the time. I told them the same thing I told Rick and Dick: coaches overreact too much in this league. I knew as a player that there were times when we'd go through a couple of rough minutes, but if the coach stuck with us we'd straighten it out. Sometimes calling a time-out just draws more attention to the fact you are struggling. It can get guys thinking too much about what they are doing wrong, instead of what they are doing right.

Anyway, we were sitting there one night, and it was a close game. I can't remember who we were playing, but Rick was sitting next to Dick and I was sitting between them and the players, and I pulled Jalen Rose over and said something to him. We were up by about eight points at the time, but the other team got hot and made a comeback. All of a sudden, we're coming down the court, and Dick and Rick are saying to me, "Time-out! We need a time-out!" I don't say anything. They start hollering at me again. "Larry! C'mon now, we got to have time!" Reggie Miller was sitting right next to me, and I was mad. I was mad at our team because they blew the cushion we had built up, and I was mad at Dick and Rick because they kept yelling at me to take a time-out. The third time they did it, I turned around and said, "Shut the fuck up! Relax!" Reggie's eyes just about popped out of his head. He couldn't believe it. All the guys on the bench were just looking at me with their mouths open, because they never heard me use language like that. In fact, I usually go out of my way not to swear too much. Anyhow, on the next play there's a jump ball, we win the tip, and we go down and score. Then we get a steal and score again. I turned around and smirked at my two coaches. I couldn't resist!

Dick and Rick never forgot it, and of course they got me back. They went out and bought some walkie-talkies, and they planted one of them in my office before the game. Then they went back into the equipment room with the other one. So I'm sitting there in my office going over something, and all of a sudden I hear this voice saying, "Larry. Call a time-out." I'm looking all over the room, but I don't see anybody. I probably wouldn't have caught on for a while except those guys started cracking up. Rick I expected that from, but Dick? I didn't know he had it in him.

I can still remember the first time I sat down and talked to Dick Harter. It was during his interview for the job. I talked to this total stranger for ten minutes, and I said, "Where have you been my whole career?" Isn't that strange? He started telling me about defense, and he was trying to be professional and all, but the more he talked, the more fired up he got. I don't know how badly he wanted the job, but I was impressed with his passion for the game. That's one thing all three of us share. When you love what you are doing, you don't care how long it takes to get it right. Sometimes parts of coaching can be long and tiring, but I've never felt that way when Dick and Rick are with me. We can be breaking down tape together and going over things, and all of a sudden I'll look up and three hours have gone by.

That's one thing all three of us agree on: how valuable the tape can be as a learning tool. Most people don't know this, but when I was a player I used to go home after a game and watch it all over again on tape. It wasn't so much to watch myself. What I'd do is zero in on plays where I had the ball, and see where my teammates were positioned. That way I could tell if I could have made a better play, or if there was someone who was open that I hadn't noticed on the floor. It also helped me make sure my teammates were going to the proper spots on the court. You can't believe how many times I'd be sitting home replaying a game I had just played, and I'd watch myself come off a pick, and I'd see Danny Ainge, wide open in the corner, and I'd say to myself, "Geez, how did I miss him?" Then I'd go in the next day and say to Danny, "Hey, you were wide open on that play last night in the third quarter. My fault. Call for me next time, and I'll get you the ball." I figure our players can benefit from the same kind of thing. I know all twelve of my guys aren't going to go home right after a game and watch the whole tape. I don't expect them to. We can show them what they need to see. Coaches can talk and talk and talk about something, but if you get it on tape and show it to them, it is so much more effective. Let's say we want Reggie to shoot the gap better than he has been. You mention it a couple of times, and he does it for a while, but then he falls out of the habit again. Because of all the video technology we have, we can break down tapes of the previous two months and put together a highlight tape, or in this case a lowlight tape, of every time Reggie didn't shoot the gap the way he should have. When you put it all together like that, it tends to catch their interest.

What I like best about Dick and Rick is that I don't have to stress to them how well prepared I want our team to be. They're stressing it to me! And we pass that kind of mentality down to the players. I've been talking to Rick about basketball for a long time. I did it that way before I became the Pacers coach—pretty much ever since he played with me. Rick is very organized. He works the game, every little detail. That's what I wanted. I wanted someone who would go after every little possible edge. When we run a play, I want our guys to know exactly what is happening. On every play. Rick feels the same way. He's not going to leave out anything. He has every angle figured. He's done booklets of information for us similar to the one he sent me when he worked in Portland. We have one booklet that tells us that if you turn a certain player toward the baseline, he will hit 28 percent of his shots. If you turn him to the middle, it's higher, like 35 percent. You show the guys all these numbers, and then you convince them that if they turn that player to the baseline he's got a lower chance of scoring than if they turn him to the middle.

One day Rik Smits asked, "How do you know the guy shoots only twenty-eight percent?" I told him, "Rik, come here." I showed him the equipment our scout, Dan Burke, uses to do our film. I told Smits, "Our staff takes every frame of a game and they break it down to a science. They go through every shot every player takes. It's a lot of work, but it's going to make us prepared." Rick goes through all that stuff after every game. He charts every single play on the offensive end. After two or three games, he'll say, "Okay, Larry. When we run this certain play, and we end up with a post-up for Mark Jackson, we score sixty percent of the time off that." Once I took one of Carlisle's sheets into the locker room and I went over to Mark and said, "Study that." It was every play we had in those three games. He looked it over and said, "Wow." I said, "That's right. You're our best option." The only thing you have to be careful about is getting enough tape to make sure you have a pattern. You have to throw out the nights when the guy who normally gives you 10 points and 5 rebounds a night busts out for 30, just like you have to eliminate games where your most reliable player doesn't show up mentally to play that night.

Even with all this information that we have and pass along to the players, I don't want them to ever lose their instincts. There are times when things happen on the floor that nobody can predict. There are situations that come up that require a split-second decision that can't be coached. I don't want to take away that kind of freedom from our guys. Rick Carlisle has devised a lot of plays—hundreds of them, actually. He's very good at calling the right ones. But sometimes I do feel we take away from Mark Jackson. Mark wants to call his own plays. I told him, "Mark, if you have something in your mind that you want to run, I don't care if us coaches are screaming at you. You just go ahead and run the play." Coaches do get caught up in the game, and we overdo it a little bit. When it gets down to the end of the game, I don't mess with the players. I've got a lot of confidence in Mark, and so does Rick. If Mark Jackson sees something he thinks is going to work to win us the game, then it's his call all the way.

While Rick is charting all our offensive possessions, Dick is doing the same thing for the defense. He's got all our players listed. He knows where we're vulnerable as a team, and what their individual defensive deficiencies are. He brings it in to me before practice, and we go through all of it, then we sit down and talk about what we need to work on that particular day. Just like with our offensive tendencies, we've got to be careful not to jump to conclusions. I remember one particular game when we played Detroit. Joe Dumars, who it seems has been around forever, killed us with four jumpers in a row. He posted Travis Best with the same move every time. Dick and I were talking about a change, but I decided to stick with what we had. I yelled out to Best, "Hey Travis, suck it up. He's just hot." Here's why I didn't alter our coverage: Travis was doing everything we asked of him. He was turning Dumars baseline and making him shoot high, which should have meant a low-percentage shot. But when a guy like Dumars—with his history and experience—gets hot, you just have to tip your hat to him.

One of the things I told Rick and Dick, and I think it

took them some time to get used to it, is I wanted everyone on our team to feel like they had the green light in terms of shooting the ball. It makes Rick nervous. I know it does. My feeling is, it's so hard to get an open look in the NBA these days, if you've got one, you better shoot. It's a completely different approach than how Rick and I were taught when we were players. I can remember one of our early games against Chicago, Travis Best came down a couple of times, pulled up for the shot, and missed both times. The next time down he had a wide-open three and—boom—misses again. Rick and Dick were sitting there all bothered by it. I was sitting there saying, "We're going to win this game." When he missed those three shots, it was because he wasn't being aggressive enough. But the point was, the shots were there.

Another time, we played Milwaukee, and it was going right down to the wire. We were playing horribly, but we were still in it. Chris Mullin had four wide-open three-pointers at the end of the game that would have put us up by three and never made one of them. Here's one of the purest shooters in the league, and he's not even close. We were in a time-out, and Chris is looking at me, and I said, "Chris, are you ever going to make a shot, or what? This is ridiculous. Just make a shot, and the game is over." Sometimes you're sitting there, and you know you're the coach, but you have this little thing about being a player again. When Reggie or someone misses three or four shots, you find yourself saying, "Hey, are you ever going to make a shot tonight? If not, why don't you come over and sit by me?" Even so, I still don't tell them to stop shooting.

One thing I didn't know about when I took the job was what head coaches did and didn't do. I had never paid much attention to them while I was a player. I had my own pregame rituals and routines, and if my coach was doing something special, I can't say that I ever noticed. So when I was mapping out my game plan for the year, I told Dick and Rick, "Here's what I want. Before the games I want you guys, and me, out there working with the players." Right away, Rick said, "You can't do that. Head coaches don't go out there and do that." He said, "You're going to make every coach in this league pissed off if you go out there." I was looking forward to that pregame work. I should have just gone out and done it anyway. I really believe I would have had more enjoyment by being able to go out there before these games and work with my guys, then come in and take my shower and get ready. But I knew I had already gotten away with a lot. We had kept it to two assistants, and we didn't have a minority, and I guess I decided we didn't need any more trouble in that regard. But I was thinking about doing it for my second year. I think it would be a blast.

I don't really care what anyone thinks, and neither does Dick at this point, but Rick is going to be in this league a long time, and I don't want to do anything that might hurt him from getting a job in the future. I think he's one of the brightest young minds in this game, and he's going to have lots of opportunities. Rick has a lot of confidence in his abilities, and the only thing I worry about is sometimes it comes off like he's too tough. You have to show these guys you are human. When I get into that locker room, I ask them to do stuff, I don't tell them. Certain guys react to certain people. Like Jalen Rose. Dick and Rick call him in all the time to talk to him about this and that. Then he'll walk by my office and I'll say, "How are you doing?" and that's about it. Jalen is an emotional kid, and he's still young, and he drives us all crazy at times.

I'll hear Dick and Rick get on him for something, and I'll wait until they're done, and then when Jalen walks by my office I pull him in and tell him, "Hey, Jalen, you're doing a great job. Just stick with what we're telling you and you're going to have an excellent year." There's no question that he needs to hear what Dick and Rick are telling him, but sometimes I feel it's my job to smooth it over when they're through.

I'm a completely different person on game night than I am in practice. I am not fun to be around a couple hours before a game. Never have been. Dick, Rick, and I have the same routine night after night. Rick goes out, does his stuff on the floor with the players, then he comes in and I ask him, "What do you think?" He says the same thing almost every night: "Aw, Larry, they don't look that sharp. We don't have a chance tonight." At that point we're in the locker room getting ready. I always put my tie on around my neck, but then Rick has to tie it for me. I can't reach all the way back there to do it, because of an old elbow injury I had. It doesn't let me bend my arm properly.

When I was a player, I was never nervous *during* a basketball game, but I'd get sicker than a dog *before* games. I used to feel like I could throw up at any time. I used to walk out after shootarounds a nervous wreck. Every day. I hated it. I was like that in college too, and it drove me crazy. That's why I always used to sleep in the afternoons, so I wouldn't have to deal with all the nervousness. The good thing was, as soon as I walked out there and stepped on that court, it was gone. One of my better memories as a player is when we used to run out of the tunnel at Boston Garden onto the court. It's awesome. I used to love it on tape, us coming up the ramp, with the camera following us from behind. We're charging out of that chute, hitting the floor, and Grant, the retired cop who guarded our bench, would be waiting, giving us high fives and low fives. It was the best.

Now that I'm a coach, it's the same thing all over again. Before the game I feel like I want to die. But once we get out there and they start playing, I feel great! On home game days I take a little nap at home. I get back from shootaround somewhere between one and one-thirty, and the kids don't get home until three, so I have time. The older Conner and Mariah get, the more they are getting into the Indiana Pacers. When the Bulls came to town, all the kids were talking about it. So Conner comes home from school and says, "I want to go to the game tonight." I said, "Well, it's a school night." He says, "I don't care. I want to see Michael Jordan." Last time Chicago came through, Conner asked me to take him in to meet Michael Jordan, but that's something I just can't do. I just remind him again about playing with Michael and his kids in Barcelona. That didn't seem to be working like it used to, though.

When we have a home game I get to the arena around five o'clock, and I always read the scouting reports on the opposing players. Then Dick comes in and says, "Larry, anyone can win this game tonight." A couple of minutes later is when Rick comes in after working out the guys and says, "We're going to get blown out by fifty." It's the same thing every night. The funny thing is, they really mean it when they say it. It's different on the coaching side than on the players' side. When I was a player I walked into every game every night thinking we would win by 20. But on this side, you just never know. There are too many variables that can affect how your team plays.

I tell our team, "If you put your mind to it, you can win any game, anytime," but if they come in and you've got two guys playing hard and three guys just sort of playing, it makes it tough.

About forty-five minutes before game time I go to the coaches' office and Dick is sitting there. I grab my chair, so I'm sitting there too. It's funny as hell. The two of us sitting there, not saying much of anything. It goes on like that for forty-five minutes. It's horrible. Once in a while one of us might say, "Well, do you think Barkley is going to play tonight?" or something like that. But mostly we're just in there, nervous as hell, getting ready for game time. At that point Rick is out on the court. When he comes in and announces we don't have a chance, that's when I know I should take a shower and get ready. Once in a while, Joe Qatado, my special assistant and equipment manager, will come in and say, "Anybody need anything?" We barely answer the guy. We're just a bunch of grumpy guys, all ticked off, and the game hasn't even started yet.

There was one time when our game was televised on TNT, and one of their guys asked if Hubie Brown, their announcer, could come in before the game, around forty-five minutes before, to talk to us and our players about matchups and stuff. I did it one time and I didn't like it. I didn't want other people in there, and because I was feeling all sick and nervous like I do, I wasn't in any mood to talk to somebody. So the next time they came to us I said, "Look, if those guys want to talk to me, tell them to come to shootaround, and I'll be glad to sit down with them." The guy says they can't do shootarounds, because sometimes they've got other meetings or whatever, and they can't be running all the way over to the arena. My feeling on that? Tough! Anyhow, Hubie got mad. He got all worked up. He didn't say anything to me, but he told Dick and Rick, "I've never been turned down by any coach in this league. This is the first time since I've started that this has happened." But it's like I told Dick and Rick: "This is how I am. You guys have seen me right before a game. I don't even want to talk to you guys. I told them I'd spend as much time as they need at the shootaround." For the rest of the season, Hubie didn't come in and talk to us. It's too bad, really. I love Hubie Brown. I always did. I thought he was a great, great coach, and I loved to play against his team because they were bulldogs. It's nothing personal against him. I think Dick, who has known Hubie a long time, has tried to explain it to him. Anyhow, I did notice once we got into the playoffs that they started coming around early to do stuff.

When I first started coaching, I might stick my head in the locker room and try to see whether the guys looked ready or not. I don't worry about that anymore. But Dick worries a lot. He'll say, "Oh, look at them. They're not moving. They're laying around in there. How are they going to play well if they're laying around in there?" But I explained to Dick that as a player, one thing I never knew going in was how I was going to play. Never. There were nights I went bouncing in there feeling ready to take on the world, and I couldn't hit anything. Other nights I'd drag myself in there and then go out and have 25 points and 15 rebounds.

The one part of my job I never really enjoyed was talking to the media. Dick and Rick get frustrated sometimes, and I do too, when people get things wrong. But I understand that talking to the media is part of my job, and really, it's not as bad as all that. I'll say one thing: it was a lot different in Boston than in Indiana. When I was with the

Celtics, there'd be a ton of reporters in the locker room before the game, looking for a quote. They were very competitive. In Boston, reporters are celebrities, just like the players. The fans know all about them. In Indiana there's not the same kind of intensity. There might be four or five writers before the games, and afterward I don't think it ever gets higher than fourteen or fifteen.

I figured out the best way to handle the media while I was in Boston. After a game I'd go in the back to the trainer's room and get iced down. I'd drink a couple of beers, wait until everyone else got done, and then I'd go out and sit on this table in the middle of the locker room. I'd answer everyone's questions, and when I could see they were starting to bog down and were running out of things to ask, I'd say, "Got enough?" Then, boom, I was out of there. I used to look at the clock when I went and sat down on that table, and then I'd look again after I was finished, and it was almost always around ten minutes. That's why I didn't get worked up about the press too much. Ten minutes isn't really all that much time. With the Pacers I pretty much did the same thing. I didn't spend a whole lot of time doing interviews about myself, because I promised my team that this wasn't about me, and I meant it. What was nice about that first season was that both Dick and Rick got their fair share of notoriety, and they deserved it.

While Rick was already one of my closest friends, I enjoyed getting to know Dick so much. He was so refreshing to me. I loved his work ethic and his enthusiasm. In the Eastern Conference Finals, when we played Chicago, Dick wanted to address the team. I told him to go ahead. He got all geared up and he got very emotional. He told our team, "It's time we showed the Chicago Bulls—it's time we showed the world—we are the better team." Hell, *I* was ready to run out there and play. I know there are no other assistants in the league who would have been allowed to give a speech to the team before a big game like that, but I think every assistant should have input. I could never understand why Boston had any assistants, because they never let them do anything, except maybe a little bit in training camp. But once the season started, you never heard boo from the assistants. It was always the head coach, and I never could understand that. When I took the Pacers job, I told Dick and Rick exactly how it was going to be. I told them I'd like them to be vocal with our team. If they felt uncomfortable about getting in and talking with some of the guys, that was fine. But both of them are so involved.

Dick in particular gets really fired up. He's fired up from the time we get there until the time the game ends, and then he's fine. Unless we lose, of course. Dick is a veteran. He's been around, and I trust his instincts. I talk to Dick a lot. I'll say to him, "Dick, do you think the guys look tired?" He'll tell me honestly. Even after a win, sometimes he'll say, "Larry, maybe we better lay off a little. These guys are beat." He's got a good feel for that.

It's beautiful, the way our coaching staff works. I've got this young guy who is as eager as hell to do well, and he wants to be a head coach so bad he can taste it. Then I've got the guy who's been there, who was the head coach, who has been in basketball forty-three years and has loved every minute of it. On top of it, those two guys would do anything for each other. Once in a while, when the offense is struggling, Dick turns to Rick and says, "Are you going to score me eighty-five points? Rick, c'mon, I need at least eighty-five." But it's all lighthearted. Rick and

Dick are in this together, all the way. Last summer, when the league locked out the players, Dick was just chomping at the bit to get back. He lives for this stuff, and he takes his part in it very seriously. Dick is ticked off if any team gets over 90 points on us. And if they get over 100, he's absolutely livid. He takes great pride in our defense, and that's why I love him. Dick and I can spend all day talking about defensive principles. Our big thing is we like to stop the pick and roll. The pick and roll in our league is major. Everybody wants to run it. When I was with the Celtics, Robert Parish and I made a living doing it. Our feeling is that if you double-team the guy looking to make the pass and take the ball out of his hands, the other guy has to come and get the ball, and now you've got a big man 15 feet from the basket, and what's he gonna do with it? All of a sudden we rotate by pulling a man over to him. At this point the shot clock is winding down, and they're stumbling around. If you get proper rotation, you can take that pick and roll away. We have guys that are supposed to sink down, and that's one of the really good things about our defense that first season. Reggie and Chris were just excellent at sinking down and helping to hold the big guy.

The pick and roll is one of the most devastating weapons in basketball. It murders people. John Stockton and Karl Malone are the two best in the league. They can do it in their sleep. Dick asked me once what I used to look for in a pick and roll, and I told him, "Coming off, I knew I'd have Parish on his way to the basket, but if I had to stay up with the ball, I made sure I was around the free throw line so I'd have a shot." That was always major. There was also always somebody standing over in the corner, wide open, whether it was Danny Ainge, or D. J., or whoever. Robert was always able to do a little extra, whether it was sticking his butt out, or moving just enough to get the big guys defending him to step out. When Robert went to the basket, all you had to do was throw it up there and he'd always catch it. People never did appreciate how well Robert executed that play.

One of the things I told Rick we needed from day one was an offense against trapping pressure. We found out we needed one during the Atlanta summer league. We played the Celtics, and they were on us. They didn't have their best players there, but they had some good ones. They just murdered us. We couldn't get the ball across half court. So Rick and I started talking about how we needed a play to break the press. We'd work on stuff, and I kept telling Rick, "Boston is going to kill us. I don't like this. I don't like how we're doing." He said, "It's good. Believe me. We just need some time, and repetition. We'll be able to handle the press. We'll put in another one about two weeks before we go up to Boston to play them. They're really the only team that presses. So don't worry." So we put in another play, and it so happened we were playing New Jersey right before the Celtics, and they were pressing us all over. We used both our plays, and we shot 67 percent against them. It was clicking like you can't believe. Then we got to Boston, and when they put on the press in the second half, we were passing to the right spots and cutting to the right places. Pitino had to back off. For the rest of the season we begged teams to press us. Mully and Mark Jackson were loving it. I said to Mark one day, "Don't you just love it when teams press us?" He said, "Hey, Coach, are we good or what!"

That kind of feeling became contagious, in our locker room as well as in the front office. When I took this job I hardly knew our team president, Donnie Walsh, at all. I laid it all out to Donnie how I wanted to do things. I told him how I'd like to handle personnel, how I was going to help players, the type of game I wanted to play, what we were going to do in practice. The one question I asked him was, "If I'm on these guys, and they think I'm working them too hard, and they come in here and whine to you about it, what are you going to say? Are you going to back them, or are you going to back me?"

I've seen that happen before, and it can be really destructive. I didn't know Donnie well enough then to know the answer was obvious. He's with us all the way. He'd listen to the players, I'm sure, but then he'd tell them to go talk to their coach. Donnie told me later the only thing he didn't really believe was that we had a good enough team to win a championship. Of course, part of that was because Chicago had Michael Jordan. But let's say Michael gets hurt for five minutes in a playoff game. The whole thing could change. Injuries are part of the game—I've always said that. If Rik Smits was down for a long time, or we lost Reggie for six months, it would kill us. But that's part of the game. It's what makes you sorry it didn't happen for us in my first season, because we had everything going for us.

The day our season ended, Dick and Rick were already talking about what we needed to do the next season. That's why I know they are the perfect guys for me, because I was thinking the very same thing.

CHAPTER 7

On Coaching Today in the NBA

I've had a lot of really good coaches during my career, and when one of them did something that had an impact on me, it stays with me. I've taken a little something from each coach I've played for along the way, and I know it's made it easier for me to understand the players I'm trying to teach.

Looking back, I can go right to my two high school coaches, Jim Jones and Gary Holland, who taught me how to establish a work ethic and to develop sound fundamentals. Jim Jones was the first person to stress to me how important it was to use my left hand. At the time, I'm not sure I understood why that was such a big deal, but the better I got and the tougher competition I played, I appreciated that advice. Jim Jones was always around in the summer when my buddies and I were playing basketball. He'd drop by to check on us, then tell us, "I'll be back around to see how you are doing." We never knew what that meant. Some days we'd play for another hour and he'd show up. Other days we'd be out there for five hours, afraid to go home until he came back, because we didn't want to disappoint him. That was something I kept up right through my pro career. I always wanted to impress my coach. When I got older, I asked Jim Jones where he went all that time, and he told me, "Hey Larry, I was playing golf!" Jim Jones is also the one who drilled the idea of boxing out into my head until I wouldn't dream of not doing it. I wasn't a great rebounder because I was stronger or could jump higher than anyone else, because I couldn't. I was a good rebounder because I knew how to get position under the boards. I was lucky to start out with someone like Jim Jones, who would meet me and my friends before school to practice our free throws. When he left in my senior year of high school, Gary Holland picked up right where he left off. Coach Holland wasn't quite as firm as Jones, but by then I was policing myself. Coach Holland let me experiment with a little more offensive freedom, and it felt great. No wonder by the time I got to the pros everyone was talking about what a sound fundamental base I had.

I'd have to say Bill Fitch, my Celtics coach from 1979 to 1983, is the best coach I've ever played for. Bill was organized, he preached discipline, and he had us in the best shape of our lives. We won the 1981 NBA championship under him, and I have a great deal of respect for him. That's why I asked him to be one of my escorts when I was inducted into the Basketball Hall of Fame last October.

Some of the guys who played for Fitch in Boston resented how hard he pushed us and how much he rode us, but they will also be the first ones to tell you he was a big reason why we were successful. Take Robert Parish. He played in the league twenty-one years and is a guaranteed Hall of Famer, but it wasn't always that way. Bill

Fitch saved his career. When Parish came over to us in a trade with Golden State in 1980, he was horrible. Fitch would have us running all day—he was killing us—but Robert would only run free throw line to free throw line. He was never involved in any of the action. Fitch taught us, "Get the ball, and go!" so somebody would take the outlet, run up the floor for a layup, but by the time Robert caught up with us at the free throw line we were already going back the other way. It was no good, and we all kept looking at Fitch, waiting for him to explode, but he never did. He just kept running and running us, until finally we got into shape. Then, all of a sudden, one day we were running down the court and we realized, "Hey, Robert's under the basket." It changed his whole game. Plus, he had his turnaround jumper. Robert discovered he could shoot fast, and sort of be falling and still be able to run down and get back on the other end. Bill Fitch is the one who did that.

The truth is, I had never heard of Bill Fitch until the Celtics drafted me. I just didn't follow pro basketball that closely. I knew of Red Auerbach, and Bill Russell and Wilt Chamberlain, but that was about it. I remember the day they flew me into Boston for my press conference. They had it at the Boards and Blades Club, which is a big function room in Boston Garden, and I was standing around waiting for everything to start. There was a lot of press around, and this guy comes up and starts talking to me. I was a little nervous about everything that was going on that day, so I was polite to this guy, but I really wasn't listening to him. Anyway, this guy was doing most of the talking, telling me how much the Celtics had a chance to contend for the title, and how I would really enjoy Boston, and then someone tapped me on the arm and said, "Okay, Larry, we're ready."

I go up to the podium, and there is Red Auerbach sitting there, and then the guy I had just finished talking with sits right down next to him. That's when I realized, "Holy smokes! That's my coach!" I knew the name, Bill Fitch, but I had no idea what he looked like. He must have thought I was some kind of jerk. I mean, there he is, talking to me about my future, and I'm blowing him off. So now I'm sitting next to him, and I think it's funny as hell. I had probably the best coach I could possibly have, sitting there talking to me, and I didn't even know who he was. I've got so much respect for the man, but you never would have known it that day.

The one scene that will always stand out in my mind was the first day we had practice. It was the same day Cedric Maxwell, Sidney Wicks, and Curtis Rowe were giving me all that grief about being the Great White Hope. You could tell those guys had their own little thing going. They were smart-mouthing everybody, and calling me the savior—here comes the savior—being really smart-ass about it. I bet we weren't in practice twenty minutes, and Fitch started killing us. He just ran us into the ground. I didn't know any better; I thought it was normal. All of a sudden Fitch blows the whistle and says, "Okay, Curtis. Why don't you go on and get dressed. They'll send you your checks. You're done here." I was thinking to myself, "What is he talking about?" But there goes Curtis Rowe, out the door. We practice another hour and Fitch blows the whistle again, and he sends Sidney Wicks packing.

Now all of a sudden the whole atmosphere has changed. I think Max was a little ticked off, but he got in line pretty quick. I didn't know what was going on, really, so I just put my head down and kept working.

So that's how I knew that Bill Fitch was going to be

demanding. A Bill Fitch practice is all movement. That's what I want our Pacers practices to be. With Bill, you always ran a lot more than you think you did, and that's what I loved about it. He just kept it coming, one drill after another. The one thing he always did was make me play one-on-one against guys after practice. In the beginning it was M. L. Carr, but as soon as he got fatigued he'd send somebody else out there. One day it might be Max, another day it would be Dave Cowens. It was just so exhausting.

In my first year, after we had played about 30 games I went to see Doc Silva, because I was losing a lot of weight. I was down to about 208 pounds, which was about 25 pounds under what I usually was, and Doc Silva said, "He's working you too hard, kid. You probably should take a week off." I was having trouble visualizing that, telling Bill Fitch I needed a week off, but Doc Silva was insistent. He said, "You can't continue to lose weight like this. Go to Florida. Put your feet up for a bit." I told him, "I don't need to go to Florida, but could you tell Coach not to run us so hard? Then I wouldn't be losing so much."

Bill Fitch was the best coach for me at that time, because I had no clue what I was getting myself into. He would put me through these grueling drills just to get a reaction out of me, but he never did get one. The truth was, I loved it when he worked us like that. He kept me hungry. He never let you know where you stood, so you kept on working so you could impress him.

The funny thing about it is that as a coach, I'm the opposite of Bill Fitch. I don't yell like he did, and I give my guys a lot more freedom, but I find myself using so much of Bill's stuff, especially when it comes to conditioning drills.

We won a championship with Bill in 1981, but you could see his ways were wearing on the team. When Robert Parish says something, then you know there's a problem. Guys like Max and M. L., they always had something to say, but Robert never said anything bad about Coach Fitch, even though there were times you could tell he'd had enough. When even he finally spoke up, then I knew Fitch was gone. All those guys respected Bill Fitch as a coach, but they had trouble not taking his comments to heart. The things he said to them when he got them in a corner, that's all part of coaching, but they couldn't separate that. Fitch would say things to Kevin McHale, and he'd get all flustered.

I was really disappointed when they let Bill Fitch go, because I learned so much from him, but I knew it was time. I truly believe three years is the max for any coach with one team. That's why when I signed my contract with the Indiana Pacers, it was for three years. I guarantee I will not be coaching for them any longer than that. Things get stale to players real fast, even more so today, and they need a fresh look at things. I'm not even sure I'll make it to three years. I told Donnie Walsh I would reevaluate things after every season.

When Fitch left the Celtics we knew it would be different with K. C. Jones, who was promoted from our assistant coach to our head coach, but we picked up Dennis Johnson that summer, and I felt we'd be fine as a group. K. C. couldn't have been any more opposite than Fitch. It took a lot to get K. C. really riled about something; it didn't take much at all for Bill. K. C. doesn't get a lot of credit for the job he did with our 1984 and 1986 Celtics championship teams, because everyone thinks we were so talented that we could just do it ourselves. That's not true.

K. C. was the perfect coach for that team, because he gave us the freedom we wanted and needed, but also because he knew when it was time to step in and make his presence felt.

K. C. didn't waste a lot of words. He'd just walk over to you and say, "Hey, you can make a better effort than that." I remember right from the beginning, K. C. said, "I don't care what you guys do off the court. When we throw the ball out there, it's time to play, and you better be ready." That's one thing that stuck in my mind. We only needed to give him two hours a day, so get to work. I've tried to treat my Indiana players the same way. I promised them I would never yell at them, and, for the most part in my first season, I kept my word. If one of my guys is doing something I don't like, I pull him aside and say, "I need a better screen from you. Don't set a lazy pick. Set a good one." And, if they don't do what I ask, I call them over a second time and say, "This is the last time I'll tell you. If you can't set a good pick, I'll go out and find myself someone who can."

One of the things that K. C. really helped me with was controlling my emotions on the court. When I was young, I could be really hotheaded at times. If something set me off, especially early in my career, I would end up with a technical, or sometimes even be thrown out of a game. I remember after one of my outbursts, when I got tossed, K. C. called me aside. He said, "Larry, you aren't thinking. You are forgetting how valuable you are to us. You don't do us any good when you're sitting in the locker room all ticked off about something. You've got to understand that when you're out on the court, we've got a chance to win every game. But when you're sitting in the locker room, and we're out there playing, we have very little chance of winning." What I remember most about that was how calmly K. C. said all of it to me. He wasn't shouting. He explained it very simply, like it was so obvious, and by the time he was done it was obvious to me he was right.

So now whenever I see my star player, Reggie Miller, getting all worked up about something, I tell him the same thing. He's a very emotional player, which is fine, but not when he gets caught up in those emotions and lets them affect his play. I sat him down early in the season and gave him that whole talk about how when he's sitting out, he's not helping us. So now Reggie knows where I got it.

K. C. was an easy guy to play for. He loved to win, but win or lose, he'd call us together after the game and say, "Okay, go in there and wash your asses, and let's get out of here." I always got a kick out of that. In fact, after one of our Indiana games, it just came to me that's what K. C. used to say, so I called my team together and told them, "Okay, go in there and wash your asses, let's get out of here." You should have seen them looking at me. They thought I'd lost it.

One other thing I stole from K. C.: not being afraid to sit back and go with the flow of the game. I remember one time we were playing the Clippers, and we were running a play called "32," for Kevin McHale (his number was 32). It's basically a play where a guy spins off from the weak side and sets a pick for Kevin. We ran the play two times in a row, and Kevin scored both times. So K. C. yells out, "Thirty-two." Again and again. He wouldn't get off it. Finally, the Clippers called time, and K. C. got us in the huddle and said, "We'll run it fifty times if they don't stop us." I love that. I don't understand why more coaches don't do that. They all want to save their big plays. But if you save it and the other team gets on a run and scores 15 points, they might have built up enough confidence to stop "32" at that point. I find myself calling out the same play over and over if it's working. Maybe not to the extent that K. C. did, but I'm with him. Why not keep coming at 'em until they stop you?

When K. C. decided he had coached enough, after the 1987–88 season, everybody knew the next guy in line was Jimmy Rodgers, who was K. C.'s top assistant and had been part of probably the best coaching staff ever in 1986—Bill Fitch, K. C., and Jimmy. I was really excited that Jimmy got the head job, because he had already been so valuable to our team, and he had very patiently waited for his turn. Jimmy had head coaching offers at other places, including New York, but the Celtics wouldn't let him out of his contract because they wanted him to be the successor to K. C. I was hopeful that things would go well for Jimmy, but his first season was the year I had surgery on my heels and only played in six games. I came back for the 1989–90 season, and it was a tough year.

People still think I didn't like Jimmy Rodgers, and that couldn't be further from the truth. It was just a frustrating season for all of us. We were running a new offense, and nothing seemed to be going smoothly. In the past what had made us so good was how quickly we could get the ball out of the hoop and move it up the floor. But as we got into the season we started playing a different way. Dennis Johnson, who was our point guard, would get the ball and control it for most of the shot clock. He'd come out, get the ball, hold it, and wait for almost 20 seconds. If I could have come off the ball and set a backdoor screen, or something like that, it would have opened up things for everyone, but to just stand there and hold the ball, that was a game I had never played.

I always thought Jimmy Rodgers was a great basketball man, and I'll always feel that way about him. But like any player or coach, we didn't always think alike. I felt at the time that our strength was ball movement, but our new offense didn't emphasize that. There was a game in Detroit, and I was told to stand out on the wing and hold the ball, to wait for things to develop. So I did exactly what they told me. I just held the ball, and I didn't shoot, even when I was open. I passed up some 12-foot jumpers with nobody around me. I was frustrated, and after the game when the media asked me why I wasn't looking for my offense, I told them I was doing what the coaches wanted. When they asked me if I liked it, I told them I wasn't a scorer anymore, I was a "point forward."

Even though I was just expressing my opinion, the media made a big deal out of it the next day, and Jimmy got all upset about it. I didn't mean to embarrass Jimmy. I wasn't trying to create problems for him, it's just that I was disappointed in the play of our team. I thought I was pretty close to Jimmy Rodgers. When he was an assistant we talked a lot. Once he got the head job, maybe he thought he had to change. His personality was definitely different as a head coach. We used to worry about him a little bit, because the stress seemed to really get to him.

About that same time, our team was starting to fall apart. One thing about the Celtics was we always had a good locker room, with guys always busting on each other, but that year it wasn't like that. There was tension in the locker room. The whole thing blew up one day after this article ran in the *New York Post* talking about our team and how divided it was.

I just remember coming in and getting ready for the game, and then all of a sudden all these reporters are at my locker asking me questions about this article. I hadn't seen it, hadn't known anything about it, but the paper said there were guys on my team who said I couldn't accept the fact I was no longer the focal point of the offense, and that my ego was causing all sorts of problems, and I was the reason we were losing. Basically, these two teammates, who didn't have the guts to put their names in there, were calling me selfish.

I had my suspicions right away on who I thought the two guys were: Jim Paxson and Kevin McHale. Paxson had come to our team a couple seasons before, and he was injured almost the whole time he was there. He was on the downside of his career, and he couldn't play the way he wanted to, but right away he was a guy I stayed away from, because he was your classic clubhouse lawyer, always talking behind people's backs. I've never trusted people like that. I've always felt that if you have something to say, then say it out loud, like a man. But Paxson wasn't like that. He and McHale became friendly almost right away, and I knew it was going to be bad news for our team. Kevin is a good guy, but he's always been a follower. The one great thing about all the years Robert Parish, Kevin, and I played together was we always had a great team— no backstabbers. But that was about to change.

The story caused a big stink. The Boston papers wrote the same kind of piece a few days later, and all hell broke loose. I didn't say too much about it, except that I felt I knew who the two guys were and one of them had a yellow streak running down his back. Everyone knew who I meant, and suddenly Paxson's name was in the paper. Right away, Paxson denied he was one of the guys. But to tell you the truth, I didn't really care. What was a lot more disappointing to me was that Kevin had said those things. I just felt that after playing so many years with one guy and going through all the battles we went through together, whether he liked me or not was one thing, but to go to a paper like that and then not even own up to it . . . I just thought it was a cheap shot. I never said anything to Kevin, but he knew.

I've always thought the world of Kevin McHale—I still do—but I was so hurt he would do something so cheap like that. But I always knew Kevin could be one of those guys. He'd come to me and say, "D. J. won't pass the ball and you've got to tell D. J. not to do that," and then he'd go to D. J. and say, "Larry is hogging the ball, you've got to talk to him," but we all knew that was just Kevin, so we sort of put up with it. The reason we did was because Kevin played hard, and he played hurt, and he won us championships, no question about it.

After playing with a guy that many years and hanging around with him some, playing golf, going out for a beer, I just couldn't get over that he did that to me. I know Paxson got inside his head and Kevin just followed along, but it doesn't make it right. It was probably one of the lowest moments of my career.

Whenever I see Kevin we say hello and all that, but it has never really quite been the same. I haven't forgotten what happened, but I'm not going to hold a grudge. We spent too much time together for that. I was with that guy every day for twelve years. I know Kevin like the back of my hand. So the best thing to do is to wish each other luck and move on.

I wouldn't say the same about Paxson. Kevin eventually admitted he was one of the unnamed players in the story. Paxson still denies it. I made up my mind that he was a guy I just wouldn't deal with anymore. He was traded at the end of that 1989–90 season, and I thought to myself, "Good. Hopefully I'll never see him again." I didn't for a long time. I retired from the game, and I started doing some work for a trading card company, and I get a call from one of the guys from the company one day, telling me they had some stuff they wanted me to sign. The guy said, "We're flying one of our new reps over. It's an old friend of yours." I said to the guy, "Tell me who it is." He answered, "It's one of your old teammates. It's a surprise." I told him, "I don't like surprises. Who is it?" He said, "Jim Paxson. He's flying in from the West Coast to Florida as we speak." I told the guy, "You better find someone else to bring me those cards. I won't see that guy." At first he thought I was joking, but he realized pretty quickly I wasn't. So when Jim Paxson landed, they told him to turn around and fly back home.

All the turmoil we had during that 1989–90 season took its toll. It made me realize how lucky I was before that to be on clubs that had good team chemistry. And now as a coach I am really aware of it. You can notice it from the sidelines, when guys make little remarks to each other on the court, or what they say to their coach when they come out of the game. I can say our Pacers team didn't run into problems like that at all. We had a really great group of guys that were interested in only one thing: winning.

I'm sure there were little things along the way, but I made a point of staying away from the locker room. That's a place that belongs to the players, and I wanted to keep it that way. Besides, I would have known if we had one of those guys who goes around trying to get in everyone else's head. They're the type of guys you really don't want on your team if you are serious about winning.

Looking back, I guess it's not that surprising we lost to the Knicks in five games in the first round of the 1990 playoffs that spring. But at the time, I was in shock. I knew we weren't playing well, but it never occurred to me we'd lose that series. Not very long after that, Jimmy Rodgers was fired. We had won 52 games that year, but the owners didn't care. They had seen enough of Jimmy. I can still remember the day he got fired. As soon as I heard the news I got myself a plane ticket, and I was out of that town. I didn't want to hear about it. I didn't want to talk about it. I felt so sorry for Jimmy. I know a lot of people think I got Jimmy Rodgers fired, but that is not true. I would never do that. I had too much respect for him.

Shortly after they fired Jimmy, the Celtics hired Dave Gavitt to be the team's CEO. We were all hoping Dave would give our assistant Chris Ford the head job. Chris was worried that because Jimmy didn't work out, the Celtics wouldn't want to go that route again. But after going after Duke coach Mike Krzyzewski, who didn't want to make the jump to the pros, Gavitt gave Chris Ford the job.

Chris and I were not only good friends, we were teammates. I always admired Chris because he got the absolute most out of his talent. But we got off to a bad start right away. On the first day, which was media day, all the questions were about how Chris wanted to get us back to a running style. I said, "Hey, I'd love to get out and run, but we hear the same story every year. Every coach tells us how he wants to run, but once the season starts, the coaches call every play, and it slows everything down." I didn't say it to be nasty. I was kind of laughing when I said it, but that's just the way it was.

I didn't think too much more about it until the next day in practice. Before we started, Chris comes over in front of everybody and jumps all over me. I mean, he goes crazy. He's yelling, "How dare you criticize me in the papers, before we've even started? Do you know what kind of position that puts me in when you start questioning me on the first day?" I just stood there, and I didn't say a word. I lost a lot of respect for Chris Ford at that moment. If he's got something to say to me, then fine, but pull me aside and talk to me about it.

Later I told him I wasn't trying to challenge him. I was just telling the truth, that everyone promises we're going to run, and then it doesn't happen. He said, "Well, that's not how it's going to be this year." So I said, "Fine," but I was still mad. I mean, it was his first year, and I was going to help the guy as much as I could, and the first day he tries to embarrass me in front of the whole team.

We ended up getting off to a great start that season. We were 28–5 in first place in the East by the All-Star break, so Chris got to coach the All-Star game. I was glad, because he is an excellent coach, a very good tactician, and he'll do anything to win the game. He was like that as a player, and he's like that as a coach. It's not about the money or the attention to him. It's about winning, and I admire that.

The other thing I learned from Chris was how to really be into the game when it's going on, but to be able to let it go when it's time to go home. That's important for the coach as well as his players. Chris always managed to maintain a healthy balance that way.

I've always said if I was ever in a position to hire a

coach, Chris Ford would be one of the first people I'd have on my list. But before I ever hired him, we'd have to sit down and have a long talk first. Chris is one of those screamers who shouts at guys on every play, and I don't think that works. I noticed when he coached the Bucks that he was a lot less like that, and I was glad to see it. In 1999, he was named coach of the Los Angeles Clippers, and he was as calm as I've ever seen him. The only other thing I would talk to him about, and I don't know if he even still does this, but when he coached the Celtics he would get mad after a bad loss and start talking about player salaries. He'd say, "For God's sake, you're making this much million dollars, and you can't throw an outlet pass?" I never liked that as a player.

I knew Chris was in a tough position, trying to coach his old teammates. The truth was, he was a screamer as a player too. But it was different when he became our coach. We had a close team when we played with Chris, and we all respected one another, but now all of a sudden Chris is screaming at us for a different reason. He thought he wasn't getting the respect, but he had the respect. He never should have worried about that.

It was a good lesson for me to learn. What I decided was that it isn't a good idea to coach guys you used to play with. My first season in Indiana, we wanted to bring in a veteran big man who would be good in the locker room, and the first guy I thought of was Joe Kleine. Joe and I played together in Boston, and I would have loved to have him on my team because he was such a positive teammate and a good guy, but I didn't sign him. The reason I didn't was because I thought about what happened with Chris, and I didn't want that to happen with Joe and me. I didn't feel so bad, because Joe signed with Chicago and they won a championship.

People make a big deal of our battles with Chicago in my first season with the Pacers, but for me Miami was almost as big a challenge, because Riley was coaching them. I was sure in my first season that we were going to have to play Miami in the playoffs, and I was really looking forward to it. But New York took care of that for us. New York has always been a tough place to play for anybody, and we turned out to have a great series with them, which we won, but I still felt a little cheated not getting a crack at Riley and Miami.

Every time we played them, it seemed that Riley had worked in something new. And then there was the stuff he always ran. It didn't matter that we saw it time and time again, because a lot of the time we couldn't stop it.

I remember playing Miami late in the season, and they had called a time-out. I called our guys over to the huddle and said, "Look, I want to tell you guys something. Just one time this season, I want to go out there and stop them after a time-out. They score every single time they get the ball out of bounds, and I'm sick of it. They run the same play every single time, and why is it we can't stop it?" They were all looking back at me, and I could tell they were as frustrated as I was, but you know what? Miami came out of the time-out and they scored. Their forward, P. J. Brown, would step out to set a pick and roll, then—pop—he'd head to the basket for a layup. Drives me crazy. The problem with stopping it, though, is that there are countless variations of what seems to be a very simple play. Someone told me once that Pat Riley never worries about what the other team does. He only concentrates on what his team does, and makes sure they do it exactly the way it was diagrammed.

The other thing I know about Pat Riley is that he's very, very demanding. I've never been to one of his practices, but I've talked to Dick Harter a lot about him. Dick coached with him in New York, and he said guys would walk into camp a little overweight, and by the time Riley was done with them in one month's time, they're thin. Dick says he works them really hard in practice. If somebody was hurt and couldn't practice, they were expected to spend the whole workout on the exercise bike, which isn't much of a break, especially the way Riley expected you to ride that thing. I'm sure some of his players get tired of all those tough practices, but if you notice, he hardly ever yells at his players during a game. It's rare that you'll see him get mad at one of his guys on the sidelines. My guess is he takes care of that stuff in practice.

As much as I respect Pat Riley, I never have really talked to him. I don't like it when coaches go out before a game and start acting like it's some kind of social hour. I can tell he doesn't like it either. Besides, to me Pat Riley will always be a Laker, and I'm sure to him I'll always be a Celtic. And the two don't mix.

I don't need to talk to Pat Riley about coaching. I see what goes on out there, and so does he. Besides, our styles are very different. From what I understand, Pat Riley is famous for his halftime speeches. People tell me he's kicked trash cans and punched blackboards, but not before he's checked those trash cans before the game to make sure there aren't rocks in them. That's not something I've done— at least not yet. I remember once when I was with the Celtics, we were playing like crap, and Jimmy Rodgers was our coach, and we got into the locker room at halftime and he was mad. He was so mad he hit the blackboard and shattered it. It was hilarious. I'm sure it wasn't supposed to be, but I had trouble looking up at him, because I knew he was mad, and I was trying not to laugh about this blackboard he had just destroyed.

There aren't very many good stories about me and my halftime speeches. I guess my feeling is if you go into the half of these games and your team is losing, you have to realize they aren't going to play great every single time. So as long as they are giving me an effort and playing hard, I'm not going to go in there and go crazy on them. The way we do it is Rick starts off with his talk first on where the offense is going wrong, then Dick stands up and chews them out if they aren't playing the kind of defense he wants, then I go in there and say, "Look, we're playing bad. We've got a chance to win this game. If we all leave here tonight with a loss, we're going to feel like idiots because we have an opportunity to win this game." Some nights, that's all you need to say. Other nights, you need to get a reaction from them, and that's when I turn it up a little bit, to make sure what we're doing wrong gets corrected. But I don't overdo it. Too many times, coaches get all riled up at halftime and start screaming at these guys, and they spend the first five minutes of the third quarter recovering from that.

That's no good. I've always felt that the third quarter is the key to the game. If you do it right, you can come out after halftime and change the whole complexion of the game. That's also when conditioning starts kicking in. Well-conditioned teams start showing themselves in the third quarter.

To tell you the truth, I don't worry much about other coaches. That's not my game. My first season, when we played Chicago in the Eastern Conference Finals, people kept asking me about Phil Jackson. He was doing a lot of talking about how crafty I was as a player, stuff like that, trying to soften me up, I guess. We had to play a little cat and mouse with the officials in that series. We both took turns blasting the refs. I don't really like to play those games, but sometimes you gotta look out for your team. I think some people were disappointed after the series that Jackson wouldn't at least acknowledge that we had played them tough and given them all they could handle, but hey, they beat us. He doesn't have to say any of that. I'm kind of glad he didn't, because it will motivate my players in the future.

There's been a lot of talk about Phil Jackson and his Zen and meditation, which all sounds like a bit much to me. You can get away with a lot of stuff when you've got the best player in the league on your team. But I really did feel for Phil Jackson. I can't understand why his organization treated him the way they did, trying to kick him out the door. All the guy did was win for them, and they did him wrong. The thing that really got me was when I heard about Jerry Krause bringing in a draft prospect for a workout and not letting Phil know about it, because he hadn't signed a new contract with them yet. That's bull. I tell you what: if Donnie Walsh ever did that to me, I'd be outta there. Who needs that? And the pressure they put on Jackson was ridiculous. One thing I'll give Phil credit for: he said he was going to quit at the end of the 1998 season, and that's just what he did, even though he knew he could probably have almost any job he wanted.

People talk a lot about Chicago's triangle offense, but the one thing the Bulls never got enough credit for was their defense. You've got Michael Jordan and Scottie Pippen, probably the best two defensive players in the league, and Dennis Rodman, who can hold his own by just playing his position all the time and not even thinking about scoring. What coach wouldn't love having those three on the defensive end? As for the triangle offense, it's great if you have the right players, which Chicago did, up until 1999. Take Jordan and Pippen out of the equation, though, and I'm not sure how effective it would be.

Next to Pat Riley, Cleveland coach Mike Fratello is one of the best I've seen. He would have been on the list of names I gave to the Celtics for their coaching job the summer they hired Rick Pitino, except I knew he was under contract and wasn't really available.

My first season of coaching with Indiana we drew Cleveland in the first round of the playoffs, and I was really concerned, because they are so well coached. I was expecting a real dogfight, but although their star forward, Shawn Kemp, played well, our team was playing great at that point. One of the things Fratello's teams do really well is flood off the weak side of the ball. All his teams, including the ones that Dominique Wilkins played for in Atlanta, did that. That's fantastic. It takes a team that is committed defensively, and one that is well disciplined. Fratello is like Pat Riley in that his teams seem to score after every time-out. It drives me nuts. Plus, he's always got his players moving exactly where he wants them to move. A lot of times he's getting ready to isolate, or pick and roll, and he's trying to string us out, and he does that better than anyone else in the league. It hurts us, because we're not real quick, and when Rik Smits is out there trying to help the guards off the pick and roll, it's hard for him to get back. That might create an opening for Cleveland center Zydrunas Ilgauskas, who is one of the bright, bright young stars in the league, although he broke his foot last February and nobody was sure about his future.

There's another characteristic that Fratello teams almost always have, and that is an ability to penetrate the defense, then kick the ball back out to the shooters at just the right time. I know he must spend a ton of time on it, because Cleveland executes that very well. I've taken some notes on it, in case I want to try to implement something like that myself. I study a lot of things Fratello does. I would not enjoy playing for him, because he's a screamer, but that's the only reason I wouldn't want to play for him. As far as knowledge of the game is concerned, I have not seen any other coaches in the league, other than Riley, who have more than he does.

When people started talking to me about possibly being named Coach of the Year, I told them that if I won, it would be a joke. I meant that. Guys like Pat Riley and Mike Fratello can run circles around me. That's where my assistants came in. I used my assistants a lot, so yeah, if you put the three of us together, we had a pretty good coaching team. But Coach of the Year is supposed to be an individual award, and that's why giving it to me was a joke.

The person who should have won that award in 1998 was Jerry Sloan. I felt his Utah team was the best I had seen all year, hands down. Take a look at how Jerry Sloan does things. He runs about four plays a game, and has been doing that for ten years. So you think, "What's so great about that?" I'll tell you. Nobody seems to be able to stop those four plays. Sure, Sloan has Karl Malone and John Stockton on his team, but hey, he makes sure those other guys chip in too. Look at how much Sloan has helped

Shandon Anderson. You post that kid up and he can't be stopped, because Jerry Sloan makes sure he gets the ball in the right places.

There are some young coaches out there who I think are worth watching. I'm a fan of former New Jersey coach John Calipari. I really get a kick out of that guy. He's a screamer too, but he got the Nets into the playoffs, and that's worth something. I like him because he's fiery, and his players always seem to play hard for him. I used to scout his college teams all the time, and you could tell they were well coached. It's just like Pitino's teams; they were always well prepared, and everyone knew where they were supposed to be. I've always liked coaches like that, who have their guys ready to go. People feel Cal screams too much, but that's his style, that's the way he coaches, that's how he gets his players to play like they're playing. He brought a lot of enthusiasm to New Jersey. He brought a lot of confidence there too.

Danny Ainge is another person I believe is going to be a great coach. We knew that from way back. He's another guy who is just 100 percent consumed by the game, and I think as a coach, even more than a player, you really have to be that way. He's got the energy, and he's always got something to say. I remember when he was with the Celtics you could hand him a clipboard and he could draw up a play he ran in high school.

Danny is the head coach in Phoenix, and he got them playing that small ball really well. His team lost to San Antonio in the 1998 playoffs, and Danny took some criticism for not double-teaming Tim Duncan in certain situations, but I don't think that's fair. If you've got a game plan, you should stick to it. Duncan scored a bunch of times in a row out of the single coverage, and people were calling Danny stubborn, but I can relate to that. We don't like to double down on teams either.

People said I couldn't be a good head coach because ex-superstars don't make good coaches. That doesn't make any sense. I'm glad I was able to prove that wrong. Now it seems like other ex-players are thinking they want to try it. Someone told me Kareem Abdul-Jabbar wants to get into it. But the one that surprised me was Robert Parish. I never thought he'd be interested in doing this, but that's what people said about me too. If Robert really wants to be a head coach, I would tell him, just like I would tell anybody, "Make sure you get yourself two good assistants, and do your research on the league." It's the little things that are major in this business. I made a lot of mistakes in my first season of coaching, but thank God I had two guys who knew what they were doing to help me through it.

I remember the first week I took the coaching job with Indiana. Chris Ford was quoted as saying, "Larry has no idea what he is getting into." Chris was right. When you are a player, if you lose a game or have a bad night, you go home and forget about it. Coaches agonize over it until the next game. The first time I did that, I knew I was just like the rest of them.

CHAPTER 8

On Coaching Philosophy

Everybody asks me how I developed my coaching philosophy. Most of it comes from things I did as a player that worked for me. The most important thing, I always felt, was to develop good conditioning habits. If you couldn't get yourself into shape, you had no chance of winning anything. I remember when our Celtics team was playing in the 1984 championship, somebody asked me if I ever got tired during a game. I said the only ones that I got tired in were the really big games, like against Philadelphia in a sixth or seventh game of the playoffs, because I used to get so hyped up and it took a lot out of me. And that was even before the game started!

But when it came to a regular game, I never got tired. The way the NBA has it worked out, you have so many time-outs, you should be able to run as hard as you possibly can, because you know another time-out is coming any second. There's no excuse for any player to say he's tired. One full game is only 48 minutes long, and nobody plays an entire game anymore. Besides, with all the extra television time-outs, you should be able to play two games.

My younger brother Eddie, who played at Indiana State, asked me once about conditioning. He said he was tired all the time. I told him that's because he had never been in shape. He got mad and started telling me how he runs and lifts weights and all that, but I said, "No, you don't have any idea what being in shape is." The only time I ever felt any fatigue was in the first two minutes of a game. That's right about when the second wind kicks in, and once that happens I could run forever. That's one thing I've always felt very strongly about. If you take pro athletes and condition them well, they'll stay away from most injuries, unless it's just a freak thing. If you get them in top shape, they will play at a higher level. I think I proved that with the Pacers my first season, when they went from winning 39 games the year before to winning 58 games and almost making it to the Finals. Also, we made it through the season with very few major injuries. I think a big part of that has to be credited to our players, who worked their butts off to be in the best shape of their lives.

I had watched a lot of Pacers games the season before, and I knew something was wrong by the way they always seemed to fall apart down the stretch. It seemed to me their conditioning was off, but instead of just telling them that, I wanted to be able to show them how important it was to be in top shape. I wanted evidence.

Rick Carlisle and I put together charts of all their games from the year before. We took a closer look at the 39 games they had won, and realized there were actually 48 games in which they were ahead going into the final quarter. Then we broke it down, quarter by quarter. In the first quarter they were ahead by an average of six points, proving they were good starters. By halftime they were usually even. In the third quarter they would be up by an average of four points, yet by the time the fourth quarter was over, they had lost by an average of eight points a game. I saw that, and I got ticked off, because it just proved what I already knew: they should have been much better that previous season.

There were a lot of reasons why they underachieved. They had some injuries. Larry Brown, who is an excellent coach, had grown stale with the players for some reason. I think some of the guys lost their focus. So now I come in, and they've come off this year where they could never get above .500, and nobody seemed to know what to expect. But I felt right from the beginning that we had a good chance to win the championship—if they would receive me well, and listen. That was the scary thing. I didn't know. How would they react to me? My gut was they'd at least say, "Yeah, let's give him a chance." That's all I could ask.

The expectation around town was for me to get the Pacers back in the playoffs. I kept saying that myself publicly, but I knew I wanted much, much more. The governor of Indiana came out and said we should win 50 games. I said I'd make sure we won 50 games if he could get us a balanced budget. I tried not to get caught up in any of the talk around the city. I just went to the office every day in the summer. Dinah and I didn't go out much. We got the papers, but they really don't write much about the Pacers in the off season. I know my friends in Terre Haute were expecting a lot, but that's because they knew how seriously I was taking this job.

The Pacers tried to get me to do all sorts of promotional things, but I told them from the beginning that I wanted the team to be the focal point, not me. That didn't stop them from asking me to do things, or me from turning them all down. I still do that. The one thing I didn't want to do was be in television commercials to sell tickets. So they got a couple of my players together, and they did this commercial where they were on a road trip to French Lick to visit the house where I grew up. That's fine. Just leave me out of it. In the summer of '98 when they had the lockout, they couldn't use any of the players so they had to make reference to me, but I still wasn't actually in it.

That was one of the first things I explained to my guys at our first meeting in Orlando, where we had our training camp. I told them, "This is your team. I don't want the attention, and I don't need the attention, so let's get that straight." I knew I would be on the cover of the media guide for my first season coaching, but I told them after that it wasn't going to be that way. The last thing I wanted was for them to think I had any plans to upstage them. The truth was, I had no interest in media attention whatsoever. I was going to do what was required of me but not much else. All the publicity was one of the reasons I considered passing on coaching. I knew once these guys got to know me, they'd see that.

When I talked to the team on that first night, I told them I believed we could win a championship. But if we were going to do it, we had to make it happen in the next two or three years. They already knew that, especially guys like Reggie Miller and Mark Jackson, who were in their thirties. Reggie will be able to play longer than Mark because of his body build, and because he knows how to play in decent shape and under control. But Mark Jackson only knows how to play a certain way—full speed ahead—and because of that, he gets hammered. I really have respect for that guy. Have you ever seen anyone compete as hard as Mark Jackson? I know he doesn't have all the ability in the world, but I didn't either, and what set us both apart is the way we competed. When I came into my first season with the Pacers, my single biggest concern was that we didn't have a leader on the team. But Mark Jackson and Reggie Miller turned out to be two of the best leaders I've ever been around.

In my first team meeting, which lasted around twenty minutes, I pulled out the charts Rick Carlisle and I had done on conditioning, and I showed them to the guys. I explained that it was important for every single player to be in top shape, not just the starters, because you never knew when you were going to be called upon. I told them about an old teammate of mine from the Celtics, Eric Fernsten, a 6-foot-10 guy who didn't get to play much. It was 1981, and we were playing for the best record in the league that season. We flew to Houston for a game against the Rockets, and we ran into a lot of foul trouble. Eric Fernsten had to go in. Fernsten was one of those guys who kept himself in good condition even though he never really got to play in the games. He gets in there, and we shoot a free throw and miss it. But Eric gets his hand up there and tips it in. It gave him confidence, and a few minutes later he got another basket. We won that game, and it helped us win the best record in the league. I told them it could happen to any one of them, just that way.

The next thing I told them was that I would not tolerate anyone being late. To me, it's disruptive and disrespectful, and it was the one thing I would not change my position on. I told them a couple of more things I expected through the course of the year, and then I got up and walked out.

I think they must have been a little startled, me getting up and leaving like that. All of a sudden, Coach was gone.

They stayed in there for a little while, and I don't know what they did. I never asked. But I knew one thing: when we started going at it, they knew exactly what to expect.

I'm sure when I first came in there and started running those guys, they weren't too happy about it. It's a lot of hard work—it's brutal, really—and I'm sure they complained, but they never complained to me.

Right from the beginning, they understood they would be running and running. One thing I believe in, and I told these guys, "As much as you hate the defensive drills, you've got to get through them." Early on, we had those guys in a stance, sliding up and down the court. The first thing that gets sore is your groin. You've got to work through that soreness, and then you're pretty good. Then you can get in shape and do all the other stuff and be able to maintain that stance. You've got to get that groin soreness out of there early, like in the first three days of camp, so you can move on. If you are fighting that, forget it. Hey, you can get out there and run and run and you might be a little sore, but if you don't get down there and defend, I don't care what kind of shape you're in, your ankles won't get you where you want to, or your legs. As hard as I worked in the off season, with my running and lifting and conditioning drills, I could never prepare for the first week of Bill Fitch's practice, because until you are with the team and doing those defensive drills, it's not the same. It's hard to really get in a proper defensive stance back in French Lick when you're not really guarding anybody.

A lot of the stuff I put them through is what Bill Fitch used on us while he was coach of the Celtics. It's hard. I know it is, because I went through it myself, but my feeling is I wasn't asking these guys to do anything I hadn't already done myself.

Our shootarounds, which are held the morning of the game to prepare for the opponent, are tougher than a lot of teams' practices. We always work for at least an hour. The last fifteen minutes of it is shooting, but for the other forty-five minutes they're knocking each other all over the court. They better be. They know that's what I want from them.

I'm sure there were times when they were wondering why we were doing that. Shootarounds aren't supposed to be like a regular practice. But I'll always remember our shootaround before playing Chicago in Game 6 of the Eastern Conference Finals. We were running plays, taking charges, telling guys to take one another's heads off. Guys were fighting, and I mean really fighting through picks. Guys were getting mad. We had to separate a couple of 'em, so nobody got punched. It was one of the best practices we had all season, and I knew we'd play well that night. We beat the Bulls 92–89 to force a seventh game, and Rik Smits, who the media was getting on for being too passive, came up huge with 26 points.

The same thing happened during our second road trip out West in February. We had a day off in Sacramento, so we held an hour-and-forty-minute practice. I called the guys together and told them, "Look, I want all-out war today. I want to see something. Show me what you got." Well, you've never seen so many bodies fly. A guy would get knocked on his butt and his sweat would be dripping all over the floor, but he wouldn't even stop long enough to dry it up. So the next time down, someone would come flying down the floor and slip. Then some guy behind him would fall, and the next thing you know, you got three guys rolling on the floor, going at it . . . I loved it. When we walked off that court, I got them together and said, "Hey guys, we've got no problem tomorrow night." And, sure enough, in the first half of that game against the Kings we played an almost perfect half of basketball. I knew it. You just can't come off a practice like that and not be ready to go into the game. We beat the Kings by 22 points on their floor.

One of the things people said about the Pacers was that they were a good, veteran team, but they weren't mean enough. I was asking them to have an edge, and that's not always an easy thing, because in some cases it's not their nature. If you take Antonio Davis, one of our young guys who plays forward and center, that kind of aggression is not a problem for him. But Dale Davis, our power forward, is nothing like that. He's just a very nice guy. You have to get him mad before he'll play that way. We have a kid, Austin Croshere, who was hurt most of his rookie season. But on this particular day, he was coming back, so I told him, "Go in there and knock Dale around every chance you get. Don't worry about fouling him." So Croshere goes in there and starts hacking away at Dale. Davis is looking over at me, but I keep calling the foul against him instead of on Croshere. He takes it about three times in a row, then all of a sudden he gets riled up, and he starts playing like a monster. He wasn't going to get into a fight, because he's been around too long for that, but he played as intense as I had seen him all year. It really worked. I was happy to see Dale playing so intensely.

You don't really want to play too many mind games with these guys, though. Most of the time I was as straightforward as I could be with them. I would tell our guys,

"Now listen, I want an hour of hard work, all-out. We could stay here an hour and a half, but I'd rather be done in an hour with you guys working your butts off." You know what the great thing was? They'd do it. I never for a minute stopped realizing how lucky I was to have guys that will respond that way. It's why I wanted to coach this team, and only this team. Because I knew they were veterans whose time was running out to win a championship. I felt as though they were competitive enough as a group to want it badly enough to make the necessary sacrifices, and I was hoping they would be willing to listen to someone like me who had been there before, who had done the work, and who had won championships.

When I told them I believed we could win a championship, I wasn't just saying it to motivate them. I truly believed it. And it wasn't just on some kind of feeling I had. I looked over their stats, and the opponents in our conference, again and again. I studied our personnel. We needed another player to take the scoring pressure off our center, Rik Smits, and Reggie Miller, but we got that on August 12, 1997, when we traded for Chris Mullin. I had played with Chris on the Dream Team in the 1992 Olympics, and I knew what kind of pro he was. We were really happy to get him, but we had to trade one of our young big men, Eric Dampier, to get him. It was hard for Donnie Walsh to let Dampier go. I didn't want to get rid of him either. Eric is a helluva talent, and he's big, and he can run. He makes mistakes, but I honestly believe, the way we did things last year, he could have been a lot better player now. But we had a lot of big guys, and it was really major to find someone who could stand out on the perimeter and hit shots like Mullin, which would stop people from doubling down on Rik Smits or trying to double Reggie Miller out on the wing. With Chris out there, they couldn't do that. Sure, we gave up a ton, but with Reggie getting older and Mark getting older, we had to play for now, not three years down the road.

One thing I told my guys from the very first day of practice was if you have an open shot, you better take it, 'cause if you don't, you're coming out of the game. I never thought one of my problems as a new coach would be to get my guys to score, but they are all so unselfish. It's ridiculous. We beg them to shoot. I don't care if they take seven shots in a row; if they're open, shoot it. That's how I approached it as a player, and that's how I wanted it as a coach.

During the exhibition season we had this one game where every time Mark Pope was in there, we took the lead. Mark was a second-round pick who had played for Rick Pitino at Kentucky, and he was doing great. He'd get us a couple of baskets by grabbing a rebound or boxing out a defender, the little things. So it comes down to being a close game against Cleveland. I've got Mark Pope in the game, and I know everyone is wondering why, because he was a rookie, but I liked what I saw out there. We're in a time-out, the score is tied, and we set up a play where Reggie is going to drive baseline and kick the ball back out to Mark. There's around five seconds left, and Reggie kicks it out to Mark, who has a wide-open 10-footer. With one second on the clock, he looks at the basket, but he doesn't shoot it. Instead he passes the ball out to Reggie, who takes an off-balance shot. He misses, and we get beat.

The next day I called Mark into my office and said, "Mark, I'm going to tell you just one thing. If you ever, ever, turn down a game-winning shot, I don't care if you are a rookie or a ten-year veteran, I will cut you on the spot. I'll get rid of you. I will not have anyone on my team who is afraid to look at the basket." He didn't say a word. He just walked out, and that was it. About two months later, Donnie Walsh told me Pope's agent called and said how his client had learned a lot, and he really likes Indiana, and he'll never turn down another shot. It's one of the best things Mark could ever have learned.

I know sometimes even my own staff thinks I take the shooting thing to extremes, but I don't care. What good is it to have a shot if you don't feel confident about taking it? Once in a while, in our tape sessions, Rick Carlisle gets carried away. He watches a play on film and says, "Aw, that was a bad shot." But here's my philosophy: any shot that doesn't go in is a bad shot, because you didn't get anything for it.

I think our team spends more time on shooting than any team in the league. We have shooting drills in practice, but then after practice they'll stay out there for hours and shoot. Dale and Antonio almost always shoot free throws. Mark and Reggie take three-pointers. I was happy to see them do that, because practicing your shooting is so important. I used to take hundreds of shots a day. Then, when my back started giving me trouble and I couldn't practice, my shooting suffered, because so much of it is all about repetition. I got to the point, at the peak of my career, when I could hit sixty or seventy shots in a row, without any trouble. You don't see as much of that today. I think it's because players seem to spend more time on jumping and dunking than working on their jump shots.

I loved most of training camp. It was fun to watch a team working together and to be part of it. But the one part I was dreading was cutting guys. It was the toughest thing I had to do. I knew we were getting close to the point where I needed to have a roster set, so I'm thinking to myself, "I know this one guy has no shot of making it, so I should just cut him." It was a veteran forward who had been overseas the past couple years. But I kept putting it off another day. I told Rick and Dick I was having trouble doing it. It was near the end of the camp, and guys were definitely wearing down, because we were running their butts off. Every day I'd talk to Dick and say, "That guy, he looks about a hundred years old," and every day Dick would say, "You're right, Larry. Pull him out, and I'll cut him after practice." I'd say, "That's the right thing to do. That way he'll have a weekend at home, and maybe a chance to pick up with somebody else." Finally, on this one particular day, practice was over and I turned to Dick and Rick and said, "I'm going to do this." Rick said, "You better do it today, because he's looking worse every minute."

So I take this veteran into the back area and he says, "Hey, Coach, how are you doing?" He's smiling at me. So I say, "I just want you to know, we're cutting our squad down, thank you for coming, and if there's anything we can do to help you out, please let us know." He puts his hand on my shoulder and says, "Hey, Coach, you're just kidding me, aren't you?" I said, "No, we've made our decision." So this kid grabs my shoulder again, and he says, "Coach, you can't do that. I'm just starting to come on. I'm just getting in shape, getting my legs under me. If you do this, it's the biggest mistake of your life. I know you're just starting out in this profession, but you don't want to start this way."

So now I'm getting a little annoyed, but I say, "Hey, listen. We decided to make cuts today, and you are the first to go because you really haven't shown us anything that would help our team out." He starts smiling again. He says, "Coach, I understand. Just give me one more day. I'll prove to you I can make your team. I'm perfect for this team. You don't want to start out by making a mistake." The guy wouldn't quit. He kept going on, and on, until finally I said, "You know what? You should get out of here."

I'm getting ticked! He's a sweetheart of a guy, but here he is—the first person I've ever cut—and he's still telling me, "I'm going to hang around another day, okay, Coach? I know you'll change your mind." I walk out of the room, and I'm shell-shocked, and I still got another guy to cut. I see Dick and Rick and I say to them, "Is this some kind of setup? Are you guys in on this?" Rick said, "I don't know what you're talking about." So I tell them what just happened, and Dick starts going berserk! He was yelling, "Bring that kid in here! I'll straighten him out! Who does he think he is?" At that point I said, "Rick, I've had it. You cut the next guy." Rick was all set to do it, but then I changed my mind. It's my job. So I brought in the next guy and I told him, as straight as I could, that he was gone. Well the next thing I know, the guy's lip is quivering and his eyes are filling up, and that really bothered me. I felt bad, because I knew it was probably his last shot at an NBA job.

That was it for the day. I couldn't handle any more than that.

Exhibition season is kind of a feeling-out process, especially when you have a new coach. In our case, it was a time for the guys to understand that I was dead serious about being on time. I laid out the rules for them: the first time you're late, it's a $1,000 fine. Strike two, it's another $1,000, and strike three in the same month and you're suspended for a game. No exceptions. That's how it was going to be.

So we have one more practice before we head out to this exhibition game against Charlotte. This is cruel, but here's how it happened. The guys are on the court stretching, and I walk onto the floor and I notice one of our point guards, Travis Best, isn't out there. I ask Reggie Miller, "Where's Travis?" He says, "He had to go to the bathroom." I blew the whistle and said, "That's a thousand dollars Travis owes us."

That wouldn't have been such a big deal, except the next day we're on the plane heading to Nashville, Tennessee, for this game against the Hornets, and Travis and Dale Davis aren't on the plane. They're late. I wait until it's exactly four o'clock, and I tell my guys, "Okay, let's lock it and go." Three minutes later, Dale and Travis pull into the parking lot, but the doors to the plane were already closed. The pilot shut down the engine, but I told him to fire it back up again. "We're not waiting," I said. As Dale and Travis began running toward the plane, lugging their bags, we took off and left them standing there on the runway. Nashville isn't the easiest place in the world to get to, and those guys had to scramble to find a commercial flight. They wound up getting a connection through Atlanta, but when they got to Atlanta they got stuck there because of bad weather. They were fogged in. That meant having to stay overnight and take an early-morning flight. They didn't get into Nashville until late the next morning, and they got there about halfway through shootaround. For Dale it was two strikes, but for Travis it was three. Three strikes, suspension. So he had to sit out the game.

I would have liked Travis to play that night, but there was no way I was changing the rules. I wanted everyone thinking about being on time, and I was prepared to do whatever it took to prove to them I was serious about it. I remember later in the season, Dale Davis had two strikes on him for the month, and we were getting ready for a game, and he was in the locker room for some reason. Dick Harter was so concerned about not having him that night that he ran in there and said, "Now Dale, remember, you've got two strikes. Hurry up and get out there. You know Larry, he'll make you sit."

It didn't matter to me who it was. The rules were the same for everyone. Reggie Miller used to get to places forty-five minutes early. I told the team, "If Reggie can do it, why can't you?" Early in the season, we were getting ready to go on a bus trip somewhere, and we were leaving at three o'clock. At three I gave the signal to lock and go, and just then, Haywoode Workman, one of our guards who was hurt at the start of the season and was really struggling, because his career might have been over, comes chugging up to the bus limping, hauling his bags, trying to get on the bus. I told him, "Woody, if you're going to the game, then you're driving there yourself. You're late." The bus driver closed the door and we left him standing there. If I say three o'clock, I mean three o'clock, not 3:01. One minute late, and it's a $1,000 fine. One second late, it's a $1,000 fine.

We had a big game at home against Chicago in March, when Reggie Miller and Antonio Davis ran into a problem and they were late. I was really upset. It's one of the few times I really chewed them out. I told them, "You just blew any chance we had of winning this game tonight. You are playing one of your biggest competitors, you're going to be battling these guys in the Eastern Conference Finals, and you're gonna show up late today? Come on!

You just don't do that." That night my team went out and got their butts kicked. I knew it was going to happen. I told them it was going to happen. The only good thing about it was it stayed in their minds after that.

When I played for the Celtics, I was never late for anything. I was usually one of the first guys on the bus. Kevin McHale was always the last guy, every time. It drove me crazy. He was hardly ever late, but he'd walk on the bus at the exact time we were leaving, with maybe a second or two to spare. I always said he was hiding around the corner, waiting until there was only fifteen seconds to go. That's Kevin. It never affected the way he played, though.

Once we finally had our roster set, the next challenge was to find enough minutes for everyone on the team. Ideally, most coaches seem to favor a rotation of eight players, but our team was a lot deeper than that. Early in the season, we really didn't have a set substitution pattern. My feeling was, "We'll go with who is getting the job done out there." Sometimes that meant in the fourth quarter of a really close game, we might have reserves like Fred Hoiberg and Mark Pope out there instead of Reggie Miller and Chris Mullin, our starters. Early on, I was playing ten guys, and I was thinking to myself, "How are you going to find time for ten guys?" It was hard to do. But I thought it would help us down the road. I thought I showed enough confidence in those ten guys so that if I went to them in a crucial situation later in the season, they'd be ready. You like to play guys who have worked all year. They've earned a chance at some time. That's not to say I didn't sweat out some of those early substitutions I made. Of course I did. I know Donnie Walsh was having a heart attack about it. I'm sure there were days he was thinking, "What is Larry doing?" But give him credit. He never said anything

to me. He told me from the beginning that when it came
to the coaching he would leave me alone.

If there was one thing that surprised me, it was how bad
a rebounding team we were. That was frustrating to me, because rebounding was such a big part of my game. I want
these guys to be aggressive on the offensive glass, even if
it hurts us sometimes. I always felt I was a great offensive
rebounder. As soon as the ball left my hand, I was after it.
I was running to it like there was no tomorrow. But then,
my rookie season with Boston we had our training camp in
Marshfield, Massachusetts, and we were playing outside,
and I took a shot and took off after the ball like I always
do, even though I was pretty sure it was going in. Well,
Bill Fitch was there, and so was Red Auerbach, and he
blows the whistle and stopped everything, and then Red
turned to me and said, "Hey, while you're going toward the
basket like that, your man is going the other way for a
layup. You've got to stay with your man." From that day
on, I was never a good offensive rebounder. Here was one
of my best attributes, chasing that ball, and now they were
telling me I shouldn't do it.

In college, when I went to the boards like that, the
guard picked up my guy. I thought it should be the same
in the pros. But once Red said that to me, I got out of the
habit of chasing the ball down. I just didn't go at it like
I used to. Red said the reason the guard could pick up my
man so easily in college was because we played a lot of
zone defense, which isn't allowed in the NBA. But I would
never get on one of my guys if he went hard after an offensive rebound. To me, it's one of those plays that is devastating to the opponent. If you get caught once in a while,
well, that's the price you pay.

I'm not sure why my Pacers players aren't better rebounders. Part of it, unfortunately, is because they don't pursue the basketball. Part of it is because they don't box out. They're usually jumping, trying to go up over people. I could never outjump anybody, so I learned very early on in my career to follow the flight of the ball on the offensive end, and to put a body on somebody and box them out on the other end. You take a guy like Antonio Davis. He jumps so well, but if you put your body into him he might still get up, but he won't explode like he usually does. I don't care who it is; anytime you stick your body on them, you take away their lift. That's what other teams did to us all year long in my first season. They took away our lift.

I used to practice watching the flight of the ball all the time. It started when I was a little kid, and I used to rebound for my brother Mark. He'd do all the shooting, and I'd try to anticipate whether it was going to be short, or long, or off to the left, whatever. I always thought it was the easiest thing to do. It was really instinctive for me, I guess. I could go out and watch a guy shoot for two seconds and be able to tell—not every time, but most of the time—whether he was going to be short or long, and then get right to the ball. The problem with guys nowadays is they just stand there and look at it. They know it's going to be short, but they don't react.

It goes back to stressing the fundamentals. Like the bounce pass. I used to throw 'em all the time, because Coach Jones, my high school coach, showed me how to do it right. With these Indiana guys, I don't want them throwing a bounce pass, because they don't do it properly. It should be done hard, with one hand. Sometimes Reggie Miller throws these soft, two-handed bounce passes, and it frustrates me, because I think every one of them is going to get picked off.

The biggest difference between being a coach and a player is that as a player you only had to worry about getting *yourself* ready to play. A coach has to prepare twelve guys. The one thing I learned real quickly was to keep these guys moving. No long speeches, no long explanations. That's when they lose their concentration. Just work them hard and don't let them stop and lose focus. Some days I might have planned a two-hour practice, but if they are really going at it and they've paid attention and got things done, then I'll consider quitting while I'm ahead. It might have only been an hour and fifteen minutes, but I'll blow the whistle and tell the guys, "Hey, we're outta here!"

The other side of it is when the practice is flat no matter how long you go, and the guys aren't moving well, and the coaches are getting frustrated. You can go either way. You can keep them there and let it get worse, or you can close her down. If I choose to do that, I say to them, "Look guys, you've got to give me something today. So far, this has been crap. We've got fifteen more minutes. I want to see bodies flying." That usually works.

There's one thing I was good at right away. I can usually sense when guys are tired or frustrated, or if something is bugging them. Dick and Rick like to push the guys, but some days I have to tell them, "Listen, back off this kid today, his body won't let him get it done today." Don't get me wrong: I get disappointed when I don't get the effort, but I'm not going to go in there and curse somebody out. It's not in my makeup. I wouldn't want somebody doing that to me. But I do spell it out for them. I say, "Reggie, I'm asking you to play thirty-five minutes. Mark, you're going to play around twenty, twenty-five minutes," and right on down the line. I say, "I'm not asking you to go out and play hard for eight hours. If you can't go for some reason, then don't insult me. Come in and tell me you can't play. Tell me before the game. Don't wait until fifteen or twenty minutes after you're in there. Don't make me pull you off the floor when you know already you don't have it that night. Be honest."

That happened a couple of times in my first season. I'd pull the guy into my office after the game and say, "Hey, you let your teammates down. Why?" Most of the time, it turns out they are having some kind of personal problem. Maybe their wife gave them hell, or the baby-sitter didn't show up, or something. You never know with these guys. But I want to know about that stuff beforehand, not when we get down by 15 points. I think these guys know by now that it's not something I'm going to hold against them.

There's something else you've got to remember in dealing with these guys. Each of them has physical limitations. You take a guy like Mark Jackson. He's a real warrior, and he'll give you everything he's got, so when Dick Harter gets frustrated with him because Allen Iverson is beating him off the dribble, you've got to step back and say, "Of course Iverson is doing that. He's a lot quicker than Mark." So then you have to realize that it's not lack of effort, it's simply lack of speed, and then you think of a way to help Mark adjust. This is something I did my entire career. I was hardly ever quicker than anyone I guarded, so I had to compensate in other ways and make up for it with smart team defense.

One thing I never had a problem with as a player was preparation. I was a self-motivated person, and I didn't need anyone kicking me in the rear to get me jump-started. The difference is, now that I'm a coach, I have to get twelve guys on the same page. That's completely different. When you call out a play, everyone has to be in a certain area at a certain time or it doesn't work. It's the coach's job to make sure everybody understands exactly what is expected of them, and to make sure they are ready to play.

So now, all of a sudden, instead of walking onto that floor making sure I'm in the right frame of mind, I've got to check with this guy or that guy, who might have had a so-so practice the day before, to make sure he's with us. You can't believe all the things that are going through my head, trying to get these guys prepared. They worry you sick.

There's another difference I've noticed since I got into coaching: I've started dreaming about winning championships. When I was a player I never had any dreams. But now that I'm coaching, I have this dream we're in the NBA Finals, and we're playing Seattle, for some reason. We usually win, and then I wake up and realize that hasn't happened yet.

Bill Fitch used to tell us, "You guys should all have to coach for a day. Then you'd understand what we go through." He's right. The one thing about being a player is if you win a game by one point, you walk out of there as happy as can be. But if you win a game by one point and you are the coach, you walk out of there and just remember all the mistakes you made.

I can't believe it, but that's what happened to me. That's why I'm on borrowed time in this coaching business. When I was playing, I always wanted to take the last shot, instead of putting the ball in someone else's hands and letting them decide my fate.

I'm not sure I'll ever get used to it.

CHAPTER 9

On Endorsements and Lifestyle

Here's something else I'll never get used to: the demand for celebrity athletes to endorse products.

When I first started doing commercials, even coming from a small town, I didn't want to do anything for a shaky company. It had to be a big-time company, like McDonald's or 7UP. I never did an ad for something I didn't respect.

Some of the commercials look like a blast when they're done, but what you see in thirty seconds can take a whole day. It's unbelievable what can foul up what you thought was a perfect take. Maybe it's because this guy doesn't like the lighting, or that guy didn't like the way one of the actors said their lines. That's my only complaint about commercials. They just take up too much time. Everything is union, so everybody has got to do their own little thing. During a taping someone might call out that they need a ladder, but if you ever touched the thing some guy would start shouting, because that's his job—to move ladders. That kind of stuff drove me crazy. Also, they make you wear makeup. I really hate that.

My first big commercial was for 7UP in 1979, the year I was a rookie with the Celtics. I guess I was a little nervous at the start, but it took so long to film the thing that by the time it was over I was just tired. I always liked 7UP just fine, but when my agent, Jill Leone, picked me up after filming that ad, I ordered a glass of milk at dinner. I drank close to two cases of 7UP during that taping, and I couldn't even look at another 7UP for a long time after that.

The other thing you have to get used to with all these commercials is the special effects they use. I did a commercial for Canon cameras in 1980, and they shot it in Boston. They wanted to create the feeling of a musty old gym, so they filled the room with all this smoke. Rick Carlisle, who was my teammate at the time, was in that commercial with me, which turned out to be a mistake, because the people at Canon wanted a shot of me dunking the basketball, and they made me stand on a crate to do it. As you can imagine, Rick had something to say about that. Back then I was dunking on guys all the time. Sometimes I see old footage and I can't believe I could do all those things, because after my heel surgery and two back surgeries I never moved the same again. Anyhow, I told the people at Canon I didn't need any crate, but after doing it about fifty times I understood why we had it there. If I had to dunk that many times for real, I would have been exhausted!

The first commercial I ever did for McDonald's took fourteen hours. I couldn't believe it. I remember thinking to myself, "You won't catch me wasting time like this anymore." My job was to say a few lines and bite into a cheeseburger. The producer didn't seem to have too much of a problem with me and how I was eating my burger, but on almost every take he found something wrong with one of the other actors. I must have bit into about two hundred burgers before we got it right. They had to keep running back and heating up fresh trays of burgers every time somebody messed up. It would have been funny if I wasn't so irritated at blowing an entire day. Jill went to the shoot with me, and that's the day I turned to her and said, "Four hours. That's it. From now on, if they take any longer than that, we're not doing it."

So after that, whenever a company called about endorsing a product, Jill would explain to them my four-hour rule. In the beginning, Jill said most of them were horrified at even considering such a time limit, but somehow she was able to convince them I would arrive on time (early, actually), ready to work. She would always send me the script and the storyboard ahead of time, so I always knew what was going to be expected of me. What it did was cut out a lot of the schmoozing and eating and chit-chat that can go on during the filming, which I never liked anyway. My way of doing business is go in, be organized, move quickly, and get it done. After a while these companies realized it was going to save them a lot of money to do it this way. What it meant for the agency handling the commercial was that they had to settle on a final script for the shoot, rather than shooting it one way, then deciding whether they liked it or not and trying it a different way.

Some commercials just seem to drag on forever. But some of them are a piece of cake. Remember that Gatorade ad that ran during the 1997–98 season with everyone singing how they wanted to be like Mike? There was no way I was going to sing anything, especially about wanting to be like Michael Jordan, not when I was hoping my team would be going up against him in the playoffs. Gatorade really wanted me in the ad, because of my connection with Michael, so we reached a compromise. I'd do the commercial, but I wouldn't sing. I ended up having to say one line: "I'm not gonna sing." It took all of a half hour to shoot it. I had on a suit and tie and I was sitting in a Learjet, and we shot it at an airport hangar in Indianapolis. Easiest one ever.

There were some offers we got that I just wasn't going to do, no matter how little time it took. One of them, back in the eighties, was for a financial services company. In the first place, I had my doubts, because I didn't like the idea of advising people on how to invest their money. They were going to pay me around $250,000, but they wanted me to dress up like a ballerina. I told Jill to forget it. All the money in the world wouldn't convince me to dress up in a tutu! I noticed they ended up getting a pro football player to do it. Good for him.

There is one guy who is great to be around when you're making commercials. His name is Joe Pytka, and he's one of the top television commercial, video, and feature film directors in the world. He organizes all the shoots, and he treats everyone like crap, and both me and Michael Jordan love him.

Pytka is a big guy, and he loves to play basketball. He could care less that we're Michael Jordan and Larry Bird, we're just two guys who will shoot baskets with him on the breaks. He'll grab two or three guys on their down time so he can get a game together.

One day when Michael and I were doing a McDonald's commercial together, we were standing there all ready to go, but we couldn't get started because Pytka hadn't finished his basketball game yet. People were all ticked off because this director was keeping Michael Jordan and Larry Bird waiting, but it's why I absolutely loved the guy. To him we were all the same.

Joe is also very, very creative. He was the director for that Nothin' But Net McDonald's commercial that Michael and I did where the ball went off the rim, off the backboard, off the roof . . . I guess the McDonald's people had a lot riding on the ad, because it was going to run during the Super Bowl, which is when television time costs you the most money. At that time, 1993, I had never done an ad with Michael Jordan before. We shot the commercial in a gym in Chicago, and I got there early like I always do. Michael was nowhere to be found. So here's this director, Joe Pytka, who I've just met, and we're waiting around for Michael, and Joe starts shooting baskets. He grabs a couple of other guys, and they all start playing. I'm not sure, but I think he was doing it to loosen me up. It worked, because let me tell you, Joe Pytka is a good director, but he's a lousy basketball player! Before I knew it, I was talking trash to this guy, telling him, "You've got the worst game I've ever seen." Michael was about two hours late that day, which normally would have really ticked me off, but I was having fun with Pytka.

One thing about Joe Pytka, though. If you didn't take the work seriously, he got really steamed. The year after the first commercial Michael and I did, which was a real big hit, they wanted to do a sequel. This time they added Charles Barkley to the script, and made it like we were in outer space. We were all dressed up in space suits, and somebody was laughing on the set, or goofing off, so Pytka says to all of us, "If you guys think this is such a big joke, I'm leaving." And he walked out. Everyone got really quiet. Nobody seemed sure what to do, so I had to follow

Pytka out into the hallway in that stupid space suit and tell him, "Joe, I've only got two hours left, and then I gotta leave. So get back in here and finish this commercial." What I remember about that filming session is that Charles was having trouble saying his lines. He was supposed to open this door, which was one of those facades you see on movie sets, and I was going to be standing there. It took Charles about eight or ten takes before he finally said the right thing. We were all thinking, "Phew, we can finally get out of here," when one of the assistant directors came over and said, "Cut. We gotta do it again. Charles isn't holding the Big Mac bag right." I'm thinking to myself, "You've got to be kidding." I looked over at Pytka and we both rolled our eyes.

Joe was one of the directors for the movie *Space Jam*. I think every little kid in America saw it. I think kids know me more from *Space Jam* than anything else. I had no idea how popular it would be.

I got a call from Jill one day telling me that Warner Bros. wanted me to be in this movie with Michael. I didn't want to have to go all the way out to Los Angeles, and I told Jill I wouldn't do it, but then she called back and said Michael would really appreciate it if I'd change my mind.

In the end it was really worth it. We had a lot of fun. Most of my scenes were on the golf course with Michael and Bill Murray, who kept every day interesting. They flew me into the Los Angeles airport and then they took me by helicopter to some place in the middle of nowhere. I still can't tell you where it was, except it was beautiful, and it had a great golf course.

The movie people really took care of us. They had this big room in the hotel filled with food, drinks, anything you wanted. One cooler had beer, another had soda, another had sandwiches. And then there was this big cooler marked MICHAEL ONLY. You weren't supposed to touch that one, because it was all Michael Jordan's special stuff they flew in just for him. So one day Bill Murray and I are sitting in there, and I go over to Michael's cooler and lift up the lid. There was this girl there, and her only job was to make sure everything was just right for Michael Jordan, and she starts yelling at me, "Larry, you can't go in there!" I said, "What are you talking about? That's bull. Everyone here is family." She was getting all red and nervous and said, "No, no. Those are all the things Michael told me he wanted, and if you take something out of there, Michael won't be able to have it, and we just can't let that happen!"

Bill Murray is laughing the whole time listening to this, because whenever Michael walked into the room he always went to one of the other coolers and pulled something out, just like the rest of us. He hardly ever opened his own cooler.

Anyhow, I waited until the girl left, then I reached in and started grabbing stuff out of Michael's cooler and throwing it out to the crew, all over the set. I threw it everywhere! Gatorade bottles, some special drink he liked, candy bars . . . She was so mad at me.

For the rest of our stay, every time I went by that cooler I took something out. And if I didn't drink or eat it, I'd just toss it to somebody on the set. That's what Hollywood is like. Candy bars by the handful, and you just toss 'em around.

We spent most of our time during the filming of *Space Jam* trying to get on the golf course. Every time there was a break, me, Michael, and Bill Murray would run out and play two or three holes. Most of our scenes revolved around the golf course, where, according to the story line of the movie, Bugs Bunny and the other Looney Tunes guys come to steal Jordan away. It was one of those times when everything clicked out there, and everybody delivered their lines perfectly. We were all having so much fun, and we were all so relaxed, we didn't miss a beat.

In fact, everyone agreed our golf course scene had gone so well that Bill suggested that he and I do one more scene together after Jordan gets snatched away by Bugs Bunny. Even though it wasn't originally in the script, everyone started nodding their heads and saying, "Yeah, yeah. Bill and Larry. Another scene." Next thing I knew, the writers, Pytka, and Bill sat down and knocked out this script in about half an hour. It's the scene where Bill and I are driving off in the golf cart, wondering what happened to Michael (the Looney Tunes needed him to play on their basketball team, and they sucked him down the golf course hole). Bill makes a crack about how he's going to give us a "2" in the previous hole, because we weren't in any kind of emotional state to putt. We're in the golf cart, and we're driving off, and he starts talking about how the NBA would need new role models now that Michael Jordan was gone, and he would love to play in the league, and was I still tight with David Stern? It was very funny, and he was making most of it up as he went along.

The last day, when our part in the filming of *Space Jam* was finally over, the production crew and Michael and everyone went back to L.A. Suddenly the whole hotel was empty. So me and Murray grabbed a beer, grabbed our clubs, and went out on the course. We played until dark, and when we got back to the hotel, it was deserted— just like a ghost town. I didn't care, because Bill Murray is one of the funniest guys I've ever been around. I loved spending time with him.

I felt the same way about Pytka. He got to be friendly with both Michael and me. Whenever the two of us did a commercial, he'd always shoot my scenes first. One day Michael said, "How come Larry always gets to go first?" and Pytka answered, "Because he's always here first." My sentiments exactly.

Pytka was working in Paris in the spring of 1998, when the Pacers and the Bulls were playing each other in the Eastern Conference Finals. Joe really wanted to see the game, so he called all over the city trying to find a place that was carrying the game on satellite television. He finally found a really expensive hotel that said they could get the game, so he booked a suite and went up to watch my team and Michael's team go at it. He stayed up until 3 A.M. looking for our game, but he never could find it.

That is the one good thing about doing commercials. You end up hanging out with someone you might not otherwise spend any time with in your life, and you can really get to know them. That happened to me when I did an ad for Frito-Lay with Kareem Abdul-Jabbar. Up until that point, the only connection I had with Kareem was that he was a Laker, and he was the enemy. I had always respected his game, but I didn't know him at all. Anyhow, the whole point of this ad was their slogan about their potato chips, which was, "Bet you can't eat just one." Kareem, who is bald, bets me I can't eat just one of these Lay chips. I take the bet, and the next thing you know I've lost the bet and I'm eating a bag of chips, and I'm bald. The way they did it was they hired the people who did the makeup for the Coneheads on *Saturday Night Live*. They fitted me with this special cap. I felt bad for the guy who fitted me, because he had to stand on a ladder to put it on my head, because that was when I was still playing and my back was really bad, and I couldn't sit down. I remember when Kareem and I walked out there with me wearing this thing, everybody started laughing. They were trying not to, I could tell that, but I guess I looked pretty funny.

I enjoyed my time with Kareem more than I expected. I have a whole new respect for him, actually. I was near the end of my career, and he was telling me to really step back and enjoy it. He said he didn't realize or appreciate how much the fans liked and respected what we do until after he was done playing, and he wished he could go back and do it differently. In retrospect, I don't think he had the kind of relationship with the fans that he would have liked. He told me to play as long as I possibly could, and to savor the moments. It was good advice, and I took it.

One of the first companies that contacted me when I retired was Miller Lite. There's a federal law that says no active athlete can work for an alcohol company, so they waited until October of 1992, two months after my career officially ended, to call me. They wanted me to be a spokesman for their responsible drinking campaign, which sounded worthwhile to me. I wanted to make sure it was done properly, so I went to a number of their sales meetings and talked with their distributors. Dick Strup, the senior vice president, international, of Miller Brewing Co., is the one who dealt with me, and I liked him right away. The first commercial I shot for them was in 1993. They had me playing basketball with a bunch of guys, and the slogan was, "Sometimes you've got to know when to shoot, and sometimes you've got to know when to pass. Don't drink and drive." I had a few problems with that shoot, because I hadn't had the fusion surgery yet, and my back tended to be a problem. One thing I remember was just before we were going to do the ad, I was stretching on the sideline, and I bet Dick Strup twenty dollars I could sink a shot from half court. He didn't know me that well then, and he took the bet. I swished it, then put my hand out and said, "Okay, boss. Pay up."

The second one I did for Miller was in 1995. I drove up in a truck with some buddies, and we all piled out and went into a bar, only I wasn't drinking because I was the designated driver. At the end of the commercial, we all piled back into the truck and I drove away, with a bumper sticker on the back of the truck that read FRENCH LICK LIMO.

I have enjoyed my relationship with Miller Lite. They're good people. They've used my image in some international campaigns that run in China, Taiwan, the Philippines, Latin America, and the United Kingdom. I can tell you that me and my buddies from French Lick only drink one kind of beer: Miller Lite. If I catch those guys drinking anything else, they know they're in trouble.

There are two places I'd rather not go: New York and Los Angeles, because they're both so congested. That causes problems, since that's where all the action is when you're talking about show business. We got a call about a basketball movie called *Blue Chips*, which was going to star Shaquille O'Neal and Penny Hardaway, and they wanted me to fly out to Los Angeles to film a cameo role with one of the other stars of the movie, Nick Nolte. I told Jill I wasn't flying to L.A. just to be in a movie. I figured that was that, but the producers called back and asked if I would be willing to shoot my scene in French Lick. I said that would be fine, so Nick Nolte came to Indiana, and while they were there they shot a parade scene and used a lot of people from French Lick for their crowd.

Although I said from the beginning that I would only deal with major companies when it came to endorsements, I did make one exception. My good friend Ed Jukes, who also happens to be my banker, had a house in Terre Haute with a great yard. He liked to keep his place nice, so he used a tractor to mow his lawn. People were always coming to him trying to sell him a new mower, but he always told them the same thing: I'm not interested unless it does a better job than my tractor. None of them ever did. So one day I get this call from Ed, and he's all excited, and he says, "Larry, you've got to come down and see this new mower I've got." Turns out some local guys had designed this mower that had a motor on the back that you drove with two sticks, like a bulldozer. It had an awesome turning radius, and Ed couldn't stop talking about this mower. He knew how much pride I took in my lawn, so he got me down there and I tried one and it was terrific. My house in French Lick had about ten acres of yard that needed to be mowed, and it used to take me, by myself, on a rider mower, about seven or eight hours to get it done. With the new mower it took half the time. I was so intrigued by those things. Mowing your yard can be a pain in the rear sometimes, but this piece of machinery was great. The guys who designed it were just starting out, and they didn't have a lot of money, so they asked me if they could take some pictures of me riding the mower and use them at parades and fairs, and so on. In exchange they would give me a couple of mowers. It was one of the best business deals I ever made. They hauled this big picture of me riding the mower all over the state, and called themselves Pro Start. Eventually a bigger company bought them

out, and those mowers became kind of expensive, but I
went out and bought myself a couple of them anyway. If
something is that good, you don't mind paying the price.

I know companies like to have successful people who
are "winners" or "champions" endorse their products, because it portrays a positive image, but just because I like
a certain mower, or hamburger, or whatever, what does
that matter to the guy on the street? I do my share of commercials, and they pay good money, but I don't understand
how people get caught up in all the glamour of it. I know
the world I live in is mind-boggling, but I can go back to
sleeping on floors if I have to. It's just the way I am.

To be honest? I don't understand the attraction of
celebrities. I always thought the whole idea of being paid
to play pro basketball is ridiculous. I mean, think about
it. You are taking that ball, running down the court, and
you've got somebody on you. You've got four guys out
there on your team, and five from the other team, and
some people on the bench, and you look up and the place
is packed, and all you are trying to do is make that ball
go through the hole. It's just crazy to me. After all these
years, it still doesn't make sense. Back when I was with
the Celtics, I used to sit there and say to my teammate
Dennis Johnson, "Can you believe this? Look at all those
people. They're in here watching us play. Isn't that just
amazing?" D. J. would look at me like I was losing it, but
it was mystifying to me. Still is. Especially all those fans
way up at the top of the arenas. You know they could see
the game better if they just went home and watched it on
TV, but they're up there sweating (in Boston Garden, at
least—our building never had any air-conditioning!), and
they're loving it. They were the real fans. I always understood that. They're the ones who had to save for their

tickets, who were happy just to be in the building. We'd
sell out every night. The fans in the nosebleed seats were
always there. I would never have dreamed, when I was a
kid, that anyone would pay money to watch me do anything. And no matter how much money I ever have, I'll
never take it for granted.

Maybe it's because growing up in Indiana we didn't
have very much, so I never got used to counting on having things. I guess we were poor, but we didn't know that.
We were just like all our other neighbors in West Baden
and French Lick—just trying to get by. We had six kids
in our family, and my mom always took a couple of us
to the store with her, because she always had to get about
five shopping carts full of stuff. You'd see all this food
coming into the house on Monday, gallons of milk and
bags of groceries, and you'd think, "This is going to last
us a year." But by Wednesday or Thursday it was all gone,
and there was no money to buy new food. We'd be down
to peanut butter and bread.

That's why I've always been careful to save my money.
Don't get me wrong, Dinah and I haven't suffered. We
live a great life. But even when I was at the top of my
game, we didn't drive a Mercedes or live in million-dol-
lar homes, things like that. When I first started playing,
we bought a nice little house in the French Lick/West
Baden area. It cost $125,000.

We didn't run out and spend all our money because we
knew there would be a time when it was over, and I wanted
to have options on what we could do with our future. I
never thought about retiring. I just assumed I would always work. Some of the guys who made far less than me
bought the $700,000 homes, and the Rolex watches, and
the big luxury cars. I used to tell them, "You're crazy, you

should be saving your money." They'd just laugh and make jokes about me stashing my money away. But I could see what they were doing. They were throwing away their future. So many of them were living for today, and not even stopping for a minute to think about ten years down the road, when their playing careers were over and the money stopped pouring in. And by the time they realized what I was telling them was true, it was too late.

I can't tell you how many ex-teammates have asked me for money. It's heartbreaking for me to say no, but I do, because I warned them. I told them to save.

Too many of these athletes get sucked in by the lifestyle. When you are on top, everybody wants to give you things. I remember one time I did a jeans commercial, and when the shoot was over they had boxes and boxes of these jeans lying around. I asked the guy what would happen to them, and he said they'd probably stash them in some warehouse or throw them away. When I heard that, I grabbed about five or six pairs of jeans and took them home with me.

It kind of gets to you—all the waste. I can remember playing in the All-Star games, and how they'd have four or five pairs of shoes waiting for you. You go in there, grab a pair, wear them for the game, and leave the other four pairs lying there. How many kids in America could have used those shoes? I would have loved a new pair of sneakers when I was a kid, but we just couldn't afford it. It's hard for me to just forget about that.

If you are going to make all this money, I feel like you should give some of it back. I have a few charities that I'm really committed to, and there are countless others that I hear about every day. Some I do, and some I don't do. I know people get disappointed, but you can't believe how many calls Jill gets. Then there's all the phone calls that come to the Pacers offices. It gets overwhelming. Some just want you to sign a ball or a jersey. Others want you to speak at different things. They get really disappointed when you say no, but if I said yes to all of them, I'd be doing three speaking engagements every day, 365 days a year, and I would be signing basketballs for the rest of my life. The bad part is, every day, I have to say no to somebody, and that's tough. People don't understand the demands on our time. They'll come in and say, "Hey, we want you to speak at this thing. C'mon, Larry, it will only take an hour." It may take only an hour to do the appearance, but what they are forgetting is it takes two and a half hours to drive down there, then another two and a half hours to drive back, and all of a sudden a whole day is gone, one that I could have spent at home with my family.

The key for me is to try and use my time wisely to help the charities that I have agreed to support. If I'm going to do it, I want to do it right, and I want to make sure I have the time that is required to fulfill the commitment.

I've picked a number of different causes to support. One thing I do every year in Naples is participate in an annual golf tournament that benefits the Hospice of Naples and the homeless in that area. I found out about that particular charity from a friend of mine who played golf with someone down there who was the head of the hospice. It wasn't that big at first, but we raised about $150,000 in one day. Now it's really big.

The other golf tournament that I've sponsored for sixteen years is in Terre Haute, and it benefits the Boys and Girls Clubs of Terre Haute. We get the same guys every year. There's about 280 of them, and we have a 98 percent return rate. And the best part about it is I don't have to bring anyone else in. Let's say they wanted me to bring Magic Johnson in. It's time-consuming for him to come all the way from the West Coast, which he would do if I asked him as a favor. But if I did that, I would know I would have to go out to Los Angeles at some point to return the favor. What's nice is that some of my old teammates come each year, just because they enjoy it. Last summer Joe Kleine, who is a great guy, was there. I really enjoy that tournament, because it's a chance for me to catch up with old friends. I know I'm going to be having it for a long, long time to come, so it's one day when I can plan on enjoying myself and spending time with people that are a whole lot of fun to be around.

The Hospice event in Florida is a great event because the people who run it aren't demanding at all. In fact, they are very understanding. As long as I show up, they are very happy with it. I don't even have to play in the tournament if I don't want to. Sometimes I just stand at one hole and each group comes around. They pay fifty dollars, or something like that. Then they have a situation where if one of the golfers hits the green on a par three, he gets an autographed ball from me. All the money goes to charity, so I don't mind.

I tend to be interested in helping charities that involve kids. What I've worked out with a number of different charities is to license my likeness to them so they can use it for their campaigns and programs. The Indiana Attorney General's office is using my likeness on a CD-ROM program that teaches kids how to safely use the Internet and avoid any kind of fraud, or pornography, things like that. Of course, I also sign tons of stuff for various charity auctions; everything from the American Cancer Society to antidrug programs. Most of my endorsement con- tracts are structured so they include charity donations. There are plenty of other causes I've helped over the years, but the problem is that for every ten organizations you help, another ten go away thinking you don't care. I guess that's something I have to live with, but I don't like it.

It happens all the time, even with people you know. You have all these people who call themselves friends, and they figure, "Hey, Larry's rich, what's a couple hundred bucks to him?" and expect me to give them whatever they need, just because I have money. What those people have forgotten is I worked for everything I've earned. Nobody handed me anything. I had to go out and prove I was worth it. It's pretty easy to spot a guy who wants something from you, as opposed to real friends who don't want a dime. The guy that never asks for anything is the one I'm going to end up helping out.

Listen, I'm still uncomfortable sometimes with all of it. Dinah and I have a house in French Lick, one in Naples, Florida, and a new home in Carmel, Indiana, that we bought when I took the Pacers job. Sometimes I think it's too much. I like to mow my own lawn and take care of my flowers, but I can't keep up with three places. I look at my children, Conner and Mariah, and I know they are spoiled. Dinah and I try to teach them to appreciate what they have. I hope they're listening. It's important to me that my kids are capable of making a living for themselves. Yes, their mom and dad have money, but I want those kids to un- derstand that they can't just sit back and coast through life. I think they realize that. As I write this, Conner is seven, and he gets an allowance, but he never spends any of it.

I asked him why. He told me he's saving his money for his family.

CHAPTER 10

On Life in French Lick

When I took the head coaching job with the Pacers, everyone kept saying how excited I must be, because I was coming home again. But the truth is, Indianapolis isn't really home for me. It's a lot different from the area of French Lick and West Baden, where I grew up. Indianapolis is a legitimate city. French Lick is a little country town. It's a beautiful place, with lots of hills and trees and winding roads, a very simple town, full of decent, hardworking people. It's the second poorest county in Indiana, but still I think it's beautiful. The people I grew up with don't have a lot. I understand that. I was one of the lucky ones to go out and do my thing, but I love spending time there, and my kids love it too, because it's quiet and comfortable. The people there leave us alone. It's definitely not someplace you want to go if you are looking for excitement. There're no nightclubs. There're a couple of family-style restaurants. We don't have a McDonald's there, but we do have a Dairy Queen. If you want to see a movie, you've got to drive to Jasper, which is about twenty miles away. The main attraction in French Lick is the French

Lick Springs Hotel. Tourists go there to play golf, have a massage, whatever. Some kids I knew worked at the hotel when we were growing up, but I never really spent much time there. For me, the attraction of French Lick was always that it was home. I have never felt more comfortable anyplace else. But it hasn't really been the same since my mother died in 1996.

The one thing I always think about is how much Mom would enjoy going to all the Pacers games now that I'm coaching. She would absolutely love it. It would have been the ultimate for her. She would make that drive up to Indianapolis for every game, I'm sure of it. It's a little less than two hours from French Lick, but she never minded driving. It was flying she hated. I think she probably only saw me play in person about two or three times in Boston Garden, because she didn't want to have to get on that airplane to get there, and it was too far to drive. I don't know why she was so scared of flying. By that point of my life, I was flying to places all the time. But my mom was a lot like me: stubborn. If she said she wasn't going to get on an airplane, then that was it. It wasn't going to happen.

I never talked to my mom about coaching. I never once told her it was something I was thinking about. But she was the first one to tell me that's what I'd be doing once I stopped playing. One day some guy was at our house and he said, "I'm sure when Larry is done playing, he'll coach." I said to him, "You must be crazy. There's no way I'm going to do that." But Mom looked at him and said really matter-of-factly, "Oh yes. Of course he'll coach." Which is funny, because she had no way of knowing. Mom loved basketball, and she got into the games as much as anyone. She knew what she was talking about too. I never keyed in on the crowd when I was playing, but people tell me she used to hoot and holler for the Celtics when we came to Indianapolis. That doesn't surprise me. I bet she yelled at the officials too.

The truth is, whatever she did, I wouldn't have noticed when the game was going on. I was never one to look up and search for people in the stands. It never even occurred to me to do something like that, because I was so focused on the game. The only time I might notice the crowd was when I would be sitting on the bench, and the place would be going crazy. But not while I was out there playing. It took me ten years before I knew there was a wives' row set aside for all the Celtics spouses. I never knew who was sitting down at the other end of the court, never mind who was watching in the stands. That's why I never knew my assistant Dick Harter, because I never looked down at the other bench. I played against him when he was head coach of the Charlotte Hornets. I told him I don't remember that, but I'm sure we must have kicked his butt.

When you are growing up and your mom is yelling at you to pick up your stuff, or wipe your feet, you don't think too much about her and what kind of sacrifices she is making for you. One thing I did appreciate even back then, though, was how hard she worked. It seemed like she worked all the time. She had to, so we could have something to eat. Mom had two jobs—one as a waitress, and one as a cook—and she did the best she could. She didn't complain; she just went out and did what she had to do. She would have never wanted anyone to feel sorry for her. Most people know by now that my dad took his own life in 1975. That left Mom with six kids, on her own. At that point it would have been easy for Mom to just let everything fall apart, but she wasn't like that. She got us all together and said, "Okay. Let's see what we're made of."

I learned to be tough by watching my parents, and the sacrifices they made for us. My dad was one of those guys who would come home one night, and he would have hurt his ankle at work. I remember one time he had an ankle that was so swollen it was horrifying to look at. It was all black and blue, and big and puffy-looking. It was the weekend, and it hurt him so much that he wasn't moving around at all, and it just got worse and worse. But by the time Monday came around, he had his boot out and he was jamming that swollen ankle into it, and he tightened it up as much as it could go and then headed back out to work.

My mother was the same way. Sometimes she would wake up sick in the morning. She'd be throwing up and feeling feverish, but since we didn't have a family car, she'd get herself dressed and walk to work. She'd walk over a mile to her waitress job at this breakfast place at four o'clock in the morning, then come back two or three hours later and get us breakfast and get us ready for school. Then as soon as the school bus took off, she'd be walking back another mile to the restaurant and work until seven, eight, nine o'clock.

My mom and I were alike in some ways. We're both proud, and we're both stubborn, no question about that, but there was one big difference: Mom loved to gossip. I hated that. I always called her the mayor of West Baden, because she had all the information. She knew everything there was to know about everyone, including me. There are a lot of people in that town who believe everything they hear, and Mom was one of them. She was always hearing all sorts of stories about me, both good and bad, and she'd soak up every word of it. I remember a few years ago, my brother's buddy had this sister, and, just kidding around, she told somebody in town, "Larry bought me a new car." Well, in about five minutes' time Mom had heard about this, and she got really mad. She was mad at me for a long time too, about two or three months, for buying this person who was practically a stranger a car, but she never said anything to me about it. She gave everyone else an earful, but not me. Then finally one day she realized I hadn't bought anybody a car. It's like I told her: "See, Mom? Don't believe everything you hear."

As much as Mom liked to talk, she was always real protective of us. You didn't say anything bad to her about her kids. That would be a big mistake. When I was home in the off season, the phone would always be ringing off the hook. She knew I didn't want to be interrupted, so a lot of times, no matter who was on the phone, she'd be looking right at me sitting on the couch and would tell whoever was calling, "No, Larry's not here. I haven't seen him." She did it to my friends. She even did it to my former attorney, Bob Woolf. The truth was, when I came home she wanted some time with me, and that was hard to come by. Once I made the pros, and built the house in West Baden, we always had an unlisted number. People don't understand, I never had a phone in my house until my senior year of high school. We couldn't afford one. My sister Linda worked, and she really wanted one, so she paid to have one put in. I hated it, because every call that came into that house was for her.

Anyhow, my mom caught on pretty early how it was all going to work. She knew when I got home that if somebody called, I would leave. So she would take a message, because she wanted me to stay. I'll never forget when we won the championship in 1984. I drove home from Boston to French Lick, all night, straight through. It took twenty-two hours. I got home around twelve or twelve-thirty, and my mom runs out and grabs me and hugs me. She said, "I know you're really tired," but she makes me a sandwich, and we go outside, and we're sitting on the porch, talking. I could tell she was really enjoying it, and so was I. But I wasn't home an hour and all of a sudden I look up and here come two of my buddies in their trucks, hauling their boats. She says to me, "You're not leaving, are you?" I said, "No, Mom, I just got here." But the next thing you know, my buddies are up on the porch, and they want me to go fishing. My mom is scolding them, telling them, "Larry isn't going anywhere. He just got home. He's been driving all night. He's tired." But the guys keep pestering me. They wanted to go up to Terre Haute, to this place they can only get into if I'm with them. I looked at them and said, "You guys really want to go?" They said to me, "C'mon, Larry, we've been waiting for you all summer." So I tell them, "All right then, let's go." Mom was ticked off. She said, "I knew you were going to leave." Even so, she still helped me pack up some stuff, because we were staying overnight. So I went up to Terre Haute and fished all night and the next day too. But Mom never stayed mad. She understood. She did warn Dinah, though. She told her, "You better know what you're getting into."

Dinah has always been great about me taking off like that. I want my own kids to be that way. I want them to be independent and be able to go out and do the things they want to do. Before we had kids, Dinah was the same as me. She'd pick up and go. She was like one of the guys. Once our children came, it changed, especially since now I'm traveling a lot during the season. Now when I'm home, I want to stay home. I want to be with my family.

We have a big backyard, and it's fun just to run around with the kids out there. Conner is really into computers, so we play solitaire almost every day, to see if we can beat the computer. In the summers, both Mariah and Conner can't wait to go down to French Lick—mostly, I think, because we have a pool there.

I loved growing up in a small town. It was all I knew. We didn't have a family car, so we weren't able to drive around to other towns or see other states. I didn't care. What was in front of me was just fine. We lived near this big hill, and whenever I was going someplace, my dad would say, "You know, Larry, if you run up that hill, you'll get there faster." So I'd go out and run up that hill as fast as I could. Who needed a car? When I was growing up I knew everyone in town. For the most part I still do. I enjoyed that immensely. Obviously it would have been beneficial for me to have more competition to play against in the summer. Those were the only times I ever wished I lived in the city, but hey, you live with what you have. One thing I did have was a lot of places to play basketball. We had courts all over town. One good thing about a small town—if someone stole the nets, you knew who did it, and you could get them back. Everyone played sports. I remember like it was yesterday my mom saying, "Will you kids go out and play ball?" I heard that over and over.

I didn't have a real love for the game until I was about thirteen years old. I never watched any basketball on TV. All I was concerned about was my game, and how I was playing. I can remember being in fifth and sixth grade, looking up at the clock in school and wondering if it was ever going to move, because I couldn't wait to get out there and play ball. When I got older, my high school coach, Jim Jones, would give us drills to work on, and I'd work on them all day, until I got them right. But the older I got, I noticed the drills seemed to come a little easier to me than to some of my friends. I was moving along a little quicker, whether it was a pick and roll, or shooting drills, or whatever. I could just tell I was improving a lot faster than my friends. I guess that's the first time I realized I might be different from them.

I knew one thing: I loved to compete. I was always trying to keep up with my older brothers, Mark and Mike. When I was little, they were always bigger and stronger, and they were constantly challenging me. I wanted so much to keep up with them. I hated to lose, and it seemed like I always lost to my brothers. It was a lousy feeling that I never forgot.

I can still remember the first time I was in a real pressure situation. I had broken my ankle my sophomore year in high school, and I came back just in time to play in the sectionals. I didn't start or anything. I was sitting on the bench. I could barely run, and the coach kept telling me, "Listen, Larry, if you don't come around, you're not going to be on this team." I understood that. Anyhow, he put me in this state sectional game, and I had the ball, and I just turned around and shot it, and it went in. Everyone started cheering and clapping and going crazy, and I absolutely loved it. I remember running down the court thinking, "This is the best!" The game came down to about four seconds to play, and we're down by one, and some guy fouls me. I go to the free throw line, and for some reason I stood there thinking, "You know, I haven't practiced all year, but I've been with this team, and I'm gonna make these free throws and we're gonna win this game." From then on, when I was in a situation where the game was on the line, I thought back to that day, and how I felt, and what I did—which was hit both free throws. The next day, the paper said, "Bird steals the show." That game changed my life. From then on I was hooked. I thought about basketball all the time. I spent hours making up drills to make myself better.

It's a nice feeling to know that the people I grew up with are proud of me. Especially Mom. She wouldn't say a whole lot to me, but other people told me how she used to brag about my accomplishments. The nice thing about French Lick was the people there didn't make too much of a fuss. When I went to Indiana State and started getting a lot of attention, people were happy for me, but when I came home in the summer I was just one of the Bird boys. Of course, that's changed some since I went to the pros. I've thought before about being the only kid from French Lick, Indiana, to ever make it to the NBA, and that's awesome. I've always said there could be another, but the chances, I guess, are slim.

People in West Baden and French Lick have gotten used to me being around, especially in the summer. I did all my off-season conditioning there when I played for the Celtics. I went through my routine every day, starting real early in the morning, and after a while the people in town just knew, "Oh that's Larry doing his workout." They'd wave or honk if they saw me, but when you start out as early as I did, sometimes at five-thirty or six o'clock in the morning, there aren't too many people up anyway.

The first thing I'd do is run. I'd run two and a half, three miles every day. Any more than three miles back then, and I'd get stiff. My back would start acting up, or my knees and my legs would give me trouble, because of all the pounding. I always felt that if I kept it to around

two or three miles, it would get me loosened up for what
else I was going to do. From there I used to go to my old
high school gym, at Springs Valley High School, and do
my sit-ups, which meant anywhere from 300 to 500 of
them. Then I'd start working on the court on ballhandling
drills, and start my shooting, and then do some suicide
wind sprints, and then mix it all in together. Then I'd go
lift weights. A lot of times I'd get on my bike and ride
through town. I always rode a loop around Route 145, and
it was about eleven and three-quarter miles, and I'd always try to make it back home in forty-three minutes. That
was always a good pace.

Once I started having really bad back problems, Dan
Dyrek put me on a special program, and it was absolutely
brutal. It was about the worst thing I've ever done in my
life. He had it set up so one day I'd run for distance, then
one day run sprints, but for some reason I always felt I
still needed to run my three miles first, because that's what
I had always done. That would get me loosened up for
my basketball drills. I just felt I shouldn't drop that part
of my workout. Dan had me lifting too, but it was different than what I had been doing on my own. His program was a tougher program. It would take me a good
two hours just to finish my lifting. It wasn't a lot of rep-
etitions, but it was three sets of twelve on every exercise.
One of his drills was one of the best exercises I ever had.
I'd be on a stationary bike, and I'd take ten-pound weights,
and ride the bike, and alternate lifting these things over
my head while I'm trying to keep my form. I'd do that
for five minutes and I'd be dying. Then I'd get off the
bike and jump rope real fast for two minutes, then hop
back on the stationary bike and start over. Dan had me do
that three times in one set. That was one of the hardest

things I've ever done. Then he'd have me run these 440-yard dashes, which I always tried to do in seventy-five seconds or less. After everything else I had already done, that seemed easy.

Once I finished all my conditioning drills, then I'd go play basketball. The basketball would last as long as I felt I could play that day, usually one and a half to two hours. I never scrimmaged. There weren't a lot of people in French Lick to choose from, but I concentrated on drills anyway. When someone like Rick Carlisle would come up to Indiana to work out with me, I'd change the routine a little. We'd still run, and we'd still ride the bikes, and we'd lift and play some one-on-one. A lot of different guys came out over the years, and I liked it when guys like Rick Carlisle came out, because he wanted to work. Rick Robey came a few times, but he wasn't going to go through all of that. Another old teammate of mine, Brad Lohaus, came out a couple times and went through all of it with me.

At the end of the summer, when it was getting close to training camp, usually the last two or three weeks I was home, I'd run up this hill. It was about a mile long from bottom to top, and the first quarter-mile is straight up, very tough. It doesn't ever level off, it's just one slow incline. It was my test, to see what kind of shape I was in. It's one of those hills where I bet Dinah and my friend Corky twenty dollars they couldn't make it to the top. Corky barely made it, and Dinah didn't make it. She would now, because she runs a lot these days. I took Brad Lohaus up that hill a couple times, and he'd start out right there with me and we'd be running real slow, because that hill goes straight up, but then you'd see him start falling back, falling back, and by the end we're barely moving, but I was still way in front.

Some days I'd run, play my basketball, and then get
on my bike for twenty-five miles. At that point I had a
regular ten-speed bike, nothing special. Later on I got me
a fancier bike with twenty gears, but you don't use but
two or three of them anyway. I rode from my house to
Wickliffe, which was around twenty-one miles. I'd take
off from my house around ten o'clock in the morning and
get there by around eleven, or a little bit after that, and
when I got there I'd get a cold beer, and I'd have my
friends from town, Sam Sanders or somebody, meet me
out there. Wickliffe is a town of around thirty people, and
we always went to this one place and got these schooners,
they call them. They are iced mugs of beer, real heavy. I
love those things. Anyhow, I'd hang out with whoever it
was that met me there, whether it's Sam, or my friend Rex
Stackhouse, and then we'd throw that bike in the back of
the truck and I'd ride home—in the front seat of the car.
By then it would feel like three in the afternoon, but it
was usually only lunchtime.

I guess it felt later because I'd always start early, and
these workouts would really last. Some of those workouts
went four or five hours. That program Dan Dyrek did damn
near killed me, and it took a lot of time. We didn't have
strength and conditioning guys back then to work out a
program for you, but I preferred to do it myself anyhow.
I never felt like I needed somebody to push me. I understand some players do, and a lot of my players are doing
programs with personal trainers and strength and conditioning people. I'm all for that. It's like I told my players: "I don't care how you do it, but I want you coming
in here at the start of each season well conditioned."

Now that I'm retired, I don't need to go through such
grueling workouts. I couldn't anyway—my back would

never hold up. But I still do use the summer to get myself back in shape. I'm an early riser, so I usually get up and put on my running stuff by six or six-thirty in the morning. I run from my house all through town and back around, but then I stop at the Honey Dew, where I know I'm always going to see some of my buddies. Sometimes I sit there for five minutes, and other times for an hour. Rex, Sam, and Jimmy Evans are usually there, talking about the news of the day. Sometimes there will be ten or twelve guys, sometimes just a couple, but there's always somebody. It's gotten so the crowd at the Honey Dew knows to expect me.

I really enjoy talking with those guys. Most of them are in their sixties, and some of them are even older than that. I don't know why most of my friends are older. It's just how it worked out. When the word gets out that I'm home, they know where to find me. When I'm in French Lick, I spend a lot of my free time down in my garage. There's a little table in there, and when my buddies drop over, we just hang out, have a beer or whatever, and talk or play cards. We don't talk about basketball. We talk about life. We talk about fishing. We tell stories of back when we were twenty. Some guys, all they talk about is their job. Most of them are big-machine operators, whether it is bulldozers, backhoes, trench lines. Rex helped lay the pipeline in Alaska. He told us he had to drive three or four hundred miles if he wanted to buy a drink. Sam is a painter, and he always has a good story to tell. Maybe it sounds boring to some people, but I just love it. I've had some of my most enjoyable times sitting there in that garage with my friends.

Sometimes I go down to that garage by myself. I take my car down there, and I go through the whole car and I clean it. I'm a very neat person, and I don't like my car to be dirty. So I get it just the way I like, then put everything away and sit down and have a beer. Next thing I know, it's three hours later. Sometimes Conner will come down, and that means Mariah is going to come down after him. People just sort of wander in and out of there.

I go down to that garage to think about almost everything. I made some of the biggest decisions of my life in that garage. When I was thinking about whether I wanted to coach or not, I went down there and just went over it again and again in my mind. Nonstop. I'd drive myself crazy like that for a couple hours, then I'd get up, go to the refrigerator, grab myself a beer, and sit down and think about it some more. My wife used to come there—she still does—and say, "Well, Larry, I guess we know where to find you. Same seat as always."

When I was younger I used to spend time in some of the local bars in French Lick. We used to go to this place called the Hoosier, but that burned down some years back. There's another bar I used to like called Jubil's, which is still there. It's nothing fancy. It's a regular bar, with linoleum floors, and I used to like to go down there to say hi to the guys. But what started to happen was I'd go in there for one beer, and then I'd say, "I gotta get going now," and as soon as I started out the door, somebody else I hadn't seen in a long time would come in there and he'd want to buy me a beer. Next thing you know, nursing one beer turned into three or four hours! I'm enjoying it, because I'm with ten guys, drinking Miller Lite, but Dinah is home cooking and waiting for me. Dinah didn't believe me for a long time, that I'd be halfway out the door before somebody else pulled me back in, but it's true. But I don't go down there anymore. After a while people like to start telling you what you need to do. Then you got guys who sit there and get their nerve up, and then they start asking you for stuff. I had this one guy I knew from Naples, who I met fishing. He was always asking me for stuff—autographs, basketballs, you name it. I'm telling you, it was nonstop. So one time he wanted to come up to French Lick, and when he got there I said, "I just want to show you something. You're always asking me for autographs for your friends, and you think you're the only one that's asking me. Well, you watch. Because almost everyone that comes up to me is gonna want something." Sure enough, about eight to ten people came over, some friends, some not, and they all wanted this, that, or the other thing. I turned to that guy and said, "See? Now you understand what it's like. You've got to stop bugging me for things." After that he stopped. If he hadn't, I probably would have told that guy to get lost, except I liked to go fishing with him.

Up until a few years back, I used to love to go hunting too. My favorite kind was deer hunting. We used to go all the time. But I've lost my taste for it. Right before I had back surgery, I was deer hunting right behind my house in French Lick. We have some really nice woods back there, and I was up in this tree, sitting there, holding my bow. I had used guns in the past, but at this point I was really enjoying hunting with the bow and arrow. It was almost dark, but all of a sudden I see some deer running down the hillside. I couldn't get a shot at them. Then I saw a ten-pointer, a real nice buck. I was getting ready to line him up, and all of a sudden I heard something, so I sat there, real still. The next thing you know, this deer walks out and stops right underneath my tree. I know it must have smelled something. That deer turns its head and is looking straight up at me. I released the bow, and I put the arrow in there, and I got myself ready to shoot, but that deer was still looking up at me. It looked almost human. It kept staring at me, standing there nice and still, and I said, "Well, that's the end of that." I put my bow away and I put my arrow away, and finally that deer just walked off. That was it for me. It changed my hunting habits forever. I haven't been hunting for deer ever since.

The summer before I talked to the Pacers about their coaching job, my friend Rex got into wine making. He'd make all different kinds of wine. He had rhubarb plants right in his front yard, so he'd make batches of rhubarb wine, and dandelion wine. I got into it a little bit, and I really enjoyed it. I made up a couple of bottles that didn't come out half bad, but once I took the coaching job, that was that. I don't really have time for anything like that these days.

There was one good thing about all the time I had on my hands during those years I was retired: I got to spend more time with Mom. Within two or three years after I retired, things had really quieted down. Dinah and I could come and go as we pleased without too much of a commotion. We spent a lot of time in French Lick, which is how I could tell something wasn't quite right with Mom.

I'd ask her, "Mom, is everything okay?" and she'd say, "Oh, I'm fine, Larry." But after a while you could tell she wasn't feeling quite right. She got real tired, and seemed to have lost some of her strength. That went on for a long time, until finally she went up to Indianapolis to have some tests done. Dinah and I went up there to pick her up at the hospital, and the doctor wasn't around. I said to Mom, "When is he coming?" and she said, "Well, he told us we could leave. I'm all done with the tests. Let's go home

and I'll call him tomorrow." I wanted to see the doctor,
but Mom was anxious to get going, so we drove home.
The doctor called me the next morning and said, "Larry,
I'm sure you want me to tell you everything, so why don't
you get the family together?" That's when I knew it was
bad. I said, "Why don't you just tell me, and I'll pass
along the information?" He said, "Your mother has probably got a year to live. She's got Lou Gehrig's disease,
and she'll have six good months, and then she'll start going
downhill real fast." I didn't say a word. Next, the doctor
started explaining to me that they needed to put a tube in
Mom's stomach so they could feed her. The doctor was
real nice, and he said, "I know it's going to be hard to
tell her. Would you like me to come down there? I could
talk to her. I could explain it." But I said, "No, I'll tell
her," because I knew I wouldn't want that kind of news
from a stranger.

I knew next to nothing about Lou Gehrig's disease until
Mom got it. The medical term for it is amyotrophic lat-
eral sclerosis, and it's a fatal disease with no known cause
and no cure. Lou Gehrig, a star baseball player for the
Yankees, died from it, so they renamed it after him. It's
really a horrible disease. It's a slow, degenerative illness
that attacks the nerve cells in the brain and the spine, and
eventually the muscles become paralyzed.

When I hung up with the doctor, I went in to see Mom.
I said, "Let me tell you what the doctor said." She said,
"Oh yeah, okay." I looked at her and I said, "Do you want
me to lie to you, or do you want me to tell the truth?"
Typical Mom. She said, "Well, Larry, I think I'll take the
truth." I told her what the doctor had said. She sat there
for a minute, then said, "Well, looks like I'm going to
have fun for the next six months." I explained the whole

thing and told her she could tell the rest of the family whenever she was ready. She was getting weaker and weaker every day. We could all see that. She was losing all her muscle definition. I stayed for a while, but when I was getting ready to leave she said, "Can you bring some of those weights over here for me?" I said, "Mom, it ain't gonna help." But I brought them to her anyway.

As much as she hated to fly, Mom got on a plane during those next six months and came down to Naples to see the kids. She did a lot of traveling around in the car, catching up with old friends. She did what she said she was going to do—she had fun.

Mom got the feeding tube, and she didn't like it at all, but she knew she had to have it. She was a guinea pig, really. She'd go up to Indianapolis every three weeks or so, and they'd have all these doctors in there, testing her, and asking her a ton of questions. She loved it. She really thought she was helping somebody else out. But then it got to where she couldn't talk anymore, and that was the end of that.

That was the worst part. It was murder on her, not to be able to talk. She could hear fine, and her mind was as clear as a bell, but she couldn't speak to us. All the muscles around her throat were gone.

It ended up going pretty much the way the doctor said. She got around some in those first six months, but she went downhill real fast. She just got so weak. She was wasting away to nothing, and it was really hard to watch. My sister Linda was with her all the time, and Dinah was with her a lot too. Poor Mom. She did the best she could, but there's no way to beat this thing.

The thing that bothered me the most was when I had to go to training camp with the Celtics that October. It was M. L.'s first year as coach, 1996, and we were headed down to Tennessee for about a week. I left on a Sunday, and I went over to see Mom before I went, and I knew it would be the last time I would see her alive. I didn't say much. Just kissed her goodbye. She died Monday night, so I had to go right back. The whole family was there. It didn't seem real at first. I knew she was going, but I guess I was figuring it would be more like a week, not just a couple of days. The thing that I wonder about, the part that must have been so hard for her, was that her mind was clear right down to the end. You wish she didn't have to suffer like that.

I think about Mom a lot when I walk into Market Square Arena and everyone is screaming and clapping and shouting, because she would have been right there with them. She followed basketball pretty closely. We had a satellite dish in West Baden, so she could watch anything she wanted. She was a big Isiah Thomas fan, and liked to watch all the Pistons games. My friend Tom Hill always said Mom was the best coach all of us kids ever had, because she was the first one to teach us discipline and hard work. Looking back, she really was amazing. I don't know how she kept track of all of us and kept us all out of trouble, but she did.

Before Mom died, she'd look after the house for us when we weren't there. Whenever we'd come home, she'd be flying out the front door, running to greet us. My kids really loved Mom. She was real good with them. I know they are young, but I really think they will remember her. I miss Mom every single day of my life.

CHAPTER 11

On Team Dynamics

I've said over and over no coach should stay in one place longer than three years. You stay longer than that and you get stale. The players don't listen as closely. So after my three years is up with Indiana, I will step down as coach. People have asked me if I'd go to another city and do this again, but I can't see it happening. I don't know. Maybe it could—it's just that I've got the best group of guys in Indiana. If I had one or two guys who didn't care about winning, it wouldn't make it worthwhile for me. I'm just lucky I have this collection of players who really want it. Too often these days it seems the NBA has a group of guys with too much going on. That's what people don't realize. If one guy is off, it can affect the whole team. When I was with the Celtics, the guy that I could never figure out was Tiny Archibald. He was a terrific player, but from one practice to the next you never knew what you were going to get from him in terms of his personality. When Tiny was in a really good mood, we'd all say, "Hey, let's live it up! Tiny is happy today." And when he wasn't, we just tried to get through that practice and get out of there.

Everybody has their own way of figuring out these athletes. I just rely on my gut. Danny Ainge has this guy he hired for his Phoenix team that can look at your facial expressions and your brainwaves and tell you what kind of person you are. It's this formula that determines if you have leadership potential or not. Danny is really into it, and he was telling me all about it last spring. I'm sitting there listening and thinking, "This guy has lost his mind." I was laughing my butt off. He said, "Larry, you are an intense, high-personality guy, a lot of serial killers have the same profile as you." I said, "Yeah, Danny, I ought to kill you for saying that."

When I first came in, we had this psychiatrist that had been with the team since Jack Ramsay was the coach in 1988. Jack Ramsay wanted him to administer this test to his players. He wanted to know who was a leader. But I'm thinking to myself, "After one month with these guys I'm going to know every one of them. We're wasting our money on this guy." I've always said you find out more about a player when things are going bad than when things are going good. Anybody can keep it together when you're winning every night.

When I looked at our roster, I knew we had some really, really good players, but no one guy who could carry us on his back night after night. Those guys, like Jordan, are rare. So for much of the early part of the year, my guys pooled from each other. That's how they managed, by feeding off one another. Like Chris Mullin. Guys were really happy for him. He had come from Golden State, where everything had fallen apart, so our guys wanted him to succeed. They would really try to get him the ball. Same thing with Reggie, or Rik, if he was feeling it. They are just so unselfish. That's how they do things. As far as leading them, I told them, "Don't worry about me. I'll handle all the bull. This team should just focus on playing basketball. If you guys want me to lead you, I'll lead you. I can't score any baskets, but I'll have you prepared to score those baskets."

My biggest concern about our guys coming in is who would emerge as a true leader for us. I asked Donnie, "Who is the leader on this team?" He said, "You've got guys who think they are leaders, but they really aren't." After a couple of months it became obvious to me that our leader was Mark Jackson. He wasn't the most talented guy on our team, but guys responded to him.

What Mark did was get these guys in the right frame of mind. He was the one who earned their respect. When he was in a huddle and he said, "Look, we've got five minutes left, and we're down by four points, let's shut them down," you could see their eyes getting bigger. That was all they needed to hear, sometimes, to get them all fired up.

People think it's an easy thing to be a leader. It's not. You have to earn the respect of your teammates. You have to be willing to challenge them as well as support them. And you have to prove you are willing to do whatever it takes. I can remember Cedric Maxwell saying once, "You can always tell when Larry's back is hurting, because the first thing he'll do at the beginning of the game is dive for a loose ball. He might not get to it, but he'll pop his back, he'll feel better, and he'll take care of any ideas that he's not ready to go." Max was right. Anytime I went down for a loose ball, and a mess of guys ended up diving for it, our team always got fired up by that. Hey, I got fired up by it. And that helped me forget about my injuries. Think about it. If I came out and it was obvious I was having a problem because I wasn't moving well, and favoring that back, then the guys would be saying, "Ah, Larry's hurting tonight. We're going to have a tough time."

You take a guy on our team like Rik Smits. You never really used to see Rik dive for loose balls. But last year I saw him flying all over the court. These guys bought into the fact that that kind of effort would win games for us. The one thing I have to say about these guys is that they truly know I believe in them, so they listen. We'd be down a few points, and we'd have a time-out and I'd say, "Look guys, don't get frustrated. We've got plenty of time left out there, let's use it to our advantage. We're not out of this game. We're gonna win this game." I'd say it real calm, like I knew what I was talking about, and they'd go out there and come back, and we'd win the game, and they'd be in the locker room afterward saying, "Man! We really can do this!"

I think that happened with Mark Jackson more than any of the other guys. He understood right away what I was trying to do with the team. Here was a player whose career had taken so many twists and turns, and I think he saw a coach that was willing to let him be whatever he wanted to be, as long as he put in the work and the effort.

Mark Jackson reminds me of Dennis Johnson. It's the way he gets the ball and knows what's going on all the time, and won't hesitate to step up and nail the big shot, even if he's missed the last ten in a row. Mark works for everything he gets. He reminds me a little of myself, in that way. He keeps plugging and plugging. Look at how his career has gone. He was Rookie of the Year in New

York, then that all went bad, and for a while he was a guy people didn't respect that much. But then he comes to Indiana, and he is the key guy. All you have to do is look at what happened to the team when they traded him the season before I got there. They lost all their chemistry. I can understand why Larry Brown did it. He thought Travis Best could start at point guard. But Travis is the perfect backup. Anyhow, it's been a long road for Mark Jackson, and I was so happy for him we had the success we did last season. The truth is, he saved our butt. He's the one who, if we lost a big game or something, would get everyone together and give them a talk. It really helped the younger guys. They definitely reacted to it.

That's why I got so frustrated with him in our playoff series against New York. He was playing great, and that's when he started doing that shimmy thing, and I just wanted to deck him. It was Game 3 of the Eastern Conference semifinals, and Mark had just caused a turnover, and then he went into this shimmy, a real showboat move where he gyrates up the court dribbling the ball. He was doing it at the Knicks bench, and even though we were up by 13 points I knew right away it was a mistake. I knew New York was a good defensive team, and I knew they were gonna make a run. They did, and they won the game. The next morning we had a breakfast meeting. I just laid it on the line to him. I felt he had put us in a position to lose that game, and I told him that. He didn't say anything, because he already knew. I wanted Mark to feel bad, because I wanted him to make it up to his team.

He did too. In Game 5 of that series, a game we needed to win to close out the Knicks and play the Bulls in the Conference Finals, Mark Jackson played unbelievably. He recorded the first playoff triple-double in Pacers history, and it was because of him that we won the game.

Not long after that I asked him, "Do you want to be remembered by doing that shake, or do you want to be remembered as the guy that came into New York and knocked off the Knicks and got a triple-double against them?" To a guy like Mark, who saved his career last season, he saw the writing on the wall.

After he got that triple-double, I made sure we got him a ball and painted it up real nice for him. We did the same thing whenever a rookie scored his first two points in a regular-season game. I think that's something every pro player should remember. The Celtics never really did that. They'd have balls for the major things, like 10,000 points or something. I still have some of mine. I know how important stuff like that can be to players, to be recognized.

The only ball I ever really wanted was in 1986, because we won that championship by beating Bill Fitch and his Houston team, and to me that really meant something. When the game ended, our backup center, Greg Kite, grabbed the ball, because he was on the court and the closest one to it. After the game I asked him for it, but he wouldn't give it to me. I was named the MVP of the playoffs, and I won a car for it, and I was thinking about trading Kite the car I won for the ball. But the more I thought about it, the more I felt Greg should have just given it to me outright. I had just finished playing a great series, and made sure he was going to have a ring. Greg knew how much I wanted to beat Bill Fitch, because I respected Fitch so much, and I feel he should have offered me that ball. I never told him, but that's how I felt. But it doesn't matter now. It's done.

It did teach me to be smarter about these things. Before they closed Boston Garden, which I thought was the greatest place in the world to play basketball, they had a special ceremony to commemorate the building, and they invited all the old Celtics greats to come back. Bob Cousy was there, and Bill Russell, who hardly went to anything at that point, and John Havlicek, and K. C. and Sam Jones, and some others. Anyhow, we all got on the court, and each Celtics "legend" passed the ball up the floor, from one to another. I was at the far end, the last player in the chain, and I shot the layup. Then I grabbed that ball, and I didn't let go until I was on the plane back home.

One of the things I loved most about being a Celtic was the tradition. I loved looking up there before the game, while the national anthem was playing, and seeing all those championship banners. So many unbelievable basketball players wore the Celtics uniform, and it was important to me that I spend my entire career there.

I would love to help the Pacers create their own kind of tradition. They have some from the days they were in the ABA, but it would be awesome if our team could bring them a title and start something. I'll tell you one thing: I don't want to be the one that trades Mark Jackson or Reggie Miller. They deserve to finish out their careers in Indiana. If the Pacers wanted to do that, I'd have to leave.

I had been watching Reggie Miller play for years, and I knew he was the guy that would make or break this team on the court. When I got the job, there was some talk in Indianapolis that he might react negatively to me, because I would be taking attention away from him. He had always been the show in Indiana—it's part of his game. I knew a lot would be said, but I also knew Reggie wouldn't let me down. If he was upset, or put off, about the hoopla over me coming here, he certainly never let on. And once he got to know me, he could tell pretty quickly I don't care about that stuff.

The thing about Reggie is he's really a scorer more than a shooter. Yet he hits really big shots, and he's got range. How many other guys do you know in the league who can take one or two dribbles and throw it up from 25 feet or longer? What I like best about him is he thrives on the pressure of the big shot. He wants to be the guy to take it with everything on the line. Sometimes he demands it. Some people are put off by all the trash-talking Reggie does, but it's all a game. It's his way of getting inside the opponent's head, and quite often it works.

What surprised me most about Reggie is that he's a good defensive player. He's so much better than I thought he'd be. Reggie could be a great defensive player, but he wants to be a scorer. I keep telling him he can be both. It's funny, really. Reggie knows a lot more about defense than he'll let on. But I admire him, because he works his butt off every day. His work ethic is amazing, and not enough people give him credit for that. I can honestly say he's been above and beyond what I thought he would be.

I remember one night during the playoffs I was trying to convince these guys they were good enough to beat the Bulls. I stood up there and pointed to Chris Mullin, and I said, "You've got a guy here who has played in some huge games. He's never been to the Finals, but if you see him open, you know he's going to pop some down for us, because he wants so badly to get there. And look at Mark Jackson, have you ever seen a guy compete as hard as him? He doesn't have all the ability in the world. I didn't have all the ability in the world, but it doesn't matter if you compete. And look at Reggie Miller over there. He's probably the greatest shot maker in the game, in the whole history of the NBA. Anytime, this guy will stick a knife in your heart." I stopped and looked at the guys, and they were hanging on every word. Later, a couple of the players said Reggie was really touched by what I had said. It meant a lot to him. I told the guys, "I wouldn't say it unless I meant it."

The guy I really felt sorry for in my first season was Rik Smits. He was having problems with the nerves in his feet, and he was in agony all season. I give him credit, because he played hurt an awful lot of nights. The littlest things, like stepping on a towel, could send pain just shooting through his feet. That's how bad it was. By January, I was really concerned that he was going to have to retire. He was trying, but there's only so much you can push yourself. Rik came to me and said, "I don't know, Coach. I don't know how much more of this I can take." I asked him if he'd be willing to see my friend Dan Dyrek, who had helped me so much with my back trouble. Rik was willing to try anything. He flew to Boston and spent a couple of days with Dan, who immediately began working on those feet. What he does is this technique called joint mobilization, which is a deep, usually painful massage that helps break up scar tissue and rejuvenate the joints and muscles and tendons in that area. Within a few visits, I could tell he was helping Rik. I knew we had no chance in the playoffs without Rik, so I was relieved that Dan had made some progress.

I hated to see Rik miss out, because he was so much a part of what we were doing. Rik Smits is like most of the guys on this team, one of the nicest people you'd ever want to be around. Truthfully? That's not what you really want. You want guys who are nasty, who have an edge, that killer instinct. Rik can't give us that, but he's very capable of scoring points and getting rebounds. He's proven that he'll play hurt, and play through pain. There's only so much one guy can do. I don't have a problem with Smits.

Besides, it's not like he was the only one who had trouble getting mean. Reggie is a great late-game shooter. I mean, he loves the pressure. I see how he's progressed the last five years and I'm happy for him, because he's a nice guy. But he's not all that mean either.

Believe me, it matters. All you need to do is go back to the 1984 Finals, Celtics versus Lakers, when Kevin McHale clotheslined Kurt Rambis as he was heading in for a layup. The networks show a clip of it whenever they talk about "playoff intensity." There's no question in my mind that Kevin didn't mean to do it, but after he did, it turned the whole series around. The Lakers never really liked physical contact, and we got them intimidated after that.

You need to find somebody who, if your opponent is coming in for a layup, every once in a while is willing to knock him down. That's just the way this league is. Guys don't like to be hit. You get a couple of them on the ground and it makes a difference, especially if you're in the game. Hey, teams used to beat on me all the time. That's why I had so many surgeries.

The Pistons were very physical. The Lakers, after 1984 or 1985, were willing to hit people. Philadelphia's teams, back when we were battling them, were always tough. They gave you a shot every once in a while. But Detroit was definitely the best. Rick Mahorn, Bill Laimbeer, and those guys, they took you right out of the game.

We had a pretty heated rivalry with them. They were very limited, and so they had to do what they had to do. The only guy I really didn't like from that bunch was

Laimbeer. I thought he was a cheap-shot artist. There's a difference between knocking somebody down, and letting him know, but Laimbeer was the kind of guy who got his shots in after the whistle blew. He'd be standing there with the ball in the air, and the whistle having already been blown, and he would take a crack at your knees or your back. Listen, nobody played any harder and hit people more than me. I hit people all the time. That's part of it. But I never tried to hurt a guy. All you need to know about Laimbeer is what Robert Parish did to him during the 1987 playoffs. It takes a whole lot to get Parish riled up about anything, but he was sick and tired of Laimbeer nailing him with those sneaky cheap shots, so during the course of Game 5 of the Eastern Conference Finals, he just leveled Laimbeer under the basket. At the time the officials didn't call anything, because they knew all about Laimbeer too, but then the Pistons took the tape to the league, and there was Robert pummeling Laimbeer on tape, so they suspended him for Game 6 of our series. It was the first time in the history of the postseason that anyone had been suspended like that. That's what I mean about Detroit taking you out of your game. We lost that game because we didn't have our center. We came back and beat them in Game 7 at Boston Garden, but it never should have come to that.

None of us made any secret about how we felt about Laimbeer. I remember one season, I got on the team bus and the writers were talking about the All-Star team, which had just been announced. I turned to one of them and said, "Did Laimbeer make it?" He said, "No, not this year." I said, "Good. Now I won't have to worry about him getting on the team bus and saying, 'Good morning, Larry,' and me saying, 'Screw you, Bill.' "

Chris Mullin, on the other hand, was a guy I would have loved to play with. He's one of those guys who understands the game. You can tell by the way he passes the ball, and is always in the right spot for the rebound, and by the way he drills his shots. I remember being impressed by the way he handled himself on the Dream Team. We never really had any serious practices, but Chris was always working on something anyway. He was a real pro, just working and working.

I was really excited when we were able to trade for him. We knew Chris was getting older. He was thirty-four years old when we traded for him. But the one thing about Chris was that he had had so many freak injuries that he hadn't played a lot of minutes over the past couple of years, so we were thinking his legs would be fresh. Chris went through some tough stretches earlier in the season with us. We were asking an All-Star player to become a type of role-player on this team, and it took Mully a while to adjust to that. But he's a team guy, all about winning. I wish we could have played together in our prime.

What happened was that Mully got to where he was sort of standing around out there, not being aggressive. One thing Chris Mullin needs to be is aggressive on the offensive end, or you might as well not have him out there. He is one of the best shooters I've ever seen. I've been around a lot of great ones, and he's right there. We needed him to be consistent for us, so we could keep defenses honest. The season before, when the Pacers didn't have Mully, teams would double Reggie on the wing and Rik in the post, and there was no outside threat to make them pay for that.

That's one of the reasons I tried to get these guys in the mentality of looking for their shots. Take the Davises,

Dale and Antonio (who, by the way, are not related). We would definitely like to have more scoring from each one of those guys, but we're limited in where we get our baskets. Some games we look at our team and we wonder where the scoring is coming from, but somehow we manage to fight through it and get enough points to win.

Dale has always thought his role is as a defensive player who will get you rebounds. I'd like to see him do more. I think he has the skills to be a low post threat, but he has to believe he can do that, and I don't think it comes as second nature to him the way it does other players.

Dale is a real good guy. You love having someone like him. My guess is basketball isn't the most important thing in the world to him. He'll do everything you'll ask him to do. He just won't do more. You look at that body, pure muscle, and you wonder about the possibilities. What I said to him at the beginning of the season was, "Dale, if you get yourself in perfect shape, where you can run, you're going to pick up rebounds, and you're going to get fouled, or you're going to get easy baskets. So just run. I'll get you the ball, and when we throw it down to you I want you to take it right at them." But he just never did, until the end of the year. He had some spurts in the playoffs where he was really kicking butt. If we could ever get him to do it all season long, look out.

Antonio is the more passionate of the two. I love it when he gets mad. He can be so good, but sometimes even he can't believe it. He's one of those guys, when he's running up the court in practice, that I have to holler to, "Hey, Antonio, pick it up." I shouldn't have to tell the guys that. I'm a firm believer that, if he started, Antonio could average 18 points a night. He has unlimited ability.

When Smits went out with foot problems, Antonio took

his spot in the middle and played really well. When Rik was getting ready to come back, everyone was wondering if I'd still start Antonio. I went to him and said, "Antonio, what do you think is best for the team? You starting, or Rik starting?" He goes, "Rik starting." So that was that. Antonio was right. We were a better team with Rik as a starter, because Antonio could come off the bench for either him or Dale Davis. Either way, Antonio was always going to play a lot of minutes. He often ends up playing more minutes than anyone I've got. But I thought it was great that he put aside what he wanted for himself for what he knew would help us win more games.

I know that starting is an issue with Antonio. I can't say I blame him. I fully expected him to come in ready to steal Dale's job away if he could. My dilemma is that I really don't have anyone else to back up Rik.

The guy I had the toughest time figuring out, I guess, was Derrick McKey. I'd see him and say hi here and there, but I knew I hadn't really connected with this guy. So I called him in one time and said, "Derrick, I played against you. I know how you play. I'm not bringing you in here to get fifteen points and ten rebounds a night. I just want you to play. If I put you in the game, don't worry about numbers. Just play." He said, "I like that. That's the way I prefer to play basketball." I said, "If any of our coaches come up and say, 'We need ten from you tonight, Derrick,' you tell them you talked to me." Then I asked him if it was important to him to start. He said no.

There are times when Derrick will really frustrate you. He's got so much talent, but what can you do? He has to want to get the most out of it. I can't talk him into that. But I always appreciated how he responded when I asked him to. We were playing Boston, and Antoine Walker was having a good night, so I went to Derrick in the fourth quarter and said, "Derrick, all I care about is that you put the stops to Walker." He went out there and was all over the kid. He shut him down, and we won the game.

A guy like Derrick McKey has been around long enough to know not to get too high or too low. With younger players, that becomes more of a challenge.

Take a kid like Travis Best. There's a guy who got a taste of success. Travis did a great job of breaking down Chicago's defense in the playoffs. We were all happy that he got some recognition. He became a free agent that summer, and we knew other teams would be after him. I was hoping to re-sign him, but if he made a decision to go somewhere else, we certainly knew we'd be familiar with his moves and be able to defend them.

I wanted Travis to stay, and I was glad we were able to re-sign him. First of all, Travis Best is a great kid. He is going to do whatever you tell him, no questions asked. The problem Travis has is that he's still developing an ability to feel where everyone is on the court. He's not really a true point guard. I considered making a change halfway through the season, and having Jalen Rose handle the ball so Travis could come off screens, where he'd have more opportunities to score. The problem with Jalen is that he sees too much sometimes. He gets all excited, and he sees something that's closing up, and he tries to make the difficult pass anyway. Jalen wants to be a point guard, and I don't blame him. That's his dream, and I think he can do it. I feel bad for both Jalen and Travis that there was a lockout last summer, because we could have worked out with them, and I think they really would have benefited from it.

Jalen Rose is very, very talented. I love that kid. He

does make me frustrated, though. We were playing Orlando in late February after the All-Star break, and we're up about 16 points. We were playing pretty good while Jalen was in there, so after a break I put him back in. He started throwing the ball all over the place. Next thing you know, our lead is gone and we end up in a real dogfight. We won the game, but Jalen knew I was disappointed with him. I chewed him out right in front of the team. I told him, "You got careless and reckless, and we could have lost this game." He says, "You're right, Coach," and then he jumped up and hugged me! I couldn't believe it. I didn't know what the heck to do.

One thing about Jalen, though. You can talk to him. I remember a game midway through the season when Jalen played really well. I took him out for a breather, and Chris Mullin got really hot, so I went with him the rest of the way. After the game, I could tell Jalen was mad, so I called him in. I said, "Jalen, you played well, there's no question about that. I took you out for a break, and Chris played great. So let me ask you. What if I took Chris out for a break, and it was you that got really hot in the fourth quarter? Should I jerk you out of the game and tell Chris to go back in there?" He said, "No, I guess not." So I said, "Then what are you upset about?" He looked right at me and said, "It won't happen again."

You wish you had time to spend a couple hours alone in the gym with each of these guys, but there's no time during an NBA season. Once we get into the thick of it, you have very few days off, which means fewer days of practice, and you are traveling all over the country. That's why when guys get hurt they get behind so quickly, first because their conditioning goes, and second because they don't have enough practice time to catch up with everyone else.

I felt very badly about how things went for our young forward Austin Croshere in his rookie season. I thought when we drafted him—and still I think this—that he can be a very good pro. He played for our summer league in Atlanta and he got dinged up a little bit, and then he broke his hand early in the season, and that was that.

I didn't say a whole lot to him. I felt he had to figure it out for himself. I will say this: he handled it as well as he possibly could. At home, I bet he was a bear. I bet he had no clue what was going on, but he is going to be a good player. He just had some lousy luck. He was finally coming along when he broke a bone in his foot. Bad enough that he broke his hand, but then this other thing on top of it, it was just unreal. The poor kid was devastated. All he wants to do is play basketball.

He didn't know. He thought he could come back from the broken hand and everything would be fine, but he was so far behind. When he came back, he struggled quite a bit over the next month. I said a couple of things to him, especially when he started playing better. I told him, "Hey, you're getting a groove now. You're starting to do the things we've been trying to implement all year." You don't need to sit him down and talk to him all the time. He doesn't need to hear from me that injuries ruined his rookie year. He's a smart kid. He knows that.

Of course you develop relationships with certain guys. Coaches are lying if they tell you that they don't. But you have to remember that it's a business. I played some golf with Fred Hoiberg last summer. He's a top-notch kid. You wish your own children would grow up like him. I think he's a good player, and there's a place for him in this league. He was a free agent last summer, and I wanted to re-sign him, but I also understood that we might have to spend our money other places. That's the business part of the job. Still, I was glad when we were able to keep him.

The hardest part for me last season was putting a guy like Mark West on the team, then not being able to find him much time. He worked hard in practice. He's a veteran, he's been around a long time, he's paid his dues. You don't find guys like him anymore, who will do whatever you ask, even though it might mean he won't play for a month. He's a true professional that way. I loved having him on our team. He knows his career is winding down, and you hate to see it finish up that way. We did not re-sign Mark in 1999.

Guys like Mark West helped develop this league, not because he was a star but because he worked his tail off and made his team better. We had a guy like that on the Celtics, Terry Duerod. He only played four years (one and a half in Boston), for a total of 143 games, but he was so valuable to us. I always said he was one of the toughest players to guard, because he was quick and relentless. He just never quit. He made our practices worthwhile, because he was always pushing us. A guy like that, you just want the best for him, but the truth was he didn't have enough talent to extend his career. Then you see all these players with natural talent and you want to kick them in the rear because they are wasting it.

Hard work does make a difference, which is why you can be happy for a guy like Mark Pope, who is really going for it. Let me tell you something: he is a lot better than people think. We drafted Mark in the second round, out of Kentucky, and he got teased a lot at the beginning because the guys thought he and Austin were both a little bit in awe that Larry Bird was their coach. After the first couple of practices, when I was running them into the ground, they got over it real fast.

I know it helps me that some of these guys played against me, and the younger guys know all about my career. It won't always be that way, if I stay in it. But if there's a guy that comes along five years from now that doesn't remember me playing, it will be all right with me. I never saw Cousy or Russell play. I just knew they were special by the way other people treated them.

I pick my spots when I talk about my career with these guys. And I try not to lecture them too much. Most of them are veterans. They've been around. But once in a while I remind them to look around and appreciate all that they've got. I tell them, "Check it out. You've got nice wives, or pretty girlfriends. You've got fancy cars, and you live in expensive homes, and you travel all over the country in luxury jets. Just think about that, because in a few years you'll be out of the league and you aren't going to have this lifestyle anymore." They nod their heads, but the truth is they all think they're going to play forever. I knew better. I always knew what I had. Once in a while I'd look at the nice house I was living in and I'd say to myself, "Here I am in Boston, playing basketball in a city where they love us. What would I be doing if I wasn't playing ball?" And that would bring me right back down to earth.

But sometimes professional athletes forget how good they have it. I know they do. They're used to first-class hotels and corporate jets. We flew commercial most of my career. We had to get up early, get to the airport, and fly on a regular plane with everybody else. That's just how it was. We might have chartered a half dozen times, but it was a regular plane, like USAir, which didn't have any first-class seats. We could move around and all, because it was just us, but those seats were so small. They just killed my back. The other thing was, the hotels we stayed in were usually like a Holiday Inn. All these players I have now, they want to look at the list of hotels we're staying at. I don't care where we stay. We're not going to be there that long. All you have to do is lay down for a while, then get up and play. But Donnie feels we should stay in the best hotels. That's fine, but I don't want it. I never stayed in a fancy hotel until I came to the Pacers. Why do we need to stay there?

There was one point during our season when I thought our guys were getting soft. I thought it would have been a great thing if we had made them fly commercial for the next ten games. For one thing, it would stop guys from showing up two minutes before takeoff. The problem with these guys is they think they're hot stuff. It would have been good for us, but we had a contract with the corporate jet we use, and it couldn't be broken. Too bad.

There are certain things I'm pretty firm on. But I want these guys to like coming to work. I don't want it to be miserable. That's why one of the things I wanted to do was develop a kind of family atmosphere around our team. When I was a player, I loved it when guys brought their kids into the locker room. During our championship season in 1986, Bill Walton's kids were running rampant in our locker room. They were wild kids. Everyone else would be saying, "Get those kids out of here," but I was having the time of my life with them. At the beginning of the season I told my guys, "Look, we're going to have certain rules. Nobody can come to our practices. I want us to be all business." So somehow they thought that meant the locker room was closed. I walked in there one time and I said, "Where's all the kids?" One of the guys said, "But Coach, you said the locker room was closed." I told him, "Hey, you got that part wrong. I want kids running around here like you wouldn't believe. Bring 'em in here. Let's go!" After that, it was great. Total chaos. It's the perfect atmosphere. These guys don't see their kids enough anyway. Now, after games, the locker room is full of kids, and they run wherever they want to run. That should be part of their growing up around it. My son, Conner, loves it. He hangs out with Chris Mullin's kids a lot, and after the game I bring him in there and he just runs around like crazy and tears up stuff. He doesn't remember me playing. He was just a baby when I retired. All he knows is I had to quit because of my back.

Mariah wasn't even around then, but she knows Daddy used to play basketball. Both of them love the Pacers, and they love to come to the games, but Dinah and I usually only let them go on weekends, because they have school. What's really sad is when they come running into our bedroom around six-thirty in the morning and Mariah will say, "The Pacers lost last night, Daddy." That kills me. She looks so sad about it. But when we win they come in shouting, "Daddy, we won last night!"

Conner is a real fan. His favorite player on the Pacers is Mark Pope. He's always telling me, "C'mon, Daddy, Mark Pope has got to play more." Mariah likes Reggie Miller. We have a picture of him on our refrigerator. Sometimes Conner gets curious, and he'll ask what I think about Charles Barkley.

What happens is kids at school start talking about Larry Bird this and Larry Bird that, and then he starts wondering why everybody is so interested in me. So he'll come home and say, "Why does everyone want your autograph,

Daddy? Are you a superstar, like people say?" I tell him, "Nah, Daddy just played some basketball, and now he's a coach." Conner has all these friends over, and they stay overnight. Conner is saying, "Let's play on the computer," and they're all saying, "No, we want to talk to your dad," but after about two minutes of seeing you, they're on to something else.

One of the other decisions I made, and I insisted on it with Donnie, is we don't let outsiders fly on our plane. We don't take businesspeople, sponsors, or any of that stuff. Donnie understands and agrees that's how it should be. As far as wives and families go, if we're on a long trip and they want to see their families out there, that's great. I'm all for it. I know each team handles that differently. The Celtics never liked our wives traveling with us, but I made sure Dinah always used to come out for the Finals.

Really, what it's all about is being reasonable. I want these guys to be comfortable. Every once in a while the guys will come to me and ask something. If it's within the realm of the team and what we're trying to do, I don't have a problem with it. One time Reggie had a restaurant endorsement he needed to do, and he asked if he could take a limo to shoot it when we landed after a trip. I said, "Fine, no big deal." But if we got off our plane one night and there were a couple of limos sitting there waiting, and my guys jumped in and tooled off without asking me, that would be completely different.

Before I got to the Pacers, the team never had a Christmas party. I wanted one that included everyone, not just the players. I wanted their wives there, and their kids there. I wanted the secretaries, and all the people in the office, but it didn't come off the way I wanted. The next one, I

promised everyone, would be better, because I would have
time to plan it out.

The other thing I made sure we had was a break-up
dinner. I couldn't believe the Pacers never had one. To
me, the break-up dinner is the ultimate. It's the last time
you're going to see anybody, maybe ever, because people
retire, or get traded in the off season, or they sign somewhere else. I know it's hard for the players at first. Whenever we had one in Boston, and we had just lost, you
didn't really feel like going. But once we all got there, it
was a chance to be together one last time. I told my guys
after we lost to Chicago, "I know we just lost, and it's
tough to come here, but I think you'll enjoy it more than
you think." My feeling was, at least these guys would
know we cared about them. The other thing was, I told
them I felt it was important for everyone to show up.

The league goes by so fast, your careers are here and
gone before you know it. Take Kevin McHale—I practically lived with that guy for twelve years, and all of a
sudden I never see him anymore. At the time you are playing, it seems like a million other things are more important. But then your career is over and there's nothing to
do. You go from this pace of driving to practice and rush-
ing to airports and getting treatment to . . . nothing. At that
point, you'd do anything to go to dinner with all your
teammates.

Even though we didn't win the championship, I felt
good about our team chemistry and my relationship with
the guys. I felt as though the respect was there. On the
day I won the Coach of the Year award, the Pacers held
a press conference. I was unhappy about the whole thing,
because I didn't think I deserved to win. So I walk in
there, and I'm uncomfortable about being up there any-

way, then all of a sudden someone is asking me a question about Mark Jackson and his shimmy in the playoffs against New York. I look over, and it's Travis Best. All my players were sitting there at the press conference. I always thought we were a different kind of team, but that's when I knew for sure. I had said from the beginning, "When someone on this team wins something, I expect everybody to be there, including the coaches." If Reggie had won something, we would have all been there. So I was happy to see them, even though I was kind of embarrassed.

There's nothing better than being part of a team. Especially when you win.

CHAPTER 12

On the Long Season

It's one thing to run guys up and down and get their conditioning just the way you want. It's another thing to get them ready to play an 82-game NBA schedule. I felt confident about getting them ready. I know the game inside out and I know how the league works, and although I had never coached before at any level, I felt my instincts would help me in crucial situations. As for the things I wasn't sure about, that's why I had Dick and Rick.

We had a strong exhibition season. I played almost every guy on our roster, because I wanted to look at everyone in a game situation. My biggest concern coming out of preseason was that we were averaging around 21, 22 turnovers a game. That was too many. I could tell the team was in decent shape, but they weren't playing that well yet. You'd like to go into your first game with a little more than that, but that's what we had. I wasn't that worried about it, because I knew that in time everything would come together. I was willing to be patient, or at least I thought I was willing. And I loved the way we were playing defense and trapping the pick and roll.

My first real game as the head coach of the Pacers was against New Jersey, in the Meadowlands. I was all excited about the game. I didn't really have a routine at that point, and I didn't know what to do with myself before the game. I just followed Dick and Rick around. I went out, watched the guys shoot, then looked at the clock for like the fourth time. The tip-off was delayed, because the Nets had all these season-opening ceremonies, and I remember standing back there just waiting and waiting, and thinking, "Come on, let's just play!" That's how I was as a player too. Let's get going. The waiting around used to kill me.

We went out and played great. Absolutely fantastic. We were up 14 or 15 points in the third quarter. We were running, and we were pushing the ball. I remember thinking to myself, "This is awesome. What a great feeling to know that all this stuff we've taught them actually works." Then all of a sudden we couldn't do anything. I started to get a little frustrated, because of course I wanted to win the game. New Jersey's best player, Jayson Williams, started attacking the boards—I think he had 18 offensive rebounds—and we ended up losing. My first game ever, and I walked off feeling like we should have won it. (I can tell you now that's how you feel after almost every loss, but I didn't know that then.) Reggie had a big night. He had 35 points, and I said to myself, "Man, Reggie gets thirty-five, and we still get beat. That's not good." So that's when I started stressing the need to spread out the scoring among everyone.

When I took this job, I promised my players I wouldn't holler or scream at them. I don't think it's a good way to communicate with your players. I hated it when my coaches did it, and I was determined not to lose my cool like that. But there were a couple of times when I needed to get through to these guys, even if it meant raising my voice. In fact, probably my worst outburst of the season was in the first couple of weeks.

It was only the fourth game of the season, and we lost a game to Charlotte, in Charlotte. I was so disappointed I could hardly talk, because it looked to me like my guys could have taken over that game anytime they wanted, and they were out there just going through the motions. They weren't aggressive, and they sure as hell didn't look like a team that was trying to win. After we lost that game, our record was 2–4. It wasn't the kind of start anyone had hoped for, and the thing that was frustrating about it was we were blowing leads in the fourth quarter—the one thing I wanted us to avoid. People were already starting to call us chokers. Charlotte scored three straight layups on us in the final minutes, and we didn't do anything about it. I wasn't about to panic, but I sure wasn't happy either. I remember Rik had two free throws that would have tied it late in the game. He goes up to the line and he misses both of them. I was just mad. After the game, I said, "I just want to tell you guys something. I'm disappointed in what happened out there tonight. You guys didn't give me the effort we needed. Charlotte has a chance to win our division, and they didn't want to win tonight. Did they do anything out there that was so spectacular that should have allowed them to beat us? It looked like three layups to me. How do we allow that to happen?" Then I said, "Rik, what do you think when you go to the free throw line? Do you think you're going to miss them, or make them?" He said, "I think I'm going to make them." So I said, "Well, then why don't you make the damn things?" Rik is sensitive. I've got to be careful how far I go with him. On that night, I gave it to all of them. I didn't get personal. I just stuck to the facts of the game, and those were bad enough.

After we lost to Charlotte, my old teammate Dave Cowens, who was coaching the Hornets, said our problem was we were running the same stuff over and over, and people were figuring it out. People were surprised. They were wondering where that criticism came from, but I knew. Before the season started, I said David Wesley, who Charlotte spent a lot of money on to sign as a free agent, wasn't a true point guard. He isn't either. But that must have ticked Dave Cowens off. Wesley played for the Celtics before he went to Charlotte. I saw him a fair amount, and I thought he was a little too offensive-minded to be a really good point. Anyway, I didn't really care what Cowens said. I was more concerned with what I was going to tell my guys.

I knew we had to be smarter with our offensive possessions. I knew if we could spread the court and get guys to start moving toward the ball, we'd be fine. I had a lot of faith in these guys, even though I got upset from time to time. I know people in Indiana were feeling let down. There was so much excitement when we started the season, and before you knew it we were 2–5. Dick Harter reminded me that it takes time when you have a new coaching staff and a new system. I knew he was right, but I didn't like how we kept blowing leads in the fourth quarter. And the one thing I wasn't going to stand for was less than a total effort.

There was one other game that really got me upset. It was in December, and we were just finishing up a road trip. We had beaten Minnesota, Denver, and Phoenix, and we came really close to beating Utah in their place, which might be the toughest place to win in the league, but we got a couple of bad calls down the stretch that cost us the game. The game with the Jazz was tight all the way through, and around the middle of the third quarter Reggie picks up two technicals for arguing with the officials. That had been a real problem with Reggie. He spends too much time bickering with the refs, and it takes away from his concentration. I'm sitting there pulling my hair out, because I know we're going to need him down to the wire, and now he's gone. Then, with about seven minutes to go, Rik fouls out. All I kept telling the guys was, "C'mon, now. Don't quit on me. I don't care about Reggie right now. He quit on us tonight. But we've got to pull together and forget about the officials. We need everybody." What really got me was we're down by one, and Karl Malone gets a call he doesn't like, and he kicks the ball up to the stands. Just pounded it up there. But the refs don't call a T. They just stand there. I was sitting there thinking, "Oh, boy. We're not going to get a break in this place." We lost the game, but I told my guys how happy I was they stayed with me to the end. Then I told Reggie he let his team-mates down.

So we're 3-1 on the trip, and we're finishing up in Portland. The one thing I told them before the game was, "Hey, this has been a long road trip, and when you play as well as we've played in our first four games, you might have a tendency to say, 'Hey, let's get home.' Well, I don't want to forget about this game. If we win it, this was one helluva road trip. If we lose, all the hard work we just did won't hardly matter." Well, sure enough, we go out for the first half, and before you know it we're down by 20. I called a twenty-second time-out. I was furious. I looked at them for a long time, and then I said, "Just who the hell do you think you are kidding? You're not kidding me.

You guys have got this game packed in. That's a bunch of crap. You aren't even trying, and that's a disgrace to this organization." I was hot, and they knew it. So what do they do? After we break the huddle, Mark stops them and gathers them back together again. I couldn't hear what he said, but he was gesturing to them and talking to them with real emotion. Next thing I know, they go out there and hustle their butts off, and they take the lead. We almost won that game, but Portland still had something left to fend us off. Rasheed Wallace got really hot, then J. R. Rider hit a three, and that was it. It bothers me a lot when these guys don't give the effort. They know I've been there. They know I know all the tricks, so why even try it? After the game, I got right to the point. I told them, "You guys bailed on me tonight." I went right down the line with each of them and told them how many minutes they played. I said, "Did I ask you to bust your butts for two solid hours tonight? No. Reggie, I asked you for about thirty, thirty-five minutes. Rik, all I needed was twenty-eight minutes." I went like that right down to each of them. I said, "I don't think it's too much to ask you guys to bust your butts for less than forty minutes." When I get mad, I get real mad, but it doesn't happen very often.

I guess what it comes down to is, I pick my spots. We had a game with Minnesota where we were up 20, but then they came back on us and started hitting everything in sight: three-pointers, driving layups, you name it. They ended up with the ball, down two, and a chance to win. We pulled it out, but it was close. In that situation, though, it was a matter of Minnesota playing great in the second half. So you don't rant and rave over a game like that. You do that too often and they stop listening.

I often wonder what it would be like if I had a young

team. Rick and Dick tell me my demeanor would be completely different. Maybe they're right. I know one thing: I'd drive them and push them. With my guys, I drove them really hard early, but once we got in the proper condition, these guys are veterans. They police themselves. It's true that I haven't had to deal with many young players with a so-called attitude. But I'm not afraid of that. In fact, I look forward to that challenge if it presents itself. Someone asked me once if I could ever coach Dennis Rodman. I don't care how many different shades of green his hair is. If he plays hard and performs, he'll always have a place on my team. The only crap I wouldn't put up with is him showing up late for practice and games. That might be where we'd part company. Rodman and I have a lot of history, back from when we played each other during those Celtics-Pistons rivalries. When I first took the Pacers job, he came out in the papers and said I was overrated as a player, and I'll be overrated as a coach. I loved it. There's not enough of that in the league anymore. That's how rivalries get started.

I'll remember a lot of different games in my first season for a lot of different reasons, but there was one in particular that was really important to me. It was the first time we went to Boston to play the Celtics. It was on Sunday, January 18, 1998, and it was televised on NBC. The Celtics were going to retire Robert Parish's number at halftime that day, so I knew there would be a lot of old faces around and the place would be jumping. People kept asking me leading up to that game if it was special. I said the stuff a coach usually says—"It's just another game"—but that wasn't really true, and everybody knew it. The part that was true was that I had no connection at all to their new building, the FleetCenter. I never played in there, and I had no feeling for the place. I'm glad about that. It would have been really difficult to go in and play the Celtics at Boston Garden. I have so many great memories of that old building, and I'm thankful we didn't have to play the game there. Walking into the FleetCenter was like walking into Reunion Arena in Dallas, for all I cared. But the minute we got there and I saw Grant, the security guard, in the hallway, and Mr. Randall, who helped out with uniforms, I started getting all revved up.

Even so, I wanted to get it over with as quickly as possible. It was a zoo that day. The place was loaded with media. Kevin McHale had flown in for Robert's halftime ceremony, and of course Robert was around, and the atmosphere was absolutely electric. It felt like a playoff game in there. If I didn't have to coach a game that afternoon, I would have been back in the locker room hanging out with Chief and Kevin, but instead I was trying to get my guys prepared for this game. Bill Walton, who was working for NBC that day, came in to talk to me. Bill and I are old friends. I told him the truth. When he asked me how big this was, I said, "It's the biggest game of my life."

The one thing I made sure of was that there were no distractions. I didn't want anybody messing with our routine. For most of the pregame I stayed in the back of the training room where nobody could find me. I remember seeing Jim Gray, the guy who does the sideline reporting for NBC, before the game. I went up to him and told him, "Jim, I'd appreciate it if you wouldn't talk to my players while they're preparing for the game." He said, "Larry, you know I don't do that." I said, "Don't make this the day you start." Truth was, I wasn't really sure I could trust Jim Gray. I knew his job was to get information, so I fig-

ured he'd be snooping around as much as he could, trying to get the upper hand on a scoop. I don't mind having television people around, as long as they understand
the boundaries. Truthfully? I'd do a lot more for those
guys if they would come to me instead of snooping around.
It's the one thing I can't stand. I don't like it when one
of these TV guys grabs one of my players and says, "Go
in there and tell me what the coach says to you before the
game." I know Jim Gray does that. If they want to talk
about it after I finished saying my piece, that's fine. But
don't send somebody in there to spy. You won't get very
far with me when you pull that crap.

When I went in to talk to the team before the game, I
knew there was no use telling them it was just another
game. The players could tell how I felt. Mark Jackson
came up to me beforehand and said, "Don't worry, Coach.
We'll win this one for you." I said, "Win it for yourselves,"
but there was no point in hiding it. I wanted this game
really bad. There were only two times all season that I
was nervous, and it was the two times we played the Celtics
in Boston.

You've got to realize, Boston was my whole life for
thirteen years. That city couldn't have been any better to
me. They made me feel like one of them. I couldn't imagine playing for any other team than the Boston Celtics. It
was so important to me for our team to win this game. I
wanted to show the fans, my old teammates, Red Auerbach, everyone, that I knew what I was doing. It may
sound funny, but I wanted them to be proud of me. I don't
think I realized how much I missed the city of Boston
until I was back there. Dinah and I loved living there so
much. The great restaurants, all the excitement, the Freedom Trail, all of that. It wasn't until my second year in

the league that I realized how much history was in Boston. After that, whenever I had friends come to town, I'd say, "C'mon here, you've got to see this, it's Paul Revere's grave . . ."

I remember the first time I was in Boston, when Bob Woolf brought us out there to meet with the team. We were staying at the Parker House, which is this really nice hotel right near the State House. So we're in the room, and before we left to go over to the Celtics offices I open the curtains and I hear all this noise going on outside. I look out there and it's just a mass of people, protesting with signs. I said to myself, "What kind of place is this?" I had never ever seen anything like that. It just blew me away. Once I had been living in Boston a few years, I got used to the fact stuff like that happened all the time. After a while, I'd have friends in from out of town, and we'd walk by some Hare Krishnas, or some group trying to ban nuclear weapons, and I'd say, "Oh, there are the protesters," like I had been seeing this sort of thing my whole life.

I hadn't been back to Boston in a while, so I was thinking about all that went on there. The night before the game, my friend Dan Dyrek came over to the hotel, and we did a little reminiscing. I was telling him how I found out I was drafted by the Celtics. I was on the golf course, but it wasn't a big deal to me, because I knew I was going back to school, so in my mind anyone who drafted me was wasting their time. I could care less. I was playing golf with a couple of friends in this real small town in Indiana, and we came back, all of a sudden the news is on, and the news says, "Larry Bird has been drafted by the Boston Celtics." It was the first I'd heard of it. Nobody from the Celtics had called me beforehand, or on the day they drafted me either. But what started happening after that was Red began showing up to our games. I remember one time Tommy Heinsohn was doing the game for Home Box Office, and Red was there, and he came back into the locker room after the game and talked to me a little bit. I always knew when he was around, because people were always telling me, but it didn't affect me one way or another.

When I started playing for Boston, that changed. We always knew when Red was in town, and it fired me up, because I didn't want to disappoint him. I guess going back to Boston that day, I was feeling some of the same things.

I saw Pitino briefly before the game, but I didn't talk to him. I haven't talked to him since I left Boston. Just like any coach, I wasn't about to go down there and shake his hand and wish him luck, because if I told him "Good luck," I wouldn't have meant it. The Celtics are Pitino's organization now. He can do whatever he thinks is right.

The game was close, which is what I expected. Our guys struggled a little with Boston's pressure in the first quarter, but by halftime they were figuring it out. I didn't have long to talk to them, because I had to go out for Chief's ceremony, but I told them I expected a much cleaner effort in the second half. I wasn't comfortable with the game at all. Both Rik and Reggie gave us some breathing room in the second half, and I put Derrick McKey in for the fourth quarter and told him I wanted him to put the clamps on Antoine Walker. He did a great job of that. When Reggie hit a big three with about a minute to go, I thought we had it, but I wasn't going to celebrate until the buzzer went off. When it did, we had won 103–96. You would have thought the Celtics had won, the way the

crowd was going crazy. They really had given me an unbelievable welcome. They held up signs for me, and they
kept running highlights of my career on the scoreboard.
I'm surprised Pitino let them do any of that.

Walking off that court that day, I had so many mixed
emotions. I wanted to win so badly. I was so happy, it was
unbelievable. I had a lot of friends and fans sitting in those
stands who watched me grow up in Boston. I was so
pumped up, I could have run all the way home. The only
thing that was disappointing was it took away from Chief's
day. I thought it was a bad choice on the part of the Celtics.
It wasn't supposed to be all about me, it was supposed to
be all about Robert, but it didn't turn out that way. Those
fans should have been chanting, "Chief, Chief," not "Larry, Lar-ry." I would have liked Chief to be given his proper
due. I would have liked to have been able to honor him in
a way that had nothing to do with me, but I had a team
there and a game to play, and it just made it difficult. I never
even really got to talk to Chief because there was so much
commotion.

I look back at what has happened to the Boston Celtics,
and I think it's a shame. They've gone through some problems, and they've made a lot of bad decisions. Whether
Dennis Johnson should have had a chance to be the head
coach or not, I can't say. But should he be a part of what's
going on with that franchise? Yes. He's earned that right.
That's my personal opinion. Kevin McHale, he made up
his mind he was going back home to Minnesota after he
retired, but they never asked him to stay. So they read in
the papers he plans on going back to Minnesota. But why
not go in there and talk to him? Why not see if there's a
way to get him to stay? He's done a great job in the Tim-
berwolves front office. He could have been a big plus for

the Celtics organization. He's intelligent, and he knows what's going on. But they just let him go. Now you hear Robert say he'd like to go into coaching, but the Celtics don't reach out to him. That's one of the things that made the Celtics so special in the first place. They were family. They looked out for each other. But you don't see that anymore. Even Danny Ainge. They traded him, which was their choice. But after he's done playing, don't you want to talk to a guy like Danny Ainge, who you know is going to make a great coach? And what they did to Red Auerbach was wrong. The Celtics are everything to him, and to humiliate him like that, to take away his title of president, why? What good did it do? I'll never forget the first time I met Red. I was playing in a college All-Star game in Atlanta, and he was going up the escalator, and I was going down. I didn't think he'd know who I was, but as we were going by each other, he reached out and shook my hand. I remember turning to one of the other guys and saying, "What's he doing here?" A long time later I found out that his friend Bobby Knight had told him about me and suggested that he go see me play.

People ask me if it was hard to leave the Celtics. Maybe ten years ago it would have been, when there were still people there who I liked and respected. But there's a whole new group of people in there now who I don't even know. They don't mean anything to me. But I'll always have feelings for Red. He taught me so much about the NBA. I just wish they would have left him alone and let him finish his life as president of the Celtics, which is what he deserved. As for me, I can't ever see going back with the Celtics and working for the owners they have now. I always liked Paul Gaston—I still do—and he treated me well, but he made a lot of bad basketball decisions.

We played Boston three more times that season. We played them six days later in our place, and won 95–88. We played them again at Market Square Arena in early March, and we won again. Our last game with them was on April 12, at the FleetCenter. By then we had won 54 games and were coming off a big overtime win in Atlanta. I was feeling as good as I had ever felt about our team. The Celtics, at that point, were coming to the end of their season, since they weren't going to be a playoff team. I'd be lying if I said I didn't want to sweep the Celtics. I never said that to my players, but they were aware of it. This is how I know. We did beat Boston for the fourth time, 93–87. A few days later, we were back in Indiana and Mark Jackson said the team had something they wanted to give me. He handed me a ball, which was painted yellow and blue, the color of the Pacers. On the ball the guys had inscribed the score of each game with the Celtics, and the dates. Then, in big letters, they had written, COACH LARRY BIRD, PACERS SWEEP OVER CELTICS, 4–0. I don't keep many of my old trophies or awards in my house, but that ball is in my study, where I can see it.

The problem with the NBA season is that for every high moment, like beating the Celtics in Boston, there're just as many low moments. There's one game during my first season of coaching that I'd like to forget forever: our March 29, 1998, loss to the San Antonio Spurs. We knew we were in trouble before the game even started, because we weren't going to have Reggie Miller that night. He had been suspended by the league for a flagrant foul against Charlotte center Vlade Divac in the game before. Reggie didn't like the way Vlade was throwing his body around, so late in the game he threw an elbow that caught Vlade in the chin, and he got tagged with a flagrant foul. It wasn't the smartest thing in the world to do, but I wasn't as upset as I might have been, because at least Reggie showed a willingness to get physical if needed. That was something I hadn't seen enough of from our team. I knew we were going to have a tough time scoring without Reggie, but I never expected what happened. We scored only 55 points, and set a new NBA record for the lowest amount of points since they started using the 24-second clock. Unbelievable. I scored more than that once in one game, by myself!

But I knew it was going to be an uphill battle, and not just because we were going to have to do it without Reggie. That night, Rik came hobbling into Market Square Arena, and we didn't know if he was going to play or not. His feet were causing him terrible pain, and he wasn't sure if he could suit up. He hadn't given us a definite answer either way, but we knew once we had our team meeting, because he took his shoes off in front of all the guys. I knew at that moment, when those guys were sitting there and they saw Rik do that, and they just dropped their jaws, that it was a lost cause. Rik didn't understand. He didn't realize that when they looked at him and thought about playing the game without him, it just deflated the hell out of them. I tried to get the guys fired up. I tried to get their minds off what we didn't have, but it was no use. The tone had been set.

So we start the game, and we couldn't buy a basket. I felt sorry for our guys. They were playing against a really good team that they wanted to beat, and they really weren't playing all that badly. We just couldn't hit anything in the first twenty minutes or so. We went into the locker room at halftime, and we had scored only 34 points. I couldn't go in there and get all over them. I'm not that type of guy, and besides, I could see it coming. To compound matters, we weren't hitting any of the shots we normally hit. We couldn't drive on them, because all of a sudden we weren't big enough, and they are such a great interior defensive team. We couldn't get any easy passes. We had trouble converting shots. It was apparent very quickly that scoring was going to be scarce. Defensively, our guys were moving and working hard, but it doesn't matter if you can't generate anything on the other end. We lost the game 74–55, and we were all pretty miserable. We shot 27 percent in that game. I wouldn't have imagined that was possible.

Two nights later we scored 128 points in a blowout win over the Clippers. By then we had Reggie back. He helps spread the court open, and then Antonio and Dale can do a little more down low. When you don't have Reggie out there and you've just got Chris Mullin working the perimeter, and the Spurs put just one guy on him, then they bring Tim Duncan over to guard Mark Jackson, that makes it really difficult. A loss like the San Antonio game would be devastating if it was football and you had a week to think about it. Thankfully, we didn't. For us it was a bad loss, so let's move on.

In preseason I told our team we should win at least 55 games. By the All-Star break we were right where I had hoped we'd be. We were 33–13, and we had the best record in the East. For most of the first half of the season, we were battling with Chicago, New York, and Miami for that right. I was happy with our position, but the last thing I was going to do was allow our guys to get comfortable with our new status. There was one thing I hadn't thought about when I was mapping out our goals, and that was that the coach of the team with the best record in the East has to coach the All-Star game.

I really wasn't interested in coaching the All-Star game. I had already booked a flight to go down to our place in Florida. I thought it was funny, in a way, that I got picked for the game, since I had never liked All-Star games as a player either. I kept telling everyone I wasn't going. I said, "I think Dick and Rick should go in my place." I didn't want to go. I needed a break. Plus, the game was in New York, and I've never liked going there. But I knew it would be really bad for the franchise if I didn't do it. For one thing, Rik Smits was on the team for the first time, and Reggie was there after being left off the year before. Donnie was really concerned that I wouldn't show up for it, but in the end I knew I had to. A couple of days after it became official I'd be the East coach, we were getting ready to go out to practice at Market Square. The players were stretching, then Dick and Rick walked out there, and just as I'm coming up the ramp, all of a sudden I hear this loud music blaring. It's that song "I Love New York." The players were howling. They loved it. It was Reggie's idea.

Anyhow, if I was going to go to this All-Star game, I wanted to make sure we won it. I could tell from the first practice we had that all the East players felt the same way. So I got them all together and told them, "We've got an All-Star team. No matter who we put in should be able to compete with the other team." Dick, Rick, and I made up a time chart and put it in the locker room. That way everybody knew how much they were going to play beforehand. And we kept to it too. That was tough. I felt bad for certain guys, like Glen Rice, who then played for Charlotte. He came out, and he was having one of those games when you just knew if you kept him in there for 35 minutes he would score 35 points, pretty easy. When that kid gets on one of his streaks, he's unconscious. But when his time was up I had to take him out of the game. He didn't say anything about it, but I felt bad anyway.

Michael, of course, was on the team, but he was sick and he missed our one day of practice. He made it for the game, though. I was the first one on the bus for our shootaround, and he got on, and I said, "How many minutes do you want to play?" He told me, "Enough to win." I said, "Okay. You let me know, because I know you're sick." He ended up playing around 32 minutes, which was more than anybody. I mixed all the other guys in around him. People asked me if it was weird coaching Jordan. I told them, "I didn't coach him. I just watched him play." We did put in a couple of plays in practice and told Michael, "All we're doing is running a basic motion offense. If you want to pick and roll, just holler."

I know one of the reasons Michael played so well was because there was all that talk of the young kid from the Lakers, Kobe Bryant, being the next Michael Jordan. Michael doesn't like to hear that kind of crap. I know Michael well enough to be able to tell you that. So the kid goes out there and tries to do it all himself, and you knew that wasn't going to work. If Bryant came out and had a hell of a game, and won the MVP, that would be different. But you can't just hand him the ball and tell him to take over without him earning it first. Guys have too much pride in this league, especially the superstars. That's why Karl Malone was upset. He wanted to play basketball. He's trying to set the kid a pick, and Bryant's waving off Karl Malone. That's no good. But that's what happens in those games. Guys get carried away. They think it's their chance at the spotlight. But the funny thing about All-Star games is they've always been the same, from high school right on up. Guards control the game. They decide whether they're going to bother to pass it, or who they're going to pass it to, and whether they're going to dribble the ball. If you're a big guy, there's nothing you can do but watch and be ready in case someone throws you a pass now and then.

I enjoyed being around the guys at the All-Star game. A lot of those young players are very talented, and I haven't been around them very much, and it's like anything— they're nice kids when you spend a little time with them. When I played in those games, the winners got $2,000 and the losers got $1,000. Last year, I think it was $10,000 and $5,000. It's the only time I've ever seen when players really want the extra money. Fans have this idea the All-Star game is just for fun, and nobody cares what happens, but believe me, that's not true. These guys care—a lot. That's why there're always arguments about who was the MVP of the game and all that. The year I coached the team, it was obvious. Michael was the MVP, and nobody disputed it.

When Reggie, Rik, and I got back to Indiana, the city was really buzzing. It was nice to see people excited about the Pacers again. There have been times when the franchise has really struggled to get support. Indiana is the best basketball state in the country, but the emphasis has been on high school and college ball for so long that the pros have always seemed to come up a little short. When I used to play for the Celtics, we'd go into Market Square Arena, and there would be so many Boston fans that it felt like a home game. The big difference was I loved playing in Boston Garden, and I always had a brutal time at Market Square. I hated that arena. The sight lines were bad, and the rims were always too tight and too high. When I became coach of the Pacers, I had the guys who run the arena measure those rims. I stood right there with them while they did it. They use a pole to measure them. I said to the guy, "I'm telling you, that rim is too high." He said, "No, look. It says ten feet." So I said to the guy, "I know it does, but have you ever measured the pole?"

Before we started the second half of the season I gave my guys a little speech about how important it was to be consistent over the final two months of the season, to get your team ready for the playoffs. If you look at what Utah and Chicago have traditionally done during those months, I think you'll find it's pretty impressive. Our guys, for whatever reason, got into a little bit of a funk after the All-Star break. We come back after the break, and we beat Orlando and Miami, two Eastern Conference rivals, and then we play Dallas at home, where they're having all sorts of problems, and we lose that game. That's how it went for a month or so. Win. Loss. Win. Loss. It drove me crazy. I told our guys, "If you want to make a statement in these playoffs, this is the time you have to be getting your game together. This is no time to go into cruise control." But my guys are veterans, and they know. Mark and Reggie helped out there. They got the guys in the right frame of mind. We won eight of our final ten games in April, and finished the regular season with 58 wins. It was the most wins the franchise had since they came over to the NBA. But as good as we were, we didn't break the all-time Pacers record. In 1970, when Indiana won the ABA championship, they had 59 wins under Coach Slick Leonard.

Fifty-eight wins was nice, but what really made me feel hopeful was that these guys had proven they could play with the best in the league. They had proven they could beat Chicago, in Chicago. They had beaten Utah at home, and nearly beat them on the road. They had beaten Phoenix, in Phoenix. They took three out of four from Miami.

There was only one test left, and that was to see if they could win it all. When you really got down to it, our team all agreed on one thing: the one guy standing in our way was Michael Jordan.

CHAPTER 13

On Jordan, Magic, and Myself

One of the most frustrating games of my short coaching career was when we played Chicago at the United Center in February of my first season. Every guy on my team was turning down shots. They were completely out of sync. It was a difficult game for me to watch, because my guys kept hesitating. I didn't know why they did that. I had never seen them do that before. Then I realized—it was Michael Jordan. My team was convinced they couldn't beat the Bulls as long as Jordan was there. I spent the rest of the season convincing them it wasn't true.

After we got beat in that February game, and looked so intimidated in the process, I called my team together and said, "Have you ever seen anyone knock Michael Jordan on his butt? Have you ever seen anyone challenge him, eyeball to eyeball? People might talk a little trash to him, but the truth is, everybody is scared of him. Including you guys." They knew I was right. The guy had become untouchable. If you took Michael Jordan somewhere else in the world, and took the name off the back of his jersey, and put him out there where nobody knew who he was, guys would be beating on him and banging him. But here, it's, "Hey, isn't he amazing?" Even the refs are afraid of him.

I told my guys, "The next time we play Chicago, I want you to knock Michael Jordan flat on his butt if you get the chance. That's part of the game, understand?" But they wouldn't do it. He had them too psyched out. Michael Jordan played the mind game better than almost anyone. He really knew how to get inside people's heads. Plus, I believe he had the second best player in the league playing right next to him in Scottie Pippen. You take Michael off that team, and Scottie moves down to fifth. But when Michael was out there with him, they were the two best in the league.

Michael did some of the things I used to do, like walk up to a guy on the other team and tell him, in a low voice, exactly how he was going to beat him. So now the defense knows what he's going to run, but Michael gets the ball, does exactly what he told the guy, and beats him anyway. Believe me, having done it to people myself, it's absolutely devastating.

Everyone was so worried about what would happen to the league when Magic and I retired, but I told them they shouldn't give it any more thought. Michael Jordan was going to be The Man. No question about it. I said, "Guys, here is your next superstar. He'll make you forget all about Larry Bird and Magic Johnson." I believed that, because I knew Michael was that good, and he had the right kind of personality to go along with it. In 1987, Jordan's third season in the league, Chicago played our Celtics team in the playoffs, and Jordan scored 63 points against us. Afterward, everyone was just in awe. I told people, "That was God, disguised as Michael Jordan."

It was a truly unbelievable performance. It was one of the greatest shows I've ever been around. We could not stop him. But to be honest, we didn't spend much time talking about him in the huddle. All we were concerned with was winning the game. At the time, we were up 2–0 against Chicago in a first-round, best-of-five series, and we wanted to sweep them. Game 3 was in Chicago Stadium, and we wanted to get out of it as quickly as possible. People forget that Michael had 48 or 49 points in Game 1. That was a close one, wire to wire. We beat them 108–104, but we weren't feeling great about it. There was a sense of, "We better get this series over with, because this guy is dangerous." We were right about that. In that 63-point game, he just kept hitting everything. Everything. But in the end we got the win. I walked out of there thinking what I always did when I saw a great individual performance like that: one guy can't beat a whole team.

From the first time I saw Michael, I knew he was very talented, but I never would have guessed he would turn into probably the best player in history. My first impression of him? Shoot, shoot, shoot, shoot, shoot. I didn't see him play much in college, but I remember back in 1984 when Michael was playing on the United States Olympic team, they had a bunch of us pros come up to Indianapolis and play against them. We showed up there all out of shape, fooling around, and we played some games against them in the Hoosier Dome. You could tell Jordan could jump, he could pass, you could see he could do a little bit of everything, but he wasn't the kind of guy that you'd just sit down and watch the whole time. There were some other pretty good players on that team, like Patrick Ewing and Chris Mullin. It wasn't like you watched only Jordan and walked away from there thinking, "I just saw the future of the league."

When he got into the NBA and I played against him a few times, I remember thinking to myself, "Whoa, this kid has got a lot of talent. I can't believe how high he can jump, and how out of control he is. He's going to score a lot of points forever." But I saw a change in Michael after a while. He wasn't on fast-forward all the time. He was more patient on the floor. Then I started thinking, "Boy if they put some players around this guy, I wonder if he'll calm down a little bit and use his passing skills." Because I always felt he didn't understand the game. Well, now I realize he always understood the game, he just didn't have the players. Simple as that. It's amazing to me that he could score as many points as he did and still play within the team frame.

The one reason I do feel badly for Michael is that he didn't have one team, or one player, to shoot for year after year, like Magic and I did. If I didn't play at the same time as Magic Johnson, I might have won a couple more championships, but I don't know if they would have been nearly as worthwhile. I loved the fact that we both spent our careers fighting each other every day for those rings. I wouldn't have traded that rivalry for anything.

But you can't say Michael didn't have anybody. There are a lot of great players out there—Karl Malone, Charles Barkley, David Robinson—it's just that he's so much better than everybody else. Is he better than Magic Johnson was at the peak of his career? No. He's the best for an overall period of time, maybe, but when you put me, Magic, and Michael at the height of our careers, I don't think you'd find that big of a difference. Yes, Michael is more spectacular, and Magic could pass a little better than both of us, and you could say this and that about my shooting or my rebound-

ing, but we all had our different parts of our games that made
us special.

What separates Michael right now is he did it over a long
period of time. You look at the championships he won over
the last four or five years, and it's just amazing. People are
always so surprised that injuries didn't come into play more,
because he played so hard. Of course, the thing is he did
have injuries, but he's one of those players who played right
through all that. People don't give him enough credit for that.
They say, "Oh, Michael was never injured." But he was injured. He had back spasms like everyone else. He had sprains
and muscle tears and all that stuff, but he went in, he got his
rest, he got his treatment, and then he went out and played.
That's the difference between Michael Jordan and a lower-
level player. The best players just lace 'em up and go.

It's funny how you get tied to certain people, because
you played at the same time. Somebody takes a picture of
a couple of movie stars, and everyone thinks they're linked
together for life. That's just the way it is. Everyone wants
to believe Larry Bird and Kevin McHale were the best of
friends. Sure, Kevin and I had some good times together,
but the truth is, Artis Gilmore and Quinn Buckner were
probably the two best friends I had on the Celtics. But
that doesn't fit what the public wants to believe. Along
those same lines, everyone wants to think that Magic Johnson and Larry Bird hang out together all the time. And
after *Space Jam* came out, people want to think that
Michael Jordan and I play golf together every weekend.

I loved to compete against Magic and Michael as much
as anything I've done in my life. But I wasn't hanging
around with those guys. I didn't want to. We were trying
to win the championship, and I'm not into socializing with
the guys who have what you want. It's funny how every-

one decided me and Magic were best friends after we did that Converse commercial back in the eighties. The commercial was shot in Indiana, at my house and on my court. The way it went was they had Magic pull up to the court in a limo and get out with his basketball stuff on, in Lakers colors of course. I'm standing there, and he challenges me to some one-on-one. It was a really popular commercial, and one thing about that shoot that turned out to be true was how Magic and I got a chance to know each other a little bit off the court.

Before that, whenever we played the Lakers I'd say hi and stuff to Magic after the game, but I don't think Magic really knew where I was from, or what I was all about. And I've got to say the same was true for me. So anyhow, Converse arranges for us to do this commercial. My mom was there, and Magic charmed her right off the bat. He was there ten minutes, and she was offering him a drink and asking him if he needed anything. She loved him right away. I knew we were going to be spending a fair amount of time together, so I let my guard down a little bit. We had a great day. We went out riding on my four-wheelers. We drove around in my truck. For the first time, I saw him in a different way—a young guy from the Midwest who loves his family. When you took away all the glitz and glamour, that's what was there. One thing people don't realize is that when I talk about Magic, I'm talking about the basketball player. When I'm talking about the person, he's Earvin. When we were in San Diego for our Olympic training, we sat around and played cards. That's Earvin. But once we got into practice, or arrived in Barcelona and there was a crowd around, that's Magic. They are two completely different people.

Magic and I are like Joe Frazier and Muhammad Ali. That's just the way it is. I knew it was going to be like that forever after I played him in college for the national championship. I never came up against anyone, other than Magic, who could challenge me mentally. Magic always took me to the limit. Michael Cooper, who also played for the Lakers, challenged me on defense, but as far as the mental game went, he wasn't on the same plane as Magic. Magic Johnson was the only player that could really get to me. He knew it too.

Magic Johnson was the best passer I've ever seen. You could never guess where he was going with the ball. You'd just have to try and react with him. It took me a while to realize that. He had a three-on-one break against me two times in one game, and I got a hand on both of them, just from sitting back and letting him make the move. A lot of guys have the tendency to come down right-handed, and pass it that way. What Magic did was come down and keep the ball on the left, then just before you could react to it he'd throw it across his body, off the dribble. That's the hardest pass to defend against.

Magic was bad for basketball in one way. He made all these great passes, and then everyone else started trying to do it. You have to be special to thread the needle the way he did, or fire off those no-look passes. Magic knew how to do it. Most players don't. I tell my guys, "Just make the play." If you've got a look at a 15-foot jumper, and somebody is underneath the basket for a two-footer, just make the play. That's all I ask. The best passers, like John Stockton, make the pass that gives you the highest percentage shot.

While it's true that Magic and I developed a kind of friendship the day he came to French Lick, and it's true we both always had respect for each other, it's not like we all of a sudden started going on vacation together. It's funny, actually. I'll turn on the television and hear Magic

say, "Larry and I were out to dinner the other night, and
we were talking about this or that." But the truth is, I can't
ever remember being able to go out to eat with Magic,
other than when he came to my house that time to shoot
the commercial, and during the Olympics. I'll tell you what
has happened a lot. Magic will come up, and there will
be a lot of people around, and he'll go, "Larry, we've got
to have lunch next time you come to L.A." I always say,
"Yeah, sure, Magic, that would be nice." But I know it's
not going to happen. We both have pretty busy schedules,
so it's hard to get together. However, we were able to do
a television interview together on the twentieth anniver-
sary of our Indiana State–Michigan State matchup, and it
was great to see him. The truth is, I've never been into
spending very much time out in public on the road anyway. Some guys like that sort of thing, and Magic is one
of them. He handles a crowd better than anyone I've ever
seen. Kids will be clambering toward him, and their parents grabbing for him, and he just smiles that big smile
and touches as many of them as he can, then keeps on
going. Even though all those people never got an autograph, they think Magic Johnson is the greatest, because
he touched them or smiled at them. He just charms people to death. That's not something I was ever very good
at.

　　Even though Michael and I have been connected through
the years, it's not like I see him every week either. We do
commercials together, and once in a while we might do
some appearances. The last time I was really with Michael,
we played in a golf tournament together. He wanted to
come to Naples the next day and play there. So we did it.
But he's another guy who has all these people around.
Don't get me wrong, the way Michael does things is fine,

that's his thing, but it's just not my style. I have the same friends I had years and years ago. I would never push them aside to bring someone else in. Michael has some buddies that have been with him a long time too. But he also has a bunch of bodyguards and people like that, and it seems as though he can't go anywhere without a crowd around him. That's the price you pay for stardom.

Michael gives back in a lot of little ways that probably don't get into the newspapers. He'll help out a sick kid or something, and he'll do it quietly, not because he wants the publicity but because it's the right thing to do. Michael would be the kind of guy you'd like to hang around with. He's a fun guy, and he likes golf. What else do you need? Now that Michael is retired, we'll probably see each other two or three times a year, at a golf tournament or some charity thing, and that will be enough. There's no question our approach is a little different. If I call a country club and say, "Hey, can I come over and play golf?" there would be people all over the place, wanting stuff. But if I have my friend call the club and have him say, "I've got a guest here, and I'd like to come over," which I've done, then we go over and play and get through there without it being too bad. When Michael wants to play, he has someone say, "I'm calling for Michael Jordan, he wants to know if he can play golf at your club." Well, when that happens, you better be ready for the circus that is going to go along with it. If you are Magic, you can handle it, no problem. If you're me, you're going to run from it as fast as you can.

I'm sure it's hard for Magic now that he's not playing. He loved the limelight, and it's never really the same when you retire. He has always been attracted to the whole idea of show business, and good for him. I think he's doing well, and he's happy, and he wants to be the greatest businessman in the world, and from what I understand, with the movie theaters he's opened up in the city of Los Angeles, he's on his way. Someone told me Magic wants to be an agent too. I hope not. He'd be very tough. I'd rather not be across the table from him. I'm just glad that his health is holding up, and he's able to enjoy his family.

I'll never forget the day I found out Magic was HIV-positive. I got a call from his agent, Lon Rosen, and I was just sick about it. Really sick. We had a game that night, and for the first time in my life I didn't feel like playing. Lon told me Magic wanted me to know before it all went public, so I said, "Is he there? Can I talk to him?" It turned out Magic was at the doctor's, so I said, "Listen, I need to talk to him." I waited a little while, and I called him back, and he sounded all right. Hell, he sounded a lot better than I did. I told him I couldn't believe it. I wanted to see him. The last thing I wanted to do was go out and play basketball.

The whole thing was so incredibly mind-boggling to me. I kept trying to shake this sick feeling I had, but I couldn't. I got to the Garden for the game, and everyone wanted to know how I felt and did I talk to Magic? I wouldn't talk to any of them except to say that my heart and prayers were with Magic and his family.

Of course we had to play the game. We were playing Atlanta, and we were up by 15, and they came back and beat us. I didn't care. My mind was somewhere else. I talked to Magic once or twice over the next couple of weeks, but it still wasn't real to me. None of us knew too much about HIV then, and I think we all thought he was going to die. It was so hard to believe that someone that fun, someone that alive, could be so sick. There was never a dull moment with Magic.

Once he got on his medication and continued to feel good, I knew Magic was going to make a comeback. When you are forced to retire before you are ready, I'm sure it's hard to put the basketball behind you. For me, it was different. I only planned on playing twelve years or so, and I played thirteen. Besides, my back was so bad I knew I could never play again. But Magic still had ideas about playing. So the first thing he does is take over as coach of the Lakers. Magic is a spur-of-the-moment guy. I'm sure two days after he said he'd coach the team, he was saying to himself, "Now what have I gotten myself into?" No wonder he didn't like it, and no wonder he didn't do as well as he would have liked. Coaching is not some spur-of-the-moment decision. I agonized over whether I wanted to do it for almost two years. That's why when people were comparing my decision to coach to Magic's, I didn't put much stock in it. It was two completely different situations, with two completely different people approaching it two completely different ways.

Magic still wanted to play when he took over as coach. I'm convinced that if Magic wanted to coach, and put his mind to it, and forgot about all this other stuff he's doing and really put the proper time into it, he'd be a good coach. But Magic thought he could get out there and play with these guys and practice with them and all that. You can't. It doesn't work.

When I decided to coach, I spent a lot of time thinking about Michael Jordan. I knew, like every coach in the league, that he was standing in the way of my team and a championship. I knew I had to figure out a way to turn that all around. For years, Michael had been playing mind games with Reggie Miller. He complained about Reggie in the press all the time. I would have loved it if I was Reggie. It's hard for me to speak for him, but I would thrive on it. I'm sure there were a lot of guys in the league who hated me. I didn't care. That was good. It was even better. Reggie does his fair share of talking, and he's rubbed a number of guys the wrong way. If my guys want to say something to someone else out there, that's fine. There were a few of our guys talking junk. But it's like I tell them: "If you're gonna talk it, make sure you back it up."

I always liked how Michael handled himself. He talked it better than anyone, without crossing the line. But there was something he did during my first season that surprised me. ESPN had just come out with a new magazine, and Michael did an interview with them. He said playing against Reggie Miller drove him crazy, and he compared it to "chicken fighting with a woman." He said Reggie's whole game was based on flopping, and he claimed Reggie had his hands on him all the time, "like a woman holding your waist." The comments caused a big stir, and they were very embarrassing to Reggie, and all of a sudden everyone was talking about how Jordan hated Miller.

I really did feel bad for Reggie. Of course I'm going to feel that way, because he's my player. I didn't think Michael should have said all those things. I understand it's the way he felt, but it seemed totally out of character for him. He knew that he and Reggie were going to meet up again. Just play. Settle it on the court. But I guess it's something he just wanted to say, for whatever reason. Here you have probably the greatest player ever in the NBA, and everybody looks up to him, and when Reggie has children they're going to ask him about Michael Jordan. That's why I felt bad for Reggie. But as bad as I felt for him, I really did like it, because I thought, "We're going to play these guys in the playoffs, and Michael is going to be guarding

Reggie." Well, come playoff time Michael didn't guard him. And it ticked me off.

I brought up all those things Michael said to Reggie as soon as we got to the Eastern Conference Finals. If someone said something about McHale, I always brought that up to him, as a teammate. I wanted it to motivate him. I know it would have motivated me.

Before we got a chance to play Chicago in the playoffs, we had to get through Cleveland. The Cavaliers made me nervous. They were well coached, and they gave us problems. I never knew what a guy like Shawn Kemp would do, which made it hard to prepare. When he was on, he was a scary player. I was worried enough about that series, but then Rik Smits came up to me on the Friday before regular season ended and said, "Coach, my uncle just died. I need to go home." I said, "Okay, we have our last regular-season game tomorrow night on the road, you can miss that, go home, and be back by Sunday night." But Rik says, "Coach, I'm from Holland, remember? It will take me a full day to get over there." I'm thinking, "Oh my God, we've got a playoff game Thursday." I said to Rik, "How close an uncle is this?" He said, "Coach, he was just like a father." So I told him, "Then you go. If anyone on this team has someone that is close to them that dies, I expect them to go. Don't worry about the team. I'll handle it." The timing was horrible, because Rik was coming off an injury, he wasn't in great shape, and he needed the work, but it was out of my hands. I brought everyone in and sat them down and told them the situation. It got even more complicated, because Rik's uncle died on an oil rig, way out in the ocean somewhere. His body was out there two or three days, and Rik didn't know when they were bringing him in. Finally I said, "Rik, you've got to pay your respects to your family and get back here." He missed three days, flying back and forth to Europe, so that left us Tuesday and Wednesday to get ready for Cleveland. During our shootaround the day of the game, we had to go like crazy. But the guys were together on this. They understood. We won that first game 106–77 and I started breathing a lot easier.

We eliminated Cleveland in four games. We had New York next, and the big story there was Patrick Ewing was coming back from his broken wrist. I knew how determined Patrick was to win a championship, so he was the one that caused me worry against the Knicks. But our guys were focused on one thing—beating the Bulls—and they took care of New York more quickly than I ever would have guessed.

After we knocked off the Knicks, Mark Jackson got all fired up and started shouting, "Bring on Chicago." I felt the same way. I really liked our chances. Of course, right before our series Michael started laying the groundwork for his mind games. He told Rick Carlisle what a great coach he was. He told Rik Smits how much he enjoyed playing with him during the All-Star game. I jumped right on it. I wanted our guys to know he was fattening the calf.

The Bulls won Game 1 by putting Pippen on Mark Jackson, and just suffocating him. It took away Mark's ability to post up, and it hurt us because he had to eat up more of the shot clock to get rid of the ball. Pippen has such long, gangly arms, and he's a superb defender. Mark had seven turnovers in that game. The other change Phil Jackson made was that he put Ron Harper on Reggie, and Jordan on Chris Mullin. It definitely disrupted us, no question about it. But I still believe that if Reggie had been able to come out and score 30 or 35 points, they would have changed things around real fast.

Unfortunately for us, that didn't happen. Even so, we

played pretty well in the first half. But then we started breaking down, and Michael took over. That was the one thing I was concerned about. I felt if we hung in until the fourth quarter, then anything could happen. Even Jordan doesn't hit every shot. But if you give him an opening early on, he's going to go for the kill.

In Game 2 Michael dropped 41 on us, and we lost again. At that point everyone was writing us off. They were saying we were being outplayed, outcoached, and we were overmatched. I'm sure it looked that way, but I knew it wasn't over. I also felt that the officials needed to recognize what was going on out there. I said I would have liked to see how Michael Jordan would make out if Pippen was guarding him the way he was guarding Mark Jackson. I said it because the Bulls were getting away with too much. I know the Chicago Bulls get their share of calls, especially Michael, but Pippen was just manhandling Mark Jackson. It was over the line. I didn't say a whole lot, but then Sam Smith from the *Chicago Tribune* came up to me and said he was writing an article about how much Pippen was getting away with. He said he wanted to talk about it. I said, "I don't really want to say much. How about you say it for me? Then you can save me some fine money." Well that got Phil Jackson going. So now everyone is talking about the officials, and I just put my two cents in here and there. I put out just a little bit—just enough.

There's no question the referees have changed since when I was playing. I've always felt the referees have tough jobs. Just let them do their jobs, and if you really do get upset about something, then realize you can get away with more by just talking to them. Cursing and swearing at them doesn't work. The problem now is that the referees let their egos get into it a lot more than before. They carry themselves differently. They want to be part of the show. Earl Strom, one of my favorite officials, was part of the show, but he never lost control of the game. And when it came right down to it, he was going to make the call because it was a real foul, not because Michael Jordan is a superstar and nobody should touch him. Earl was fair that way. If you were the twelfth man, and you got clobbered, you got the same respect as the star.

Who knows if it made any difference, but we did get our share of calls in Games 3 and 4. Just before we tapped off for Game 3, I told my guys I still thought we were a better team than Chicago. I reminded them we hadn't lost home court yet, and if we won the next two games at our place, we were right where we needed to be. We won both of those games, mostly because our guys finally started playing physical, and because they played like they finally believed they belonged. Reggie, meanwhile, was heating up. He was playing on a sprained ankle, but there was never any question whether he'd go or not. This was the playoffs.

Reggie probably hit the biggest shot of his career in Game 4. We were down to the final seconds, and he pushed off Jordan, spun, and nailed the jumper. The game was in Market Square Arena, and the place just exploded. It was pandemonium. But I just stood there. The reason I didn't show any emotion was because I had seen the six-tenths of a second go up on the clock when Reggie shot it, so I was waiting to see what they put on the clock. I've seen Chicago win too many games on last shots with six-tenths of a second. I felt at that point we were going to win, but I can't show emotions out there. It's like another game we had in April that season. We were down eight against Atlanta, and made a great comeback, and Reggie hit this unbelievable shot. It was one of those amazing, lunging, turning, falling-out-of-bounds-and-I'll-toss-it-up jobs. That put us into overtime. When the ball went through the net, Dick Harter was standing next to me, and I turned to him and said, "Can you believe that?" He said, "I don't believe it either." That's all he said. So the guys come running back, jumping all around, and I said, "Okay, sit down. We've got a lot more minutes to go." Because that's my job, to make sure they stay focused on the game. As a coach, I know guys are looking at me to see how I react a lot of the time, so they don't need me jumping around. Somebody's got to be calm. People kept talking about my lack of reaction to Reggie's shot, but that was the kind of response my team needed from me.

As it turned out, Jordan got a shot off at the buzzer that missed. The series was suddenly tied, 2–2. What Reggie had done was huge, because he had deflated the whole Michael mystique. Just the idea that Reggie would go after the ball that hard, like he really wanted it, and didn't think twice about going through Michael Jordan to get it, was just huge. I really believed we had the upper hand. Meanwhile, it was Bulls coach Phil Jackson's turn to get on the officials. He said his team was robbed, and compared it to the Olympics in Munich in 1972. I thought that was ridiculous. I warned our guys not to get too happy with themselves. I warned them that Jordan would be out for blood. And we had another problem on our hands too. Jalen Rose, who had been playing really well for us in the postseason, was suspended for Game 5 by the league because they said he left the bench when a little shoving match broke out on the floor. I know it may have looked that way to people watching the game, but that wasn't what happened. On tape, Jalen jumps up from the bench and looks like he's running toward the court, but what really happened was I told him I wanted him to check into the game, and fast. I thought the way NBC covered it was bad. They're supposed to report the game, but they made it sound like we committed murder. It was a big blow for us, to lose Jalen. I don't blame it on him. It was my fault he wasn't already in the game. I told him to go in right as all that stuff was happening. The way he took off, running down the court, it looked like he was going in to get involved, but the reason he went tearing off like that was because I was screaming at him to get into the game.

Coming into Game 5, I was thinking, especially with Jalen out, that this was the sort of game where you find out what your team is made of. I couldn't wait to see who would step up and get the job done in Jalen's absence. Who would emerge as the guy on our team who had what it takes? I couldn't wait for that game to start. So what happens? We go out and we get killed in Game 5, by 19 points. I was so disappointed. I thought my team had understood the urgency of that game. I sat them down the next day and made them watch the first half of that game all over again. It looked like we were playing in slow motion.

I don't know if they could tell, but their performance in that game broke my heart. Here was a team I knew we could beat, and we let them walk all over us. At that point I began wondering again whether our guys were slipping back into that mentality of "Nobody beats Michael." That was really going to make me angry. We had nothing left to do but to go back home to Indianapolis for Game 6 and force a seventh game. Having Jalen back helped. So did the crowd. I've never heard Market Square Arena that loud. I liked what I saw in the first few minutes of the game, but I've found that's not really a true indicator with our team. What does tell me something is when Rik Smits has a really good game, we almost always win. And Rik came ready to play for Game 6. He scored 25 points in 32 minutes, and he was 11-of-12 from the floor. But, when the game was over, the guy everyone was talking about was Travis Best.

I had been playing Travis Best in the fourth quarter, because he was having success breaking down Chicago's defense with his quickness. On another team, it could have been a problem, because there's Mark Jackson, who had been our leader all season, sitting on the bench for crunch time. But Mark was great. I didn't have to say anything to him. He handled it so well, so professionally, and I know it wasn't easy for him. But he knew it was all about winning. In Game 6 I went with Best for the entire fourth quarter. With the score tied 87–87, he beat Steve Kerr with a one-on-one driving one-handed runner. Then, in the final seconds, with our first option, Reggie, sealed off, Best took on Jordan, got a step on him as he drove toward the basket, and drew the foul. Travis is a really excellent foul shooter, and he hit them both. That put us up two, and Jordan had one last crack at it, but he slipped trying to take it to the lane. The Bulls were crying foul, but we didn't hang around. I got our guys off the court and in the locker room before the officials changed their minds.

Before Game 7, I wanted these guys to understand what it would be like to be a champion. I talked about the respect they would get if they accomplished that. Hell, all they had to do was look across the court at Michael Jordan to understand that. I told them, "Even though we would have to play Utah in the Finals, if we win today, I'm convinced this is our championship, because I know we can beat Utah." Maybe that wasn't the politically correct thing to say, but I wasn't going to lie to those guys. I told them a little story about what I felt the first time we won a title in Boston, and how all the fans came to City Hall to cheer us on, and how the whole city had this new respect for us. It was my second year with the Celtics, and we had a great team, but in the Conference Finals all of a sudden we were down 3–1 to Philadelphia. But we never thought about quitting. We still believed we were the better team, and we proved it when we came back to win that series. Well, I knew we were going to win the Finals after coming back down 3–1 to Philadelphia. I knew we were invincible then. I told my guys I wanted them to feel the same way. I told them winning a title would change their lives. After I won one, all of a sudden I'd be walking down the street and people would say, "Wow, he's Larry Bird. He won the NBA championship." I said to my players, "Look at Reggie. Now he's a great, great player, but if he ever won a championship, the way people would look at him and perceive him and feel about him would be completely different than how they felt before, no matter how many game-winning shots he has hit. Once you're labeled a champion, you are in a whole new category." I was getting kind of emotional about it, and I looked over, and two of the guys were crying. I walked over to Dick and said, "Geez, there's no way we're gonna win this game." Dick said, "Why?" I said, "Dick, our guys are crying before we go out there." He said, "Larry, it shows they really want to win."

I was really wound up before Game 7. I was trying to hide out in the locker room, away from everyone. That's when I realized Jim Gray, the NBC reporter, was even more pushy than I thought. Before Game 7, we had to turn our play board toward the wall so no one would be able to see it. Sure enough, there's Jim Gray in our locker room, trying to turn the board back around so he could see our plays. Then, during the game, we're in a time-out and our public relations guy, David Benner, is standing there, and Gray is trying to listen in on our huddle. After the players went back on the court, I quietly told Benner, "David, you tell Mr. Gray if he sticks his nose in my huddle again I'm going to pull him over those seats and kick his butt in front of twenty thousand people."

Game 7 went the way I expected. Both teams played with the kind of urgency you would expect in a game that big. Someone said it was the biggest game in the history of the Pacers franchise. It was hard to disagree with that. Michael had already publicly guaranteed his team would win, but that didn't faze me. Of course he did that. I would have done the same thing.

In many ways, all our old problems came back to haunt us in Game 7. We got into early foul trouble. We missed a lot of key free throws. But the most unbelievable statistic of all was we were outrebounded on the offensive glass 24–4. We were the worst offensive rebounding team in the league during the regular season, but that kind of margin was pathetic. You look at the film and it really turns your stomach. In spite of all that, we were playing great defense, and we were in a position to win it. In fact, midway through the fourth quarter we were up three when Derrick McKey knocked the ball loose from Jordan and forced a jump ball between Rik and Michael. Obviously, this was a tip we should have won.

When the jump ball was called between Rik and Michael, I remember wondering if Michael would do what I used to do when I thought I couldn't win a tip, which was jump into the guy a little bit. We went through jump ball situations a few times, but we don't spend a lot of time on it. We did spend a lot of time on out-of-bounds plays, shots with maybe two or three seconds to go, but when I was standing there watching that whole thing unfold, I said to myself, "Damn, we didn't spend enough time on jump balls." Because in the end, the season really did come down to that. I knew Rik would get the tip, but the way they were lined up I didn't think that he could jump and tip it back over his head, because I had never—ever—seen Rik Smits do that. If he's going to tip it, he almost always tips it forward, and when I looked forward, there was Scottie Pippen and Reggie. And Reggie was sort of on the side and a little bit behind Scottie, and I started thinking right then, "There's no way we're going to win this tip." I knew it was a turning point of the game right there.

The worst part is Dick Harter said, right when they were lining up, "I think we should get a time-out right here." Initially I looked and I sort of thought, "Well, Rik will get the tip," and then I'm thinking, "Well, the way they're lined up, we'll get a layup off it." But as soon as that thought was finished, that's when I realized about Rik and how he never tipped it back, and by then I was putting my hands up to signal time-out, but the ball was already up in the air, and boom! It was over. It was too late. Smits tipped it forward, Pippen intercepted it and tossed it over to Jordan for a jumper. Michael missed it, but Pippen got the rebound and found Steve Kerr for a three-pointer. So now, instead of us going up by five, the game is tied. There was still six minutes or so left in the game, but that one sequence cost us the game, and I was sick about it, because it was my fault. I just felt so bad for the team. I wanted to beat the Bulls so bad for these guys. I was so ticked off at myself for blowing that jump ball, and then I had to go in that locker room after it was over and look at our older guys and know they were five minutes away from the Finals, and they would have to wait a whole year to get their chance again. Horrible.

After the game I didn't feel like talking to anybody. I couldn't believe we had come so close and ended up losing anyway. I felt the same way I felt in that very first game against New Jersey: I walked off thinking we should have won the game. Because the game was televised on NBC, Jim Gray was waiting outside our locker room, and he wanted me to come out and talk to him. My initial reaction was to say no. I had no interest in saying anything to that guy. But Brian McIntyre, the vice president of public relations for the NBA, came in and asked me if I would mind doing it for him, as a favor. Brian is a great guy, so I said yes. I don't even remember very much of what Jim Gray asked me. I do know the last thing he said was, "Do you think Chicago can beat Utah for the championship?" I looked right at him and I told him, "I don't really care."

Because I didn't.

CHAPTER 14

On the NBA Today

I tried not to let one lousy jump ball ruin my first season in coaching, but it's been a hard thing to shake. I watched the tape a couple of days after it was over, and it breaks your heart. I don't ever need to watch it again. That game will be in my mind forever.

I know people are surprised that I did so well coaching. I wasn't surprised. I wouldn't have done it if I didn't think I could succeed. The one thing I always felt was that I was a leader, and with the career that I had, if I picked the right team and the right players, they would listen to me. And that's what happened. I've got a group of guys that respect me, and if I have something to say, I say it, then I get out of there. I don't need to elaborate on it for two or three minutes. It's funny. I'll give them a talk before the game, after the game, in the huddle, whatever, and all eyes are focused on me. You watch other coaches talking, and you'll see one guy wiping his leg or fixing his socks. I picked this team because I knew this group would give me the respect you need to get the job done.

After one season, I can't tell you how much I've respected them in return.

I will say this: I learned more about the game of basketball in one season of coaching than in all my years as a player. As a player, everything I did was based on reaction. And once I learned the fundamentals, I could see how to improve my game by practicing. In coaching, I learned through other people, whether it's the coaches or the players. You have to learn about time-outs, and substitution patterns . . . there are so many things going on, and you have to make these spur-of-the-moment decisions. Yes, you have to do that as a player, but it's more reaction. As a player, you are worried about taking care of your responsibilities within the game. As a coach, your responsibility is the entire game, including the five guys you put on the court.

The best example I can give is that jump ball in Game 7 of the Eastern Conference Finals. It was a major, major mistake. I knew it when it was happening. I knew I messed up as a coach. The difference is, if I saw the same thing as a player, and I didn't like how we were lined up, I would have grabbed my teammate and put him where he should be, and I'd yell at the other guys and get them to their proper spots. But coaching on the sidelines, you don't have that kind of input, or control, over the game.

I can't say coaching gives you the same thrill as a player, but it's pretty close. There are some monotonous parts of the job—I forgot, for instance, how much I hated the travel—but I really do like the action. I like the games, and I love the practices. I know I'm not what you would call a typical NBA coach, but I'm not trying to be. I'm not really interested in whether I fit in or not.

I'm not ever going to be part of the Fraternity, as I call

them. There's a group of coaches out there who all look out for each other, and hire one another when one of them gets fired. They're the ones who are gossiping about this guy and that guy. I'm just not into that, and I think it ticked people off. I don't really care. There were a lot of coaches that wanted to see the Pacers get beat so bad, because I'm not part of their Fraternity. They all like Rick and Dick, because they've been around, but they don't feel the same way about me. The worst thing for the Fraternity is a guy like me coming in, an ex-player, and succeeding without going through the ranks. Not to mention that I came in and hired just two assistants. I understand that. But I'm not a schmoozer. If that is what it takes, count me out.

I'm sure my take on this league is a little different from some of these old-school coaches. To me, one of the funniest things that happened was how everybody got all worked up about how long the players were wearing their shorts. The league actually fined teams because their guys had their shorts below their knees. If these guys can play, I could care less. They can wear whatever they want, as long as they come to play.

There is a difference from when I played, though. No question about it. A young kid comes into the league all fired up, and after about five years he's horrible. How does that happen? How do you let it happen? I always loved playing. But I loved working out in the summer almost as much. I enjoyed trying to get better. But that's where the change comes in. To me, the NBA has become the MTV league. The All-Star game started a lot of it. Before, the game was the show. Now, the show is the stuff all around the game. There's more hype than there is game, and the sport can't possibly live up to that. It's not if you win, or how you play, but how you look when you play, or where you play. Then there's all the loud music in the middle of the game, and the bands, and the acts, and the cheerleaders. It's almost like theater.

I started noticing a major change during the 1986 All-Star game in Dallas. It was supposed to be a basketball game, but they had the music cranked up like some kind of video. It was more like a dance than a game. It was the first year of the three-point contest, and even though I won my share of them, I didn't like it. I felt the three-point shot took away from the way the game should be played. And then there was the slam dunk contest. That had turned into some kind of rap contest. I knew what they were doing. They were trying to satisfy the young people and the corporate fans, who want to be entertained. I guess they had identified the future of their league. I can understand all the marketing. That's how we all make money. I always felt they did a fantastic job of promoting the league, but somewhere along the way it got bigger and bigger, and then the NBA went corporate. Like in Boston Garden. In my later years I'd look up in the stands and see a bunch of people in suits and ties. Those aren't my type of people. What I loved was when you looked up during the playoffs, and it was June, and it was hot and sticky, it was eighty-five degrees, and everybody was up there in tank tops and shorts. Those are basketball fans. But they're gone now. They can't afford the tickets, because the salaries are so out of whack, and the prices keep going up. So then it carries over to the players. They get used to a certain standard. If you asked them to have roommates on the road, like we used to have, they'd be horrified. They fly chartered planes. It's just a whole different ball game now.

That doesn't mean it's all terrible. There are still guys who work their butts off, who want to be the best. I wish they would stay in school longer, because I think they would be more mature and would have better fundamentals, but some of these kids come out early because they want to provide for their families. Think about it. If you know by going pro you'll get millions of dollars to make sure your mom has someplace safe to live, or your brothers or sisters will have nice clothes and something to eat at every meal, that's a hard thing. I had a chance to leave school early for the pros, but I promised my mom I'd graduate from school, so that's what I did. I have never regretted that decision. If I had gone, Indiana State never would have gone to the championship game, and Magic and I wouldn't have had all that history.

People ask me all the time who I think will be the next superstar, now that Michael has retired. To me, the next great player is Shaquille O'Neal. He's big and he's strong, and he uses his muscles to get away with certain things that make him almost impossible to stop. I truly believe his time is going to come. I don't know him at all, but I've got him marked down for four or five championships. He's sort of like Michael was early on. He hasn't figured it out yet, but he will. People harp on how he should be a more dominant rebounder, but rebounds can be a misleading stat, depending on what kind of system you are playing in. Personally, I think Shaquille is a great rebounder.

Kobe Bryant is an interesting young player. He could be very good. It all depends. You look at all these guys, and as talented as they are, it still is going to take them about four years. It takes time to become great. You can't hurry that along. Your body is not made to get beaten up

and banged all the time, and that's an adjustment. You
need time to mature and to understand what you are after.
There's been added pressure on Kobe because he came
out of high school to such a good team, but he's got a
presence. He just needs to be reeled in a little bit.

It's hard not to like Tim Duncan and his game. I can
remember coming back from the Atlanta summer league,
and people were saying Duncan had looked awful. I was
laughing, saying, "Yeah, right." How ridiculous is that? I
didn't know he'd get 20 and 30 points in the playoffs, but
don't even try and tell me that kid can't play basketball.
He has a chance to be a great one too.

I know the Celtics were worried about paying Antoine
Walker, but he was worth keeping for one reason alone:
he rebounds, and he can dribble down the court. That's
major. There aren't too many guys anymore who know
how to rebound and push it out. The high school kid we
drafted in 1998, Al Harrington, has that skill. He doesn't
have a lot of range, but we can work on that. Same with
Walker. His shot selection is pretty suspect, but he's still
young. He'll figure it out.

It's funny, but Kenny Anderson, who Boston traded for
in 1998, has always been one of my favorites. A kid with
his talent, it's too bad he's not healthy every night. We
had a chance to trade for him just before the 1998 dead-
line, but I didn't like their asking price. They wanted Mark
Jackson, and I wasn't about to give him up.

There are a couple of other point guards I really like.
One of my favorite guys I love to watch play is Rod Strick-
land. He can score anytime he wants to. I'm convinced of
that. He can also get the ball to anybody. I think I would
have a hard time coaching him, though, because from what
I understand, he's always late. I wouldn't put up with that.

The other thing is he evidently doesn't like to practice. That doesn't mesh with me either. I think practice is key if you plan on winning anything significant. The other kid I like is Allen Iverson. He's a basketball player. He just gets out there and plays, and I love that. I know he's a little undisciplined, but you take a guy like him and you can tell him forever what he can and can't do, or what he should and shouldn't do. Or you can set up a few parameters and say, "Do your thing, but stick to these couple of guidelines." If he still doesn't do it, you put it all on tape and you sit him down and show him what you mean. He's such a talent, he's worth the effort. He's a fun player, and he makes people around him better. A lot of the older NBA stars jumped on him because he said some things about how he doesn't have to respect anyone on the court. Like I've said before, what's wrong with that? The only difference between Allen Iverson and me, or Magic when he was on top, is Iverson is saying a lot of the things we were just thinking.

People are constantly asking me what I think about Dennis Rodman, because the guy is always ripping me. I'll tell you this much: I wouldn't want Dennis on my team, but what he did for Chicago was mind-boggling. Everybody is different. I could never put up with the stuff Rodman got away with when he was on the Bulls, like blowing off practices and staying out all night before a game, but there's no question Dennis Rodman is one of the greatest rebounders in the last ten or twelve years, and what he brought to the Bulls was championships. They don't win without him. Period. When Rodman first came into the league, I thought he'd be a great scorer. He could shoot the ball. I remember when I was with the Celtics we played Detroit in a playoff series, and Rodman took a really poorly timed three-pointer at a really bad point of the game, and after that someone must have said to him, "Hey, stick to rebounding." Too bad. Rodman could have been a complete player if he wanted to be.

Certain guys you see play, and you'd love to have a chance to work with them. Vinny Baker, the power forward who plays for Seattle, is one of those guys. He's going to be a terrific talent. I also love Gary Payton, Baker's point guard. I love the way Payton goes at it on the defensive end. He's one of the few that gives you everything on both ends. It's got to be a dream to play with that guy.

Although it's interesting to watch the young guys develop, it's sad for me to watch some of the older players come to the end of their careers. Guys like Karl Malone, who has never gotten enough credit, because he's played the bulk of his career the same time as Michael. The one I hate to see go without a ring is Patrick Ewing, because I know him better than any of them, and I know how hard he has worked over the years. He's a warrior, and I hate to see him leave without a championship. I feel the same way about John Stockton. People think because these superstars have made all this money, they'll leave the game satisfied, but I know talking to Patrick that it isn't true. He won't be happy unless he wins an NBA title, and he knows his time is running out. There's another reason I have respect for those guys. Karl, Patrick, and John played their careers all in one place. That, to me, is really significant. I am so glad I did the same thing. Like I said at my Hall of Fame induction, one of my biggest worries about this league over the course of the next ten years or so is that we won't have but one or two players who will stay in the city they started with. I think that's a shame, and I hope it's something the league addresses soon.

You have to realize how that stability helps the league. I remember meeting this Celtics fan once. He was telling me how his dad used to take him to the games when he was seven years old. For ten years that kid followed the same team, and as a result he grew up with the players on that team. I think that's important. In this case, the guys that little kid followed were Kevin McHale and me. By the time Kevin and I finally retired, that little seven-year-old kid was in college, but Kevin and I were still Celtics, and he was still a Celtics fan. Of course, the reason these players move around so much today is because they can make a lot of money doing it. There's no question the money in the NBA has gotten out of control, but I'm not going to sit here and criticize the players for that. I always said, "Work hard, and get what you can get." The guaranteed money is a good thing, but it makes guys soft. It makes them lazy. It happened when I played too. The only difference is now they're being lazy for millions, instead of hundreds of thousands of dollars. That's why I believe you need some guys on the end of your bench who are hungry, who are fighting for their lives every day, because they keep all your fat cats honest. That's what Mark West did for our team in my first season, when he wasn't injured. That's what Joe Kleine did for Chicago, and what Greg Kite did for our Celtics teams.

Greg Kite was one of the most hardworking people I've ever seen. Rick Carlisle is another guy who survived a lot of years in the league because of the way he worked. You know who else was a damn hard worker? Kevin McHale. He liked to come off like he was an easygoing guy, without a care in the world, but when we got into practice he

was there for the long haul. I'll never forget the first time
I saw him. He had been a holdout with Boston, and his
agent was threatening to send Kevin to Italy if he and the
Celtics couldn't work out a deal. When McHale finally
signed and reported to camp, Fitch nicknamed him
Spaghetti Man. What I remember most about him is that
he blocked my shot three times in practice. The first time
he did it I thought "beginner's luck," but he kept on doing
it. He even blocked some of them left-handed. His timing was unbelievable. He was already one of the top defensive players in the league as a rookie. And he worked
so hard on his low post moves. He'd be there after practice for an hour, maybe more, thinking up new ways to
beat people on the block. In 1986 he was at his best, and
I told him, "Kevin, if you keep on playing like this, you're
going to be the MVP of the league." But the problem with
Kevin was, he'd get bored. He'd score 20 on someone,
just scorch the poor guy, and we'd be up by 15 points,
and Kevin would say, "Aw, he's had enough." That's when
I'd be thinking about putting the dagger in the guy, but
Kevin wasn't like that. He truly was the best player in the
NBA that year, until the last month of the season, when
he lost interest. I said, "Kevin, but you could have been
MVP." He said, "Larry, I don't care about that stuff." My
answer was, "You don't now, but you will twenty years
from now, when it's all over."

The other part that made you love McHale was how
great he was in the locker room. He was really patient and
helpful with young players. He'd spend a lot of time with
them after practice—all the time they wanted. He worked
with Greg Kite, and Joe Kleine, and Stokjo Vrankovic,
when he was with the Celtics. Most of those guys, they'd
be ready to stop before Kevin would be ready. He'd play

all day if he had someone to work with. You just don't see too much of that anymore, and that's a shame.

My own playing days seem far, far away. It's over, and it has been for a while. It's funny. Once you stop playing, it doesn't seem that important anymore. Sometimes I feel like I never played before. Sometimes you walk into different arenas and you'll have flashbacks of a big play, or a big win. That always happens when I walk into the Forum, or Madison Square Garden. But a lot of these new arenas don't mean anything to me, because I never played in them. I miss the old Chicago Stadium. And I will never understand why they tore down Boston Garden.

In the week or so before the lockout hit, Donnie and I started talking about how we could improve our team for the next season. We had such a great chemistry among our guys, and we were grateful for that, especially after all the crazy things that had happened, with Latrell Sprewell and his reported attempts to choke his Warriors coach, P. J. Carlesimo, at the top of the list. That was terrible—uncalled for—but I'd be lying to you if I said we didn't have some interest in trading for him.

I feel sorry for P. J. Carlesimo. He was my assistant coach on the Dream Team, and both Rick and Dick worked for him, and they have a lot of respect for him. What Sprewell did was wrong, there's no question about that. He deserved to sit out a year, which he did. But it wouldn't have stopped me from taking him. I know that seems like a contradiction to some people, based on how I stress discipline and togetherness and all that. But I took a look at the group of guys we had, and I felt they would make him change. He would have to fall in line with our group. And if he didn't, we'd have to find someplace else for him to go. To me it was worth the gamble. When a guy messes up like that, he's either made a big mistake or he's got major problems. We would have needed to find out which one it was right away. And I never would have traded for him without going to Mark and Reggie and Chris and getting their opinion, which is what I did. I told them, "If you don't want him, it's your team. This is your chance to speak up."

I wanted to help these guys out, to improve their team, but they've been together awhile, so I put the ball in their court. I said, "Hey, a couple of improvements and we could do this. Or we might be able to do it just the way we are, because we're good enough. I don't know what's going to happen to Chicago, but we can't worry about that. We've got to worry about ourselves." They all agreed we should go after Sprewell. He was exactly the kind of player we needed. He was a young, athletic scorer. I think we could have gotten him if we really wanted to, but in the end I felt the price was too high. Golden State wanted one of our big guys, and I didn't want to do that.

I'll always wonder how it would have worked out. I know Sprewell has talent. That's not the issue. But is he capable of understanding that some nights, when he's really rolling, he might get 20 shots, but on the nights he's not, he might be on the bench while someone else does it? Guess we'll never know.

I learned an awful lot about the game in my first season of coaching. If I went to another team I'd do a lot of things differently. I really enjoyed having my assistants, and giving them a lot of influence on what we're trying to do, because they're part of it too. But the second time around, I'd probably have my thumb on things a little more. You don't want to take back some of the power you give people, but there will be some changes in Year Two.

I'll still have Rick draw the plays in the huddle, because he's the best at it. If something works, don't change it. But if I ever do go to another team, I'll draw all the plays myself, because now I have the confidence and the experience I need to be effective.

In terms of personnel, we have a pretty good nucleus, but I would love, like everyone, to find a guy who can throw in 12 to 15 every night from the low post. Rik isn't really a post man, and that's the one thing we really need. I know one thing: things are going to be even more organized in my coaching future. My big thing is conditioning, and it will continue to be. So, okay. A player gets injured. That will no longer mean he's sitting out. If he breaks his ankle, he'll work out his arms. If he's got a broken arm, he can run. We hadn't had injuries all season, and then all of a sudden Rik went out with his foot problems and we didn't have anything for him to do. We didn't have the right weight machines. We didn't have a swimming pool where he could go every day. My feeling is that you should make it so miserable to be off the court that guys will be fighting like hell to get back on the court. I learned that lesson from Rik. We thought he'd be out two or three days, but all of a sudden he's out two weeks and he's losing all his conditioning. That's our fault. We didn't have the proper mechanisms in place to keep him sharp.

The Pacers are paying me a lot of money to coach. But Donnie knows better than anyone that I didn't do this solely for the money. I've saved my money. I don't need this job to feed my family. I know there must be some nights that Donnie goes to bed thinking, "I wonder if he'll come back." It's not just up to me. It's up to my players too. If I went to that first break-up dinner that night, and those players came to me and said, "Look, Larry, we appreciate all you did, but our careers are winding down, and we think we'd be better off with a different coach," I wouldn't be mad at anybody. It was a hell of an experience. I did it, and if it's time to move on, then so be it. My only regret would be we didn't beat Chicago. I never stopped believing we could do it. I was hoping Michael Jordan wouldn't retire, because I wanted another crack at the Bulls at their best. At the same time, I knew when he did retire everybody would be watching our team to see if we could do it. That's good. I liked the idea of having that kind of pressure on my team.

I'm not sure what will happen when my coaching career is up. There's been some talk about me going into the Pacers front office, but we've got Donnie Walsh, and he's the best I've seen. Why should he get out? I know he's been telling people he's going to retire, but what would he do? A guy who works twelve to fifteen hours a day, what will he do then? Go off and just sit somewhere like I did? He could learn from me. I'm not saying I have no interest in that part of the business. I guess I'd like to go in the front office if they didn't have the salary cap. It's incredibly frustrating to me that I can't take one of my players and trade for one of your players, even though I've got the money to pay your guy. I understand why they're doing it. But you need more room, and more freedom to move players. Right now any team is so limited in what it can do.

It was a real downer to have dealt with a lockout in my first off season as a coach. I had all these ideas about how we could help this guy and that guy by giving them specific drills, or working with them on certain things. Instead, I couldn't talk to anyone. I know some teams didn't pay attention to the league's rules, which said you couldn't have contact with any of the players while they were locked out, but I took the rules seriously. If one of my players tried to call me, I hung up on them. When it got to be October, I still wasn't talking to our guys, because I wasn't allowed to, but I kept hearing how they were all working out together as a team. That made me happy.

The funny thing about the lockout was that both sides kept talking about this issue or that issue, but the issue has always been the same: it's all about money. I remember early in my career, our owner, Harry Mangurian, coming in and telling us we were going on strike. He said, "The players want this, and the players want that, and they're going to ruin our game if they strike." I said to him, "Look, I'll be your model player. I'll show up, even if nobody else in the league does. But do I get paid if I come in here tomorrow and play?" He just looked at me. Because it was about money and he knew it. Everyone felt sorry for Scottie Pippen because he was underpaid, but I didn't feel sorry for him. He signed the contract. If he was so sure he was going to be that good, why didn't he put an escape clause in there? And suppose he got hurt? He wouldn't be complaining about the contract then.

When I was a player, I never looked at so-and-so and said, "He's making five million dollars a year. I should be making more than him." I always believed your talent would take care of all that. When I first came in I was the highest-paid rookie ever, so I had a hand in helping these guys get what they get today. I'm all for the players earning as much as they possibly can, but the one thing I can't stand is when guys get paid before they earn it, and then they don't want to come out and play. It makes me want to throw up.

The Larry Bird exception was in the news a lot during the lockout. When I signed the contract that put that rule into motion, I had no idea the ramifications would be so huge, but my attorney, Bob Woolf, did. I remember him telling me, "Whatever you and Magic do will help the whole league." Then, when my contract was up, he said, "You've got to make sure this contract is the right thing for everyone." At the time, I didn't understand that. But what Mr. Woolf meant was that if I made a big jump in salary, then the sixth man who was making $100,000 before could now make $250,000. After the Larry Bird exception became official, Mr. Woolf told me, "You've just changed the entire financial landscape of the NBA." He knew. He could see it coming. But even he couldn't have known how far this would go. Having been on both sides of it now, I think it's time to realize that things aren't like they were before. It was time for both parties to agree on what is best for the league, not what is best for themselves. You keep hearing how certain teams are losing money. I've been hearing that since I came into the league. There's something wrong when the same teams have the top five draft choices, year after year. It's ridiculous. Teams like Sacramento and the L.A. Clippers, do they really deserve franchises?

The players didn't want to take a pay cut, and I don't blame them. But I also wonder about the agents and the influence they have on this league. Too many guys forget the agent works for them, not the other way around. Yes, Bob Woolf was my attorney during my playing days, but when it came down to negotiating a contract, I usually did most of the work myself.

I remember the contract I signed in 1984, just after we won a championship. Red Auerbach called me in the sum-

mer and said, "Come down and let's get this contract done."
I said, "Should I bring Bob Woolf?" He said, "You can if
you want." So Mr. Woolf and I go down to the Celtics
offices, and Red's got his general manager, Jan Volk, in
there, and it's going fine, but then we start getting down
to the numbers. At the time, Moses Malone was making
$1.8 million. I said, "Red, I'm just going to tell you. I
want to be paid the same as Moses Malone." Red said,
"That's one point eight million. We can't pay you that. It's
too much." At the time, that was the highest salary in the
league, but I had just been named MVP, so I said, "That's
what I want, Red." So Red turns to Jan, who was their
salary guy, and Jan says, "We can't afford that." At that
point, Mr. Woolf jumps in, and he and Jan are talking back
and forth, and Red looks at Mr. Woolf and says, "Look,
we don't need you in here." So I turn to Jan and say,
"Look, we don't need you in here." And you know what?
They left. Red and I kept at it, and it got down to a difference of $25,000, on some bonus clause. I don't re-
member what it was, but I would have sat out the whole
year before I'd let Red hold me up over $25,000. I ended
up getting my $1.8 million, and the $25,000, and I was
happy with that. I didn't want $2.3 million, or $2.5 million, which is what Mr. Woolf wanted me to ask for. I
knew Moses had a contract coming up the next season,
and he'd probably get more than I was getting, but I didn't
care about all that.

The one thing I hated was when contract talks got into
the papers, but once in a while it couldn't be avoided. I
remember in 1988, my contract was due to be up after
one more season, so the Celtics told me they wanted to
get an extension done that summer, before the 1988–89
season. Red said, "You and Jan work it out, okay?" I said,

"Fine, but I want it to be done before training camp." That summer, Jan was calling me every three weeks or so saying, "We're going to get this done soon." I kept saying, "Let's stop talking about it and just do it and get it over with. I don't want to spend the summer thinking about this." I was getting ticked off. The next time he called I said, "Jan, stop screwing around. I want this done." Jan said, "Okay, Larry, here's what I'll do. I'll fly in to Indianapolis and we'll meet there." So Jan flies in, and I pick him up at the airport, and he says to me, "How far away is that hotel you own?" I say, "About seventy-five miles." Jan says, "I've got some time, let's drive over and have lunch."

On the drive there, we don't discuss the contract at all. We have lunch, and still we haven't talked about the contract. I'm thinking, "Well, on the way back, we'll probably do it. We'll have a good hour." We drive back, and still nothing. I pull in, and I'm getting mad now, and Jan gets out of the car and says, "By the way, we've got to get this contract thing settled." I couldn't believe it. I said, "We had all day, Jan." He said, "Well, I'll call you." By that time I was livid. I called Jill Leone, who worked for Mr. Woolf at that time, and had become the person I trusted to handle my affairs, and I told her, "I'm so sick of them treating me this way, I'm going to play the year out." She said, "I would too." I didn't want to leave Boston—I always told Red I'd never go anywhere—but when I showed up for training camp I told reporters I was done with Jan, and I would only deal with Red. I told them, "They sent a boy out there to do a man's job." It was the wrong thing to say at the wrong time, but it was how I felt. And it was effective. Before you knew it, Red was telling reporters, "We'll take care of this within the week." Sure enough, a

few days later Red comes to practice and tells me, "Alan
Cohen wants to meet with you. Tonight."

Alan Cohen was one of our owners, the most knowl-
edgeable basketball guy among them. By this time the
Celtics knew I was upset about this. I can remember Dinah
saying to me, "Don't you go down there and get mad. Kill
him with kindness." I had all my stuff. I had everything.
I had every contract in the league printed out on my sheet.
So I go up to Longfellow Place and Alan says to me, "You
want a beer or something?" I said, "No, I'm fine." All of
a sudden Alan starts going at me. He's yelling and cursing at me for criticizing Jan in the papers. He said, "How
dare you talk about our general manager like that?" I told
him, "Alan, all I did was tell the truth." He finally calmed
down a little bit, and he said, "You know we want you to
stay here." Then he starts talking dollars. It wasn't even
close. I knew what I wanted when I went down there. So
I started running down these contracts, starting with Patrick
Ewing. Cohen said, "We can't pay you Patrick Ewing's
money. He's in New York. They always pay more than
guys are worth." We go down the list to Michael Jordan,
and he says, "Aw, c'mon, Jordan is a young star on the
way up," and then we get to Magic and he says, "You
can't count Magic. That's L.A., Showtime and all that." I
said, "I don't care what it is. We're talking about players
here. You average them in, and that's what I want." Now
I had talked to Bob Woolf before I went down there, and
he said, "If we get around three point two million a season, you should be satisfied." But I got so mad at Alan
Cohen, I started thinking to myself, "The heck with this.
I want a million dollars more." I wouldn't budge until I
got that and we agreed to it. I walked out of there thinking, "When I take this back to Bob, he's going to die, be-

cause I got a million more than he would have asked for."
I was feeling pretty good about myself until I got into that
car and started thinking, "I probably could have got ten
million. Cohen is probably sitting up there laughing his
butt off. He got me." But I was happy. I got what I felt
was fair.

Truth is, I loved Alan Cohen. He was one of those owners who not only loved the game, he really understood it.
He knew talent. The year the Celtics took Michael Smith
in the draft, Alan Cohen wanted Tim Hardaway. I always
remembered that. The last time I really dealt with him, I
was retired, and was helping the Celtics evaluate talent for
the draft. Cohen said to me, the night of the draft, "How
do you like Nick Van Exel?" I said, "I love the kid. I know
he's got a shaky background, but as a player he's got all
the heart in the world, and he's fearless." So Cohen says
to me, "Let's get him." That was the year we took Acie
Earl with the nineteenth pick. We didn't have a second-
round pick, but my friend Quinn Buckner, who had been
named Mavericks coach, had three of them for Dallas. We
thought Van Exel might slip to the second round, so Cohen
said to me, "Call up Quinn." I called Quinn ten times after
our first-round pick and he kept hanging up on me. He
kept saying, "Don't call me anymore. Who are you after,
anyway?" I said, "I'm not going to tell you." Then he'd
hang up on me again. I said to Alan, "He won't do it."
At this point everyone else on the Celtics has gone home,
because they weren't figuring on us having another pick.
So Cohen says, "Call him again." I did, but that darn
Quinn. He wasn't going to help us.

The thrill of trying to make moves was one of the parts
I liked best about my brief time in the front office. I had
input with the Pacers too, and it was frustrating to go all

the way into December of 1998 without any training camp or signings because of the lockout. I was anxious, and bored. But it did enable me to enjoy my induction into the Basketball Hall of Fame, which came about in October of 1998. I really had no idea what to expect. I really didn't know that much about the Hall of Fame. Jill Leone gave me as much information as she could, but I still wasn't sure what kind of feel it would have. I had never seen it on television. I found out later that's because our induction was the first time NBC televised it.

You get to choose someone to present you to the Hall of Fame, but he or she has to be a Hall of Famer themselves. Then you can also have an escort who was influential in your career. My choice as my escort, Bill Fitch, was a no-brainer. He was the first and best pro coach I had. I learned so much from him, and I'm still learning. The day of the induction, he came up to my hotel room and we diagrammed a few plays. My choice to present me was Bill Walton, my friend and teammate who played with me on our 1986 championship team.

I always used to say, "Thank God Bill became a Celtic. Now we have someone to pick on." Bill brought a different energy to the team. Usually we had guys who would come and just try to fit in. Not Bill. He came in with a lot of personality, and it seemed he had something to say about everything. He was very vocal about being ready to play, and he was constantly talking about winning a championship. We thought about all those things, but nobody talked about them much until Bill came along. Then all of a sudden we were talking about it all the time. Bill's words held weight, because he was a guy who had been there. His 1977 Portland Trail Blazers team, which won it all, was awesome. They were the epitome of basketball, and Bill was the center of it. The more I got to know Bill, the more I liked him.

I had no idea what to expect of Walton when he came to the Celtics. I had been following him his entire career, even back to college. I knew he was a tremendous passer for a guy his size, and I knew he could throw perfect outlet passes. I remember very clearly when Notre Dame beat UCLA, Bill's college team. I was happy about that, being an Indiana boy, but what I remember more was how dominant Bill was. What I loved about him was he wasn't mechanical, like so many big men were back then. If you watched him closely, it was almost like you could see the play developing in his head. And I never saw anyone close up the middle and front the way Walton did. He was an outstanding defensive presence.

One night, during that great '86 championship season, Bill, Quinn, and I drove down to French Lick after a game, because we had the next day off. We stayed overnight. We got up, ate, and went down to the basketball court I had built in our backyard. We were messing around down there, and Bill said, "Do you have a jar?" I said, "What for?" He said, "I want to take some dirt home from the court of the famed Larry Bird and sprinkle it on my own court in San Diego." I thought Bill was kidding. He wasn't. So I got him a jar and I said, "Go take some dirt out of the neighbor's yard. We don't have very much good topsoil around here."

Bill was pretty excited when I called and asked him to present me to the Hall of Fame. Later he told people he was surprised I chose him. He said he had no idea I thought that much of him. I guess I'm not the best at telling people. I just assume they know. There were some of my friends who were a little surprised I didn't choose Red

Auerbach. He would seem like a logical choice. Some of the media speculated I was snubbing him because of our so-called disagreement, but my feeling was, Red has done it a million times, and I really wanted to have someone that played with me. Bill Walton was not only a good teammate, he is a very good friend. Red ended up there anyhow, because he presented Lenny Wilkens.

At my press conference I tried to keep it light. People asked me lots of questions, including asking me to rank the best games, the most memorable, and so on. Those are impossible questions to answer. Everyone kept asking me to pick my favorite championship, but I told them you can't ever say one was better than the other. They're different, with special meaning for special reasons. When we won in 1981, it was our first one, so obviously that was incredible. In 1984 we beat Magic, so that was a little revenge from college. I wouldn't have considered my career complete if we hadn't ever beaten the Lakers in the Finals. As for our third championship in 1986, that was considered one of the best teams ever, so hey, we should have won. What I always think is so great was that Magic won a title in his first year, and I won one in my second year.

People were asking me if Magic and I resurrected the NBA. I told them, "I don't believe that's totally true. I'm sure there was more excitement by Magic and me coming into the league together, after playing each other for the national championship, but two guys didn't change this league around. There were plenty of players before us and after us." I truly believe that. People have put that Michigan State versus Indiana State game on some sort of pedestal, but I admitted at that press conference, "We met our match in Michigan State. They were the better team. If we played them ten times—and you know me, this is hard for me to say—they would have beaten us eight times." I told them I appreciated that I was joining an elite group of athletes, and what an honor that was, and that growing up as a kid I didn't even know what the Hall of Fame was. But when you go through your career and have success and accomplish things, this is the way you know it's all worthwhile. I reiterated what I had been saying since I took over for the Pacers, which is that I had no plans to coach in Indiana beyond my three-year contract. Someone asked me what was in my future, and I joked, "Oh, I don't know. Maybe I'll work as vice president for Bill Gates at Microsoft." I quickly added, "But I sort of hope not. Then I'd have to go into the office every day." Later that afternoon a representative from Microsoft contacted Jill by fax and asked her to thank me for the mention, and to offer their services to me should I have any interest in the company in the future. You forget, sometimes, how closely people monitor your words. That was an interesting reminder.

The actual Hall of Fame induction was in an arena that held about 6,000 people. It was sold out. The crowd got a little rowdy, which surprised me. I didn't mind the fans cheering and yelling about the Celtics and all that, but when the actual induction started and some of the spectators shouted things during the presentation of the other inductees, I thought that was pretty awful. I was inducted with a pretty impressive group: Lenny Wilkens, who coaches the Atlanta Hawks; the University of Texas's Jody Conradt, who has won more college games than any other women's coach in history; Arnie Risen, who starred for the Celtics in the fifties; Marques Haynes, an amazing ball handler who used to play for the Harlem Globetrotters; Alex Hannum, who was the first guy to win an NBA and ABA championship; and Aleksandar Nikolic, who is known as the father of Yugoslavian basketball. I knew all of their names, and I remembered Nikolic very well from following Olympic basketball, but the only one I had ever really talked to was Lenny Wilkens. Right away I could tell things were going to be a little one-sided, and I felt bad about that. Here were all these people being honored, on one of the most important days of their lives, and there was all this commotion around me. The last thing I wanted to do was take away from their day, but they were all pretty good-natured about it. We had a press conference before the induction during the afternoon, and Lenny started off by saying, "I want to thank you all for inviting me to Larry's party." That kind of stuff is embarrassing, but what can I do?

The problem was, whenever any of the speakers made reference to Boston or the Celtics, the place would go crazy. I started getting really uncomfortable. My feeling was, "Let everyone have their say. Then, when I get up there, you can do whatever you want." The fans gave me an incredible ovation. I really did appreciate it. But it went on and on and on, and here this thing was on television. Every time I tried to talk and say my speech, they cheered some more. Dinah and the kids were sitting in the front row, and I could tell Conner and Mariah were kind of overwhelmed by the whole thing. I'm sure they were wondering, "Why are all these people clapping for Daddy? 'Cause he's coach of the Pacers?" I didn't talk very long. I thanked my coaches and my teammates. I said I wished my mom could have been there, because I know she would have enjoyed it. Then I thanked Bill Fitch and Bill Walton, and that was that. We went backstage for some pictures, and Mildred Duggan, the coaches' secretary from the Celtics, came back to say hello. It was great to see her. I always loved seeing all the old people from the office, and remembering how nice they treated me twenty years ago. I had seen Millie off and on, and she always made me smile. She was a really nice lady. She did my fan mail for about six or seven years. She was the one who went out and bought all the presents for the kids at Christmastime. Bill Fitch really liked her too, but K. C. Jones was her favorite. Whenever he came to town he'd take her to lunch. I was so glad Millie came to Springfield for the induction. I really enjoyed seeing her. A few weeks after the ceremony I got a call from someone in the Celtics office who told me Millie had died of a massive heart attack. I couldn't believe it. I had just seen her, and she looked great. They told me how much she had enjoyed the induction, and I was glad she made it.

Looking back, the whole thirty-six hours or so I was in Springfield was a blur. I didn't have a whole lot of time to sit down and think about what was happening. We had the press conference. I also had a number of private receptions I had to attend, one for General Mills, and another for the Basketball Hall of Fame Properties. Dinah, the kids, and I were walking from one function to the next, when the doors swung open, and about a hundred people were standing there, staring at us. Conner just stopped in his tracks. I knew how he felt. I could tell by his eyes he was thinking, "What are we getting into here?" He's kind of shy. He snuggled up kind of close to me. I took his hand and said, "Just stay with me. You'll be fine."

While we were attending all these functions, they were unveiling a statue of me in Springfield. From what I understand, a large group of people gathered there because they thought I would be present for the unveiling. And when I wasn't there, a lot of them went home angry and disappointed. That's happened to me constantly in my career. I'll see things in the paper where I'm going to be here or there, and I've known nothing about it. There's one thing about me you can count on: if I say I'm going to show up at something, I'll be there. Later I found out we were told about the statue, but since we had booked these meetings and receptions months in advance, we made it clear well in advance we wouldn't be able to attend the unveiling. Besides, I'm not big on those kinds of things anyway. I don't know why anyone wants a statue of me, and I certainly wouldn't have been comfortable standing there getting my picture taken with it, or whatever.

The best part about the Hall of Fame induction was it put an end to my playing days. I can remember after I retired, somebody said to me, "Five years from now, you'll go into the Hall of Fame." It wasn't something I had ever considered, but when I stopped to think about it I said to myself, "Wow, that's a long time. I wish I could just move it up so I can get it over with."

I just want to move on. Everywhere I go, people are still asking me about my playing days. In a lot of ways, it seems like it's getting worse instead of better. I'm hoping my Hall of Fame induction will close the book on it once and for all.

I thought I would miss playing basketball when I retired, but I've never looked back.

I've got too many other things happening to live in the past. I know the only way people are going to forget Larry Bird the player is if Larry Bird the coach can win a championship.

I'm betting my guys are going to get me there.

CHAPTER 15

On the 1999 Playoffs Debacle

There was no doubt in my mind 1999 was going to be our year. I really felt we were going to win the championship.

What happened instead is one of the toughest things I've ever had to deal with in basketball.

We got back to the Eastern Conference Finals, just like we said we would, but we lost to the New York Knicks in six games. I still can't believe it. That series was our worst nightmare, all come true. Nothing went right for us. We couldn't drive and penetrate and kick out to our shooters, which is so important for us to be successful. We couldn't score down low, because Rik Smits was having so much trouble. And, on top of all that, Reggie Miller couldn't hit any shots. I never thought that was something we'd ever have to worry about.

I was really down when we got eliminated. I still am. It is just a very, very tough thing to take, because we should have beaten the Knicks. I know that, and my players know that, and we have to live with it. Believe me, it isn't easy.

Looking back, all the warning signs were there. Against the Knicks, we just never put together any sustained stretches where we were playing great basketball, night in and night out. Nobody stepped up with the big play the way they had last year. Something was missing, and we could never seem to find it.

At first, when the NBA announced we were going to play a shortened season, I was excited. Fifty games in eighty-five days sounded fantastic to me. I kept thinking back to when I was a player, and how much I would have loved that. But once we got into it, I realized it wasn't as great as it sounded. The pace was so fast, so nonstop, that I said to myself, "Wow, this is going to be a strange year."

During the lockout, our guys had stayed together in Indianapolis, working out together every day. Of course I was happy about that, but to be honest, I expected nothing less from them. I knew how much they wanted to win the championship. I also knew that even though they were going at it every day in the gym, it was going to take them a while to get into game shape. I figured we'd be there after around eight or nine games, and we'd be all right.

Well, when we got to that point, I could see they were in shape, but we weren't playing any better, and that concerned me. We didn't seem to have the killer instinct we had the previous season. The beauty of the year before was that whenever we needed a big play, or a big basket, it was someone different almost every night who stepped forward and delivered. That didn't happen in the 1999 season.

Reggie Miller didn't have a very good year. I kept thinking he was going to find his rhythm, but he never really did. He hit so many big, big shots for us the season before. This year, he had the same opportunities; he'd be looking at some wide-open game-winners, and he'd miss them.

Reggie wasn't the only one who was off. Our whole

team took a step back. The only guys who played as consistently as the year before were Dale Davis and Jalen Rose.

During the regular season, we lost six games by one point. Six games! That, more than anything, really bothered me. We'd get a lead, and instead of putting the hammer down and closing out teams, we'd relax. We just aren't a powerful enough offensive team to do that.

If I could do anything over again, I probably wouldn't have put so much pressure on them to win the championship. I think it got to them. Maybe I shouldn't have said anything to them about it. I should have told them they had to win the division, and go from there. I shouldn't have kept saying, "This is our year to win it all." But they're smart guys. They've been around. They knew this was our best chance, especially with the shortened season.

We had some struggles during the regular season, that's for sure. My honeymoon from year one was definitely over. For the first time, guys were complaining about their roles. Minutes became an issue. Guys like Mark Jackson wanted to be on the floor in the fourth quarter, but the way I had it set up, Mark played the first and third quarters and Travis Best played the second and final quarters, primarily because he's the better defender of the two. I know it was hard for Mark and Chris Mullin and Dale, veterans who have been around a long time, to have to sit for stretches of the game. I never liked to sit as a player either. If you are any kind of competitor, you want to be in the game. But like I explained to Mark, I was doing what I thought was best for the team. Besides, like I told those guys, once we got into the playoffs, I wasn't going to make them sit and watch from the sidelines.

I took a lot of heat from people for starting Chris Mullin in the playoffs. I don't care. When you are a veteran, and you have paid your dues, you have a right to be out there. There was no way in the world I was going to take that away from him, or Mark, or anyone else. But Chris also knew that if he wasn't hitting, I was going to go to the bench to bring someone in.

We got things in order in the final couple weeks of the regular season. Derrick McKey, who had missed most of the year because of a knee injury, was back in action and gave us a defensive stopper to put the clamps on the high-scoring shooting guards or small forwards. We won four in a row to close out the schedule, but I still wasn't entirely happy because we weren't going into the playoffs on a roll like we had done the previous year. I remember telling the press at the time, "I don't know if this is sufficient enough." I know that with any championship team I played on, we went into the postseason on a big high.

I was nervous about the playoffs. We played Milwaukee in the first round, and I was scared to death of them because they had the kind of team that shot very well from the outside, and they were always changing their defense, so I didn't know what to expect. I never expected we'd sweep them, and I sure as hell didn't expect us to sweep Philadelphia in the second round. They were young and energetic, and they had Allen Iverson, but our guys played so well, none of that mattered. We got to the Eastern Conference Finals without losing a game, and I was feeling really good about our team.

Our players were feeling it too. They were enjoying practice and playing together, and I liked our chances, even though I knew New York was on some kind of roll of their own and they were tough defensively and would want to take it to us with their athleticism. I always had faith that when you put New York's starting five on the floor, and then ours out there next to them, we should come out ahead.

I knew coming into this job that this team had some liabilities. I knew we wouldn't conquer the world every night, but I wouldn't have imagined we could play as badly as we did against New York. It seemed like we could never get three guys to play well on a given night. They exploited our lack of athleticism. We didn't take advantage of the obvious size advantage we had underneath. I can remember telling Rik Smits, after Patrick Ewing was declared out of the series because of a partially torn Achilles tendon, "They don't have anyone who can guard you." Why couldn't we take advantage of that? I don't have the answer.

When you look at it, you realize what a great opportunity we missed. First, New York lost Patrick, who was playing on one leg because of his Achilles. I'm friends with Patrick, and I wanted to see him out there. After he went out, there was all this talk about how New York was a better team without him because they could play up-tempo and all that, but there's no way I'm going to buy that. That's B.S.

We didn't take advantage of Patrick being out. Then, when Larry Johnson sprained his knee in Game 5, we didn't take advantage of that either.

There's no question all the controversy surrounding the Knicks brought them together. There was all this talk of whether Jeff Van Gundy would keep his job or not, and I think all the controversy helped their team. It gave them something to rally around. I think Van Gundy is a good coach. I didn't like it, though, when he went to the press and claimed we had put a bounty on Marcus Camby's head. I thought that was garbage, and I felt it would backfire on them big time.

When you look at the series, the turning point was definitely Game 3. The series was tied 1–1 at that point, and we were going to New York with plans of winning both games. There's no doubt we should have won Game 3. That's obvious. But the big call at the end of the game killed us. Just killed us.

We were up by three with the game clock running down to single digits, and the Knicks inbounded the ball. Their plan, I believe, was to go for a quick two, but Jalen deflected the inbounds pass, so whatever play they were running was busted. Antonio Davis was guarding Larry Johnson, who ended up with the ball in the corner. Tony made a stab at the ball and that put him off balance. Tony hit Johnson, who took another step, then shot the three-pointer. The shot was good and the refs called a foul. We lost on a four-point play, which is impossible. I told Antonio not to worry about it, because the guy should have been shooting free throws. There's no way that foul was in the act of shooting. It was well before the shot.

But I understand you should never put yourself in that position. We were trying to protect the lead again, and we have to take responsibility for that.

Antonio was pretty upset after the game. He had his head down, like we all did. I was ready to do anything it took to get them to concentrate for the next game, but it really wasn't a problem. They were ready. They understood they HAD to win Game 4 after what had just happened.

Game 4 was a gut check game for us. Jalen Rose stepped up and made some really big plays. Chris Mullin hit some key jumpers. Reggie had another quiet night— he was three for 10—but we got scoring from Antonio too, so we managed.

But then they got to Game 5 and they let down again.

What happened in Game 3 took so much out of them, and then they expended all this effort to even it again in Game 4, it was like they ran out of gas or something. I still have a hard time with that. Here was this major monster game, one of the biggest in franchise history, on our floor and half our guys didn't show up. It made me sick to my stomach.

I've always said Game 5 is the most important game in a series. You have to have that one. I told reporters before that game that Rik Smits was going to have a big game. I wasn't just saying it—I truly believed it. He hadn't played well at all up to that point. He had broken his toe and it was giving him trouble. It was painful for him to plant his foot and pivot. On top of that, his chronically sore feet were giving him problems again.

Every once in a while I'd ask him how he was doing. From all indications he was all right. He said the toe was hurting him but his feet were actually okay. I was relieved to hear that. I worried more about his feet. The broken toe, I figured, he could play through.

Leading up to Game 5, he looked pretty good in practice. He was running and jumping around. I remember saying to Dick and Rick, "Wow, I think he's going to be okay after all."

I don't know why Rik couldn't get it together in Game 5. He really couldn't do anything. We needed him so badly and he just wasn't there for us. I didn't have to tell him that. I'm sure it was one of the lowest days of his life.

His big problem was getting into early foul trouble. When you have to pull a guy after 30 seconds because he has two quick fouls, that causes all sorts of problems. Imagine sitting all day thinking about the game, and getting yourself mentally prepared, then going out there and finding yourself back on the bench in less than a minute.

Smits finished with eight points and six rebounds in Game 5. The media was all over him. For the first time I can remember, Rik ducked out without talking to reporters. He knew how devastating it was. Our crowd, which had seen us go ahead by as many as 14, was stunned. Reggie scored 30 that night but couldn't knock down the big ones down the stretch. Suddenly, we were in deep trouble and we all knew it.

I really challenged Rik before Game 6. Sometimes he responds better when you do that. I told him, "Rik, if I can't get anything out of you tonight, we can't win."

Then I turned to the rest of the team and told them we needed people to step up and give us more. I said to them, "There's one guy in this locker room who I know is going to go out there and bust his ass, who is going to give us absolutely everything he has. He's never going to stop playing hard. I know Dale Davis is going to do that for us. Now who is going to follow him?"

Rik Smits played pretty well in Game 6. But that game went like all the others. Not enough of our guys came to play. Chris Mullin didn't score a basket. Mark Jackson didn't give us much. Antonio Davis didn't either. I think he had only one rebound. He's one of those guys that when Smits gets into early foul trouble you can say, "Tony, Rik's not with us tonight, bail us out, okay?" And he'll go out and do it.

In spite of all that, with 6:58 left in the game, it was a tie score. We had the ball, our whole season was on the line, and what happened? We got called for two traveling violations. The turnovers in that game killed us. We had 26 for the game. That explains it all.

When I watched the Knicks, I saw them make the kind of big plays that turn games around. We did the same thing to opponents the previous season. Marcus Camby is the player who killed us. He had energy and lift, and those tips that he kept slamming down on us were the daggers in our heart. You watch him on film and he has excellent timing. He waits, and waits, then darts in just at the right time to make the play.

Latrell Sprewell played well for the Knicks too, but he didn't kill us. Someone asked me, looking back, if I wish we had pulled the trigger on the Sprewell trade, but I don't. The price—one of our top big guys—was too high. I don't have any regrets about that.

I know what people were saying about us. They were saying our guys couldn't handle the pressure, but I've seen Reggie and Mark in way too many situations where they've come up with big money baskets to believe that.

In retrospect, it all comes back to Game 3. We blew that game, then came back and fought like champions in Game 4, but couldn't follow through in Game 5. I guarantee you one thing: if we had won Game 3, we would have won Game 4 too. It's disappointing it didn't turn out that way.

You can't expect that to happen when you turn it on and off the way we did. You have to show up for every play, every night, if you want to win a championship.

I think our team, including the coaches, were all waiting for Reggie to go off and have one of his amazing games. We all sat back and said, "Reggie's going to have it the next game," instead of someone else stepping up and saying, "Let me try and get this done."

The one thing I won't listen to is people saying we were too cocky, or that we didn't put in the effort to win. It's not like these guys didn't try. I never questioned whether they wanted it or not.

All you had to do was walk into our locker room after Game 6 to see that. Mark Jackson took it harder than anyone. He knows this was our year. He understands there may never be another opportunity like the one we just let get away.

For me, the hardest guy to face was Donnie Walsh. He worked so hard and for so long to build this team, and I know it was crushing for him how things ended. He usually comes into the locker room after every game, but he wasn't around much in that last series. It was too hard for him. My pal Slick Leonard was the other guy who was really down. He wanted so much for us to get to the Finals.

Reggie wasn't around for very long after it ended. I didn't really see him to talk to him, but I know he felt bad. Reggie was three of 18 from the floor in that final game. Unbelievable. I did find Rik Smits and told him he played with a lot of heart in Game 6. A few days later, he was quoted in a foreign magazine as saying he was thinking of retiring because he was tired of playing in pain. I hope that's just his frustration and disappointment talking. I'm expecting him to be back next season.

We had our break-up dinner, but I didn't want to be there. Neither did the players. We all sat around and moped and felt sorry for ourselves. Actually, I'm still doing that. I know we had a good ball club, but the bottom line is we didn't get it done. People tell me, "There are twenty-seven other teams that didn't win it," but that's supposed to make me feel better? And then there're the ones who say, "Well, at least you got back to the Final Four." That's total B.S. That means nothing to me, or my players.

I know what we need next season. We need younger players. We're going to have to make some pretty tough decisions this summer. I said in my first season I would resign rather than see this team trade Reggie Miller or Mark Jackson. But now I realize sometimes you have to make difficult business decisions like that, for the good of the team. I'm not saying we're going to trade those guys, but my guess is, Donnie is going to look at everything. One thing is obvious to me: we can't come back with everything the same as last season.

That's why, on draft day, we traded Antonio Davis for Jonathan Bender, a high school star from Picayune, Mississippi. It wasn't easy trading Tony. I hated to do it. He's a great guy and was a big part of our team. He was also our best defender. But Tony wanted to start next season and we couldn't guarantee that. Donnie felt that for the best of the franchise we needed to be younger. I didn't know much about Bender when we traded for him—only what I've seen on tape. But Donnie's convinced this kid is going to be a star. I have to admit, though, if Lamar Odom was there at number five (the Clippers took him with the number four pick), we would have grabbed him. By trading Tony, we now have Tony's money ($4.2 million) to go out and sign a free agent, someone like Lorenzen Wright.

I'm sure that's not the only move we'll make. There might be other big changes, and some other little changes as well. Little things like moving Chris Mullin out of the starting lineup, or featuring Jalen Rose in the offense more. I don't know right now. It's too hard for me to even think about.

As a coach, when you lose a game, you go back and look at the film and see what you could have done differently to help your team, whether another defensive strategy would have worked, or whether a different play call in a certain situation would have made sense. I haven't been able to do that yet.

I haven't felt this low about basketball since I played for the Celtics and we were swept by Milwaukee in the 1982–1983 season playoffs. Back then, the way I handled it was that I went home to French Lick and played basketball all summer and vowed to be better than I ever was. But as a coach, I can tell you that there's a much bigger feeling of despair.

I've never been one to take games home with me, but this series has been brutal for me. After two straight sweeps, I was so convinced we'd be focused enough to beat New York. But when it was finally over, it felt like we were a complete and utter failure.

I told Donnie I would decide my future from year to year, and that's what I've done. He wants me to come back and coach next season, and I guess that is probably what I'll do. I'm not a quitter. But I will stick to my original promise of coaching only three years. That will be more than enough for me.

It's hard to say what our team will look like next season. We're all still a little raw from what's happened. The younger guys were disappointed, but they know they've always got next year. For the older guys, who are at the end of their careers, it's more personal. It hurts more, because they can sense it slipping away from them.

I know exactly how they feel.

Index